Computational Techniques for Intelligence Analysis

Vincenzo Loia · Francesco Orciuoli · Angelo Gaeta

Computational Techniques for Intelligence Analysis

A Cognitive Approach

Springer

Vincenzo Loia
Dipartimento di Scienze
Aziendali—Management & Innovation
Systems (DISA-MIS)
Università degli Studi di Salerno
Fisciano, Salerno, Italy

Francesco Orciuoli
Dipartimento di Scienze
Aziendali—Management & Innovation
Systems (DISA-MIS)
Università degli Studi di Salerno
Fisciano, Salerno, Italy

Angelo Gaeta
Dipartimento di Scienze
Aziendali—Management & Innovation
Systems (DISA-MIS)
Università degli Studi di Salerno
Fisciano, Salerno, Italy

https://doi.org/10.1007/978-3-031-20851-5

This Springer imprint is published by the registered company Springer Nature Switzerland AG
The registered company address is: Gewerbestrasse 11, 6330 Cham, Switzerland

Preface

This book is about *Computational Techniques for Intelligence Analysis* that belongs to the macro-area of risk management. Risk management is the process focused on identification, measurement, assessment, and processing of risks within an organization and should allow the right balance between the costs of protection measures and their benefits for such organization. In such a context, intelligence is the phase of risk management dealing with the prediction of anomalous (malicious, harmful, etc.) events in some specific domains: security, safety, emergency, surveillance, infrastructure resilience, etc. Terrorist attacks, cyber-attacks, plane crashes, accident at sea, fake news diffusion, and spread of pandemic are all examples of events that can be considered by intelligence analysis.

In particular, the commitment of intelligence is multiple: determining critical assets, identifying and evaluating existing countermeasures, defining possible threats, determining system vulnerabilities, and defining potential losses in the case of a probable anomalous event. From the information processing viewpoint, intelligence includes methodologies, activities, and tools aimed at obtaining complex (often structured) information from a set of isolated data (often raw data) gathered from an individual sensor or a sensor system. Such information is used to increase knowledge and awareness of situations occurring in a given scenario.

Despite numerous existing methodologies and practices supporting Intelligence analysis, this book focuses on the definition and implementation of computational tools, mostly data driven, supporting decision-making processes along several and heterogeneous intelligence scenarios. In particular, the aforementioned tools aim at increasing the level of situation awareness of decision-makers through the construction of abstract structures on which it is possible to reason in order to foster the chance of the human operator to make qualitative decisions.

This book will appeal to students, professional, and academic researchers in computational intelligence and approximate reasoning applications for decision-making in intelligence analysis. It is a comprehensive textbook on the subject, supported with lots of case studies and practical examples.

The readers will understand how to face the definition of decision support systems for the intelligence analysis through the concrete application of the Endsley's Model of Situation Awareness and the well-known paradigm of granular computing for information processing. The authors show how to build the aforementioned systems by adopting a cognitive approach, i.e., defining computational solutions replicating human ways of problem solving. The didactic approach of the book is mainly based on case study analysis that is conducted through the definition of a clear solution methodology, based on cutting-edge computational methods and techniques, and a practical implementation using Python code. In this way, the reader will get the solution approach as well as the related implementation issues.

Definitely, the book emphasizes practical applications and computational methods, which are very useful and important both for reducing the cybersecurity skills shortage and for the further development of the field of intelligence analysis. Focusing on rough set and fuzzy logic theories, three-way decision models, and different reasoning methods, the authors have built and adopt a didactic approach that allows to deep analyze and understand problems and computational solutions and try these solutions with the support of hands-on laboratory based on Python code.

According to the content structure, the book focuses the first chapters on the concepts of situation awareness and decision-making in intelligence analysis and on a clear background on the main theoretical computational methods which are used. Next, it moves clearly and efficiently from concepts and paradigms to case studies, methodologies, and implementation. The book ends with the description of a technological framework for the real-world implementation and deploy of techniques and methods described in the various chapters.

Fisciano (SA), Italy
June 2022

Vincenzo Loia
Francesco Orciuoli
Angelo Gaeta

Contents

About the Authors

Vincenzo Loia received the master's degree in computer science from the University of Salerno, Fisciano, Italy, in 1985, and the Ph.D. degree in computer science from the University of Paris 6, Paris, France, in 1989. He is currently Rector of the University of Salerno (from November 2019) and Full Professor of computer science with the University of Salerno where he held the position of researcher from 1989 to 2000 and as an associate professor from 2000 to 2004. Since the beginning of his career, he has shown a deep and operational research interest, in particular in the use of innovative approaches for solving complex problems through new paradigms of software design and programming, that of agent and multi-agent systems; in the design and testing of systems for approximate reasoning, through the synergistic use of standard semantic technologies, description logic, and fuzzy logic; in the definition of original conceptual data analysis methodologies for the extraction of knowledge from unstructured resources; in the creation of decision support systems conveyed by artificial intelligence models, cognitive architectures, computational intelligence, and granular computing. Precisely with respect to the latter, it demonstrates that it has the sensitivity to understand, apply, and contribute to research on models, such as granular and cognitive computing, which strongly base their principles on aspects concerning the study and analysis of human cognitive processes. These research interests have characterized his path of international dissemination through which he has established a rich network of scientific collaborations with researchers worldwide (including the close relationship with the founder of the fuzzy theory, Lotfi Zadeh). The pillars that characterize his scientific research over the years have been reflected in various application domains, from medical to legal, and more recently in the field of cyber-intelligence. Precisely in the latter area, he shows his great predisposition to multidisciplinarity, coordinating the scientific committee of the "Multidisciplinary Observatory for the fight against organized crime and terrorism" which implements a continuous scientific research activity applied to the thematic areas of computational intelligence and countering terrorist activities spread on the Web and Deep Web, in support of information analysis projects for crimes under the responsibility of DNA (National Anti-Mafia and Anti-Terrorism Directorate). Vincenzo Loia is:

- Editor-in-Chief and Founder of the international journal *Ambient Intelligence and Humanized Computing*, Springer.
- Editor-in-Chief of the international magazine *Evolutionary Intelligence*, Springer.
- Editor Responsible for Special Issues of the international magazine *Soft Computing*, Springer.
- Co-Editor-in-Chief of the international journal *Information Processing Systems.*
- Associate Editor of the *IEEE Transaction Systems, Man and Cybernetics: Systems journals*; *IEEE Transactions on Fuzzy Systems*; *IEEE Transactions on Cognitive and Developmental Systems.*

Francesco Orciuoli received the master's degree cum laude in computer science from the University of Salerno, Fisciano, Italy. He is Associate Professor of computer science with the University of Salerno. His scientific activity, since the beginning of his career, is aimed at defining methods and techniques for supporting human cognitive processes (learning, decision-making, reasoning, and problem solving). In this regard, in recent years, he is investigating how the paradigms of granular computing (implemented with methods for approximate reasoning such as, for example, probabilistic rough set theory) and cognitive computing (e.g., three-way decisions) can be applied in synergy with other computational approaches to offer an adequate formal framework for human–data interaction applied to different domains such as, for example, intelligence, surveillance, and emergency management. He is Co-author of more than 130 scientific publications indexed by SCOPUS, Co-founder of a university spin-off involved in several R&D project related to e-Health, and Co-author of a patent in the e-health sector. He is Member of the IEEE and the IEEE Computational Intelligence Society. He is Associate Editor of the *International Journal of Big Data Intelligence (IJBDI)* and serves as Reviewer for numerous international journals such as *Knowledge-Based Systems* (Elsevier) and *IEEE Transactions on Cybernetics and Applied Intelligence* (Springer).

Angelo Gaeta received the master's degree cum laude in electronic engineering and Ph.D. degree in Management and Information Technology from the University of Salerno, Fisciano, Italy. He is currently Research Assistant in computer science at the University of Salerno. His research interests relate to situation awareness, approximate reasoning, and computational intelligence for decision-making and intelligence analysis. He is Co-author of more than 50 scientific publications indexed by SCOPUS on these topics. He is Associate Editor of the International Journal*Ambient Intelligence and Humanized Computing* (Springer) and serves as Reviewer of several international journals.

Part I
Foundations

Chapter 1
Introduction

This book has the ambitious purpose of presenting computational techniques to support the discipline of Intelligence Analysis. This discipline is approached in an innovative way by integrating its main concepts with the cognitive model of Situation Awareness for which the phases of an Intelligence Analysis activity are contextualized in an operational construct which is called situation and made computationally tractable through techniques based on approximate reasoning and decision making.

The book represents the synthesis of several years of study by the authors on these issues and, therefore, tends to balance theoretical and modeling aspects with practical applications to case studies. This last part has been called *Hands-on Lab* to underline the laboratory nature of the different tutorials in the book. Moreover, One of the greatest strengths of the book is to accompany the reader to build decision support systems by using a smooth multi-views approach going from concepts and paradigms to concrete Python implementations throughout mathematical methods and scenario analysis.

The book is recommended for students, researchers, and practitioners interested in the application of rough set theory and computational approaches in intelligence analysis.

1.1 Book Content Structure

The book is organized in three parts.

The first part is theoretical and devoted to introduce the discipline of Intelligence Analysis, the background concepts of Situation Awareness and computational techniques such as Granular Computing with formal settings of rough and fuzzy sets and Three-Way decisions models, and lastly an innovative model defined by the authors to integrate Intelligence Analysis and Situation Awareness. This content is included in Chaps. 2, 3 and 4.

V. Loia et al., *Computational Techniques for Intelligence Analysis*,
https://doi.org/10.1007/978-3-031-20851-5_1

The second part consists of case studies related to Intelligence Analysis and how these case studies can be implemented with the innovative model previously mentioned and the computational techniques described in the book. Specifically: Chap. 5 presents an application of the well-know what-if analysis to a vessel surveillance scenario, Chap. 6 discusses how to reason on graphs modeling large scale infrastructures and make decisions with respect to the level of resilience of such infrastructures under intentional attacks, Chap. 7 shows an analytic method to attribute hypotheses of terrorist attacks to terrorist groups starting from open source intelligence data and Chap. 8 presents the adoption of structures of opposition to reason on information disorder phenomena, such as propaganda, that can lead to opinions change in communities. These chapter are all concluded by a series of practical tutorials allowing readers to practice with the adopted computational techniques.

The third part of the book consists of chapters that provides some detailed insights on how to deal with issues related to implementation of probability-based rough set operators in Chap. 9, data streaming scenarios in Chap. 10, optimization of thresholds for Three-Way decisions models in Sect. 3.6.1 and rough set approaches based on continuous variable in Chap. 11.

The book is accompanied by topics maps that graphically describe the main topics of the first two parts of the book to help the reader in identifying the main topics of discussion and their relationships. A topic map of the entire book is shown in Fig. 1.1. Topic maps, together with Learning Objectives and Python code, are a tool designed for teachers, practitioners and learners to guide them within the contents of the book.

1.2 Didactic Aspects

This book is suitable for supporting learning and teaching activities based on Active Learning methodologies (Bonwell and Eison 1991). Active Learning is *a method of learning in which students are actively or experientially involved in the learning process* and, in computer science, there are several techniques of Active Learning such as (McConnell 1996) modified lectures, algorithm tracking and demonstration software.

Hands-on Labs in this book share the basic ideas of demonstration software techniques. In fact, the tutorial of this book allows students and researchers to implement and execute the computational techniques improving the comprehension of the theoretical methods.

Starting from the following section, having the objective of showing how to set the programming environment, this book proposes a concept very similar to that one of a learning factory (Jorgensen et al. 1995). The Hands-on Lab tutorials are, in fact, organized as a production factory providing a complete environment for education, training, and research.

With regards to the Learning Objectives that readers can achieve following the didactic method adopted by this book, the definition of these objectives follows the

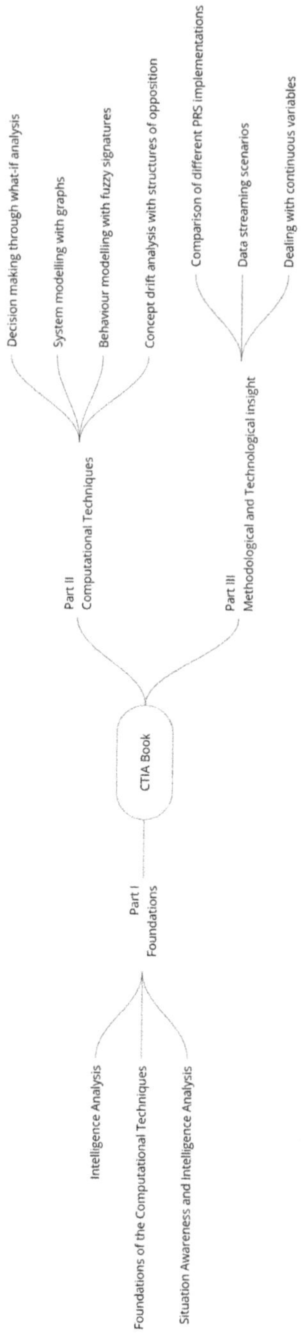

Fig. 1.1 Topic map of the book

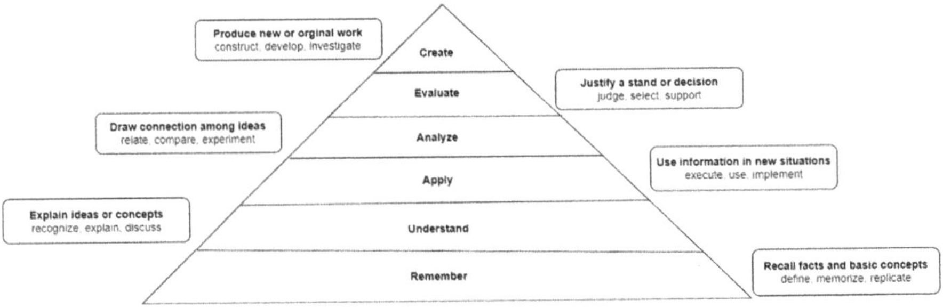

Fig. 1.2 Revised bloom's taxonomy

approach proposed by Bloom's taxonomy, as revised by Anderson and Krathwohl (2001), that is shown in Fig. 1.2. In brief, the revised taxonomy identifies six categories in the cognitive process dimension from the recognition of facts and basic concepts (see the bottom of the taxonomy) through more complex and abstract processes such as creation and development (see the top of the taxonomy). As it can be observed at the right-hand side of Fig. 1.2, a set of verbs is correlated to each cognitive process level of the taxonomy. When instructors have to plan Learning Objectives, a basic formula for creating a Learning Objective can be: *Students will be able to + Action(verb)+ Skill/Knowledge/Ability* where verbs are to be considered among the ones of a specific set proposed by the taxonomy.

For instance, for a computer science course a Learning Objective can be: Students will be able to *recognize* a sorting algorithm. This Learning Objective falls into level 2 (Understand) of the taxonomy that is related to cognitive processes of comprehension of concepts. Moving to level 3 (Apply), an example can be: Students will be able to *use* a sorting algorithm in a more complex algorithm.

Following this approach, particular attention has to be paid in using verbs or expressions such as *know* and *knowledge* if these actions can not be properly measured.

The primary educational goal of this book is to support readers in achieving levels 1, 2, 3 and 4 of the taxonomy. In particular, (a) recalling and understanding concepts of the Intelligence Analysis also in relation to Situation Awareness and Granular Computing; (b) applying Rough and Fuzzy Sets tools and Three-Way Decisions to Intelligence Analysis processes; (c) analyzing the outcomes of a process by experimenting with the hands-on tutorials. These objectives will be achieved also with the support of the case studies presented in the book that illustrate the development of the computational techniques. Users of this book will get the opportunity also to develop and reinforce skills in using Python libraries and tools.

In summary, the general Learning Objectives for this book are outlined as follows:

- Recognize and understand the basic concepts of Intelligence Analysis, Situation Awareness and Granular Computing (and its formal setting such as Rough and Fuzzy Sets).

- Identify proper computational techniques (among the ones described in the book) to support an Intelligence Analysis process.
- Apply the computation techniques to develop new analytic techniques to be applied in Intelligence Analysis processes.
- Experiment the different computational techniques for Intelligence Analysis processes and assess the outcomes.

1.3 Using Python and Google Colaboratory

At the end of Chaps. 3, 5, 6, 7 and 8, the reader will be involved in hands-on lab experiences for implementing and executing the methodologies explained in those chapters and also applying the adopted techniques to both the same or different data. In the context of such experiences, the reader can execute guided tutorials in order to achieve a deeper understanding of the concepts covered in the book and to mature basic skills for developing decision support tools. The readers do not need to re-write the source code of tutorials cause it is published on https://github.com/ctiabook/firstedition-tutorials.

The selected programming language is *Python*[1] that provides undoubted advantages. Python is open source, supported and adopted by a wide community, comes with a huge amount of libraries, can be used as a didactic programming language, and it is well known, together with the *R* language,[2] as the most important language for data analysis. Moreover, a plethora of tools and resources are freely available for developers.

The tutorials provided by this book mostly make use of a set of simple Python classes[3] (described in Chap. 3) developed by the authors and build, on the top of them, new functionalities by also using third-party libraries (which will be introduced and explained as needed).

The reader will interact with the aforementioned classes by copying and pasting the related source code into the programming environment. Moreover, the reader will acquire knowledge on used third-party libraries by accessing the subsections `helpful resources` to get links to Web resources or books related to libraries and tools exploited by the tutorials.

The suggested development environment to run the source code indicated by the tutorials is *Google Colaboratory* (Colab)[4] that allows to access interactively to cloud-based Python run-time engines without any local installation. Figure 1.3 reports the home page of Colab.

In order to exploit also the storage space offered by *Google Drive* it is needed to sign-in Colab through a valid Google Account. Once signed-in it, is possible to

[1] https://www.python.org/.

[2] https://www.r-project.org/.

[3] In the sense of Object-Oriented Programming.

[4] https://colab.research.google.com.

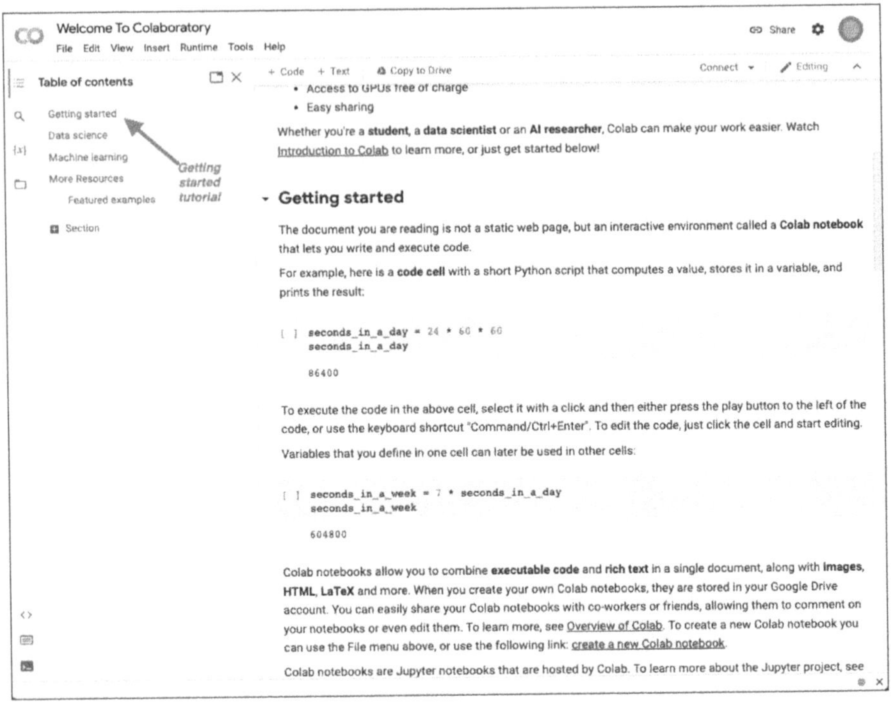

Fig. 1.3 Welcome to colaboratory

read the documentation provided by Colab. We suggest to read at least the `Getting started` tutorial.

To start the work in Python through Colab, you need to create a notebook by selecting the File menu and clicking on New Notebook. The screen corresponding to a new notebook is reported in Fig. 1.4 where you can change the name to the notebook (1), adding code or text cells to the notebook (2), writing source code (3), manipulate (e.g., delete) a cell (4). A notebook can be saved by selecting the File menu and clicking on Save. Note that a copy of the notebook will be saved into your Google Drive space.

But let go to see how to execute a code fragment in Colab. In order to do this you need to: write one or more Python instructions into a cell, click on the play button on the extreme left of the cell or pressing a combination of keys (i.e., shift+enter).

Let do an example. In Fig. 1.5, the first cell contains three valid Python instructions (1). Once the play button is pressed, the above instructions have been evaluated and the resulting value is printed below (2). Lastly, a new cell is automatically created (3) for writing additional code. New cells can be explicitly appended to the notebook by selecting the Insert menu and clicking on Code cell or Text cell.

Text cells are very useful to enrich the notebook of comments explaining better the instructions and results obtained.

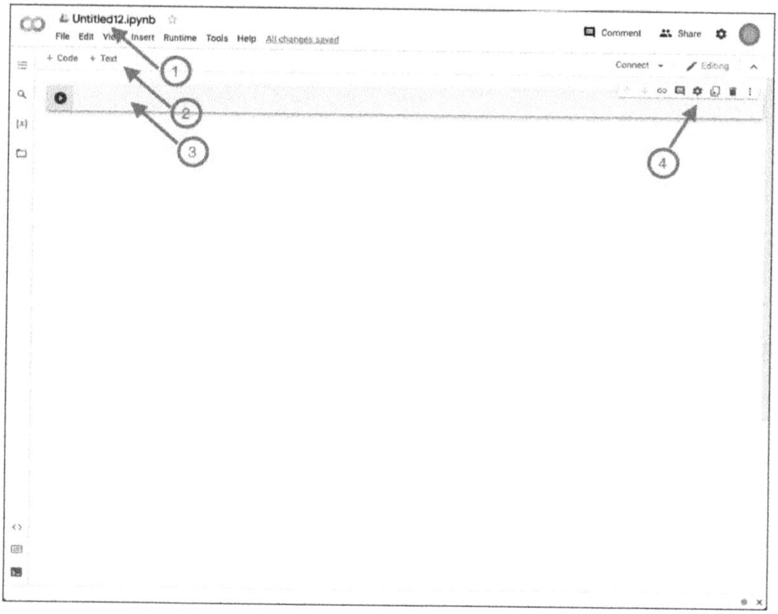

Fig. 1.4 New notebook screen

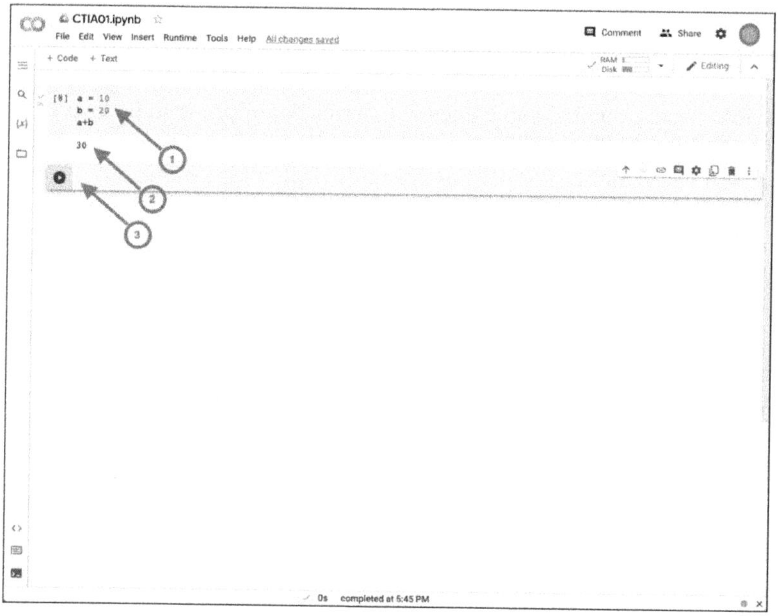

Fig. 1.5 Writing and executing python code in colab

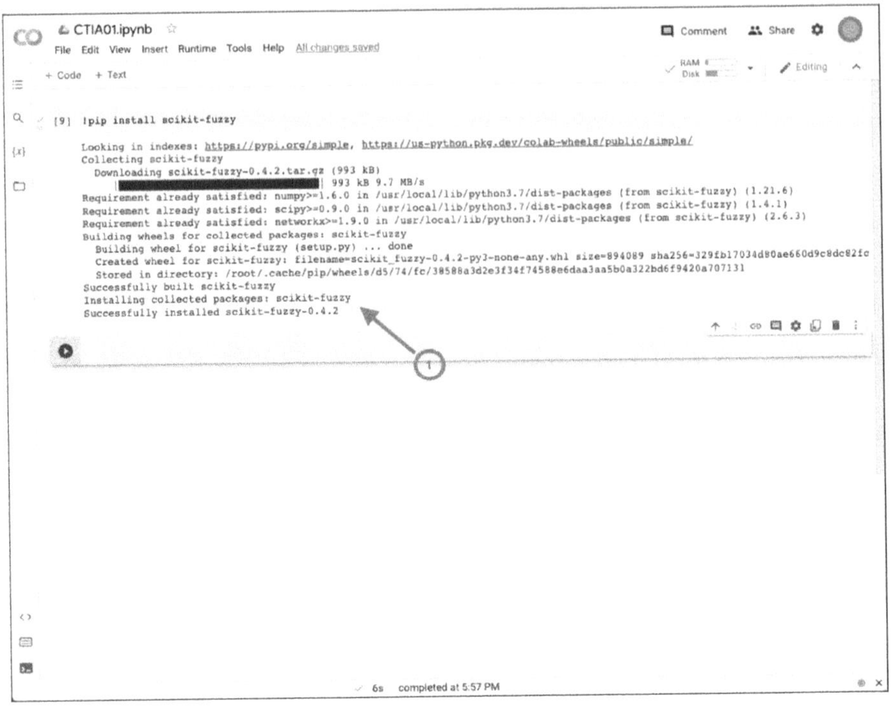

Fig. 1.6 Installation of scikit-fuzzy package

Take into account that Colab comes with a rich set of pre-installed packages like, for instance, Pandas, NumPy, NetworkX, etc. while other packages used in this book tutorials will be explicitly installed by using the following command:

```
!pip install <package name>
```

Assume that the package `scikit-fuzzy` needs to be installed, then you can do what is shown in Fig. 1.6. If the installation is successful the system provides us with a message (1) like *Successfully installed scikit-fuzzy-0.4.2*.

Take care that Colab maintains users' installations only for the current session. If you restart the engine or the session ends, all the installed packages will be dropped. Therefore, if you open a saved notebook you will need to execute again all the preliminaries operations: package installation, data loading, etc.

1.4 Useful Resources

- Python Community Site, https://www.python.org/. Go here to download any available version of the Python engine and to learn the Python language.
- Python Practice Book, https://anandology.com/python-practice-book/index.html. Go here to find Python source code samples useful for learning.

- Python Programming, https://upload.wikimedia.org/wikipedia/commons/9/91/Python_Programming.pdf. This is a free e-book for learning Python.
- Google Colaboratory (tutorials), https://colab.research.google.com/. Go here to read tutorials on Google Colaboratory.

Chapter 2
Intelligence Analysis

Intelligence Analysis is a wide discipline that, today, goes beyond its military origins to cover areas such as homeland security, law enforcement, commercial organizations. As Clark (2019) emphasizes, Intelligence is about "*reducing uncertainty in conflicts*", where the concept of conflict does not refer only to warfare but includes any competitive or opposition action resulting from the divergence of two or more parties.

To reduce uncertainty, Intelligence must collect data and information that the opponents want to hide, combine this information with other sources (including open sources) and processing them. In this perspective, Intelligence can be thought as a process of comprehension of the meaning of information. Intelligence, however, differs from similar processes (such as market research) since aims at reaching a specific objective: to establish facts and infer hypotheses, assumptions, predictions to support strategic and operational decision-making and planning.

The chapter begins with an introduction of the fundamental concepts of Intelligence Analysis and continues with an explanation of the Intelligence as a process. Then, the chapter presents some analytic techniques supporting the analyst. The chapter concludes by discussing some challenges of data-driven Intelligence Analysis and on how they can be afforded.

2.1 Learning Objectives of the Chapter

This chapter is devoted to explain the key concepts of Intelligence Analysis. At the conclusion of this chapter, the reader will be able to:

- Recognize, describe and discuss the main concepts of Intelligence Analysis.
- Recognize the phases of an Intelligence Analysis process.

V. Loia et al., *Computational Techniques for Intelligence Analysis*,
https://doi.org/10.1007/978-3-031-20851-5_2

- Describe and classify the main analytic techniques to use an Intelligence Analysis process.

The above defined objectives impact on the level 2 (Understand) of the taxonomy shown in Fig. 1.2.

2.2 Topic Map of the Chapter

The topic map of this chapter is shown in Fig. 2.1. The chapter mainly focuses on two primary topics of Intelligence Analysis: The Intelligence Process and the Analytic Process. With respect to the first topic, the chapter reports the definitions of the different types of intelligence processes and provides details on the intelligence cycles with which the processes are carried out. With respect to the second topic, the chapter details which are the structured analysis techniques (SAT) dividing them by categories and families and describes the main cognitive and perceptual biases related to the analysis processes.

2.3 What Is Intelligence Analysis?

Intelligence analysis is the process by which information is collected, processed, analyzed and disseminated in the communities of interest. It makes extensive use of individual and collective cognitive methods to collect and evaluate evidence, formulate and assess hypotheses and scenarios. As a practice, it develops mainly within government agencies (i.e., Intelligence agencies) aimed at analyzing information for purposes such as homeland protection but, today, is adopted also for business purposes (e.g., business Intelligence). Intelligence Analysis differs from other processes devoted to collect and analyze information because of its focus on operations such as military operations, cyber operations, law enforcement. Besides the process (that is the objective of Sect. 2.4), other key concepts of the Intelligence Analysis are the *customer*, the *analyst* and the *product*.

The primary customer of the Intelligence is who will act on information such as a decision-maker, a commander, an officer. It may be defined as a plurality of individuals, such as an Organization, and it must be identified at the beginning of the Intelligence process. The customer relies on Intelligence to reduce uncertainty in decision-making.

The analyst is in charge of managing and executing the analysis process and can be considered as the link between the customer and the Intelligence community. Usually, analysts work in teams where each analyst can have a different role and different competencies. In any case, an analyst must have logical and thinking capabilities and other soft-skills as well as experience in the adoption of sounded analytic tradecraft.

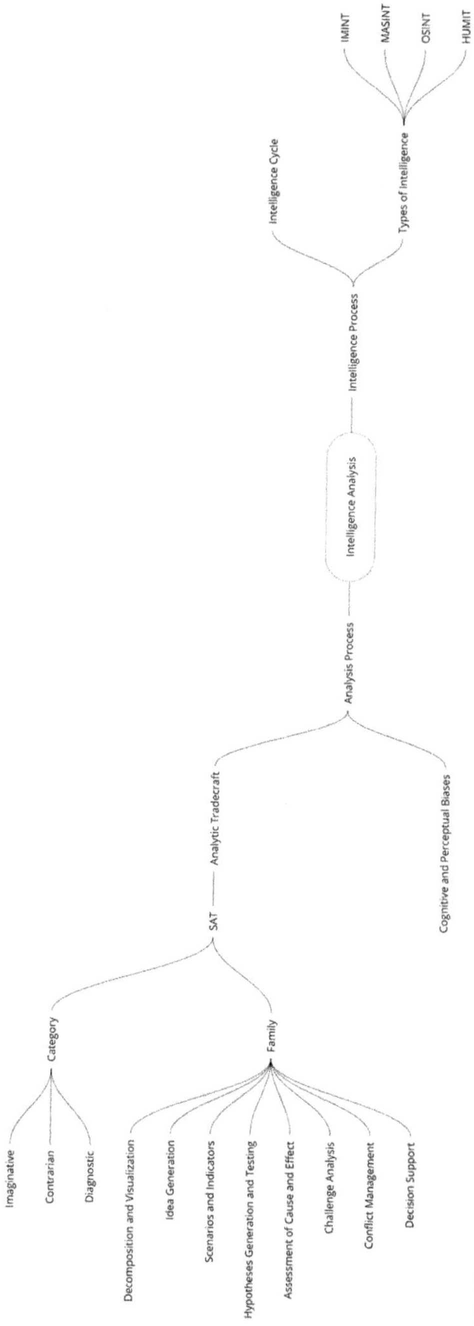

Fig. 2.1 Topic map of the chapter

The product of Intelligence is, in general, actionable information. However, not all the actionable information is Intelligence (e.g., a business report can be actionable information but not an Intelligence product). Clark (2019) considers three broad classes of products: Intelligence Research, Current Intelligence and Indications and Warnings. The first looks at long-term and refers to Strategic Intelligence used to make policy decisions and long term plans. Current Intelligence, instead, covers fast-breaking events to support on-going operations. Indications and Warnings, lastly, refers to the most common product of Intelligence involving detecting and reporting time-sensitive information.

Intelligence Analysis, at a top level, can be defined by its nature as (Clark 2019): *(i)* Strategic Intelligence that deals with long-time issues, *(ii)* Operational Intelligence that covers the Intelligence required for planning and executing an operation and *(iii)* Tactical Intelligence that support on-going operations and is, usually, a quick-reaction Intelligence. Intelligence Research is usually the product of Strategic Intelligence. Current Intelligence and Indications and Warning can be associated to both the other natures of Intelligence.

Intelligence analysis has as its primary objective the refinement of data and information, often partial and incomplete, in order to make them "*intelligible*" and therefore give them meaning to support informed decision making. This activity usually takes place within a process called the *Intelligence Process* and which is described in the next section.

To gather information, usually, there are several types of classified and unclassified sources. Depending on their nature, there can be different (but complementary) types of Intelligence. Some examples are given in the following:

- Open Source Intelligence (OSINT) that, according to NATO[1], refers to Intelligence derived from publicly available information, as well as other unclassified information that has limited public distribution or access.
- Measurement and Signature Intelligence (MASINT) that refers to Intelligence derived from the adoption of technologies to detect, track, identify or describe the distinctive features (or signatures) of target sources. MASINT is closely related with similar types of Intelligence such as Signal Intelligence (SIGINT) focused on electronic signal as sources of Intelligence.
- Imagery Intelligence (IMINT) (Beitler 2019) is focused on image (e.g., satellite or aerial photography) analysis to derive Intelligence in combination with MASINT.
- Human Intelligence (HUMIT) defined by NATO as Intelligence derived from information collected by human operators and primarily provided by human sources. As the name suggests, this type of Intelligence is mostly based on human sources and can be adopted in combination with more technical oriented ones such as OSINT and MASINT.

[1] Readers can refer to the offical NATO terminology database https://nso.nato.int/natoterm/content/nato/pages/home.html?lg=en for NATO definitions of terms.

2.4 The Intelligence Process

The Intelligence process is described with a series of steps that, in their most common form, are placed in circular succession to form the so-called *Intelligence Cycle*. The Intelligence Cycle is the process of developing raw information into finished Intelligence for policy-makers to use in decision-making and action[2]. Intelligence Cycle is a representation of how the contemporary Intelligence is organized and proceeds. Although, when compared to reality, such representation does not seem very accurate, it certainly helps to discuss on Intelligence Analysis and on how to support its different phases (Phythian 2013). The Intelligence Cycle is typically structured into five phases: Planning/Direction, Collection, Processing, Analysis/Production, Dissemination (see Fig. 2.2). More in detail, the roles of the five phases are the following ones:

- **Planning/Direction**. This phase is the beginning of the process because needs and requirements for Intelligence products are specified. Such phase is also the end of the process (which underlines the start of a new process) because the Intelligence products could generate new needs (and/or requirements).
- **Collection**. In this phase, raw data is gathered from several and heterogeneous sources (open sources, secret sources, technical collection as electronic and satellite photos, etc.).
- **Processing**. Such phase foresees the transformation of the (huge) amount of data collected to meaningful representations that are readable and usable by the analysts.
- **Analysis/Production**. In this phase, basic information, coming as a result from the previous phase, is converted into finished Intelligence. It includes integrating, evaluating, and analyzing all available information (which is often fragmentary and even contradictory) and preparing Intelligence products. Information reliability, validity, and relevance are also checked during this phase. Moreover information fragments are integrated into a coherent whole and opportunely contextualized to produce the finished Intelligence.
- **Dissemination**. This is the last step of the cycle and logically feeds into the first phase. Dissemination is the distribution of the finished Intelligence to the consumers, i.e., the ones who provided needs and requirements. Finished Intelligence is now used to support decision making and elicit further requirements triggering the Intelligence Cycle.

In other terms, the Intelligence Cycle is enacted to reduce the uncertainty in order to support and inform decision-makers (from the operational to the political level). Adopting a data perspective, Collection, Processing and Analysis/Production phases provide a pipeline in which multiple raw data are firstly collected from relevant sources (Collection) and subsequently organized and enriched in useful structures (Processing) that, in turn, become information needed to be integrated, contextualized

[2] Definition from CIA Factbook on Intelligence, Office of Public Affairs, Central Intelligence Agency (October 1993).

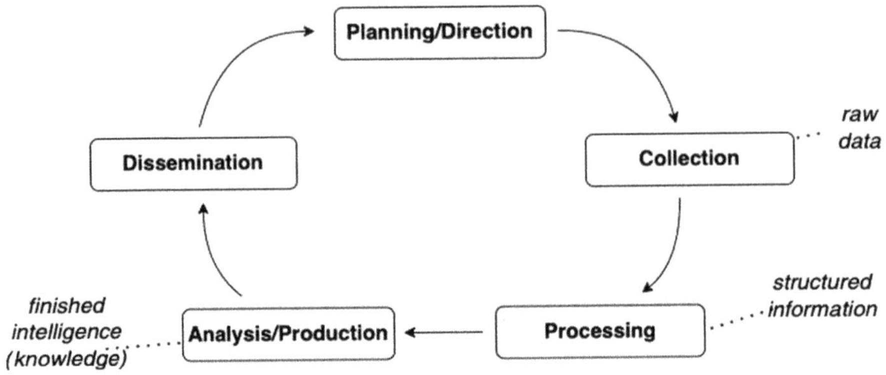

Fig. 2.2 Intelligence cycle

and further analyzed (Analysis/Production) to form Intelligence products (knowledge) able to reduce uncertainty in decision-making processes (Lim 2011).

As mentioned, the Intelligence Cycle is the most common view of the Intelligence process. However, there exist alternatives that can be considered both as alternative or complementary.

Starting from the consideration that Intelligence is always concerned with a target, Clark (2019) defines a target-centric approach to the Intelligence process. In his work, Clark argues that the traditional cycle model is limited with respect to opportunity for contributors or customers to ask questions or provide feedback since it separates collectors, processors and analysts. According to Clark (2019), Intelligence is a non-linear, interactive and target-centric process where analysts, collectors and processors collaborate and concentrate on the target and on the issues of the target. Therefore, the target is the focus of Intelligence (e.g., a terrorist organization) and it can be modeled as a complex systems since it is non-linear, dynamic and evolving. A target can be usually structurally represented as a dynamic network that is opposed to another network, i.e., the analytic network of the Intelligence community. Depending on the specific target, a target-centric approach foresees the adoption of one or more of the Intelligence sources mentioned in the previous section.

2.5 The Analysis Process and Analytic Tradecraft

The analysis process starts from the understanding of the customer issue that, in case, can be decomposed in less complex sub-issues. In a next phase, the target of the analysis is identified, modeled and populated with the information gathered from sources of Intelligence. During these activities, the analyst is supported by a set of methods and techniques.

The set of methods and techniques used in Intelligence analysis activities is typically called Analytic Tradecraft. An example of this body of methods is the Structured Analytic Techniques (SAT) described by Heuer (1999) and Pherson and Heuer (2020).

In general, four kinds of analytic methods can be distinguished: (i) *Expert judgment* is a traditional form of individual analysis based on the analyst's expertise, (ii) *Quantitative methods using expert generated data* that rely on data generation through modeling, simulation, Bayesian inference and so on, (iii) *Quantitative methods using empirical data* such as data generated by sensors, and (iv) *Structured Analysis* that is a collaborative process. This last one is the category to which SAT belong to.

A Structured Analysis is a step-by-step process for analyzing incomplete, ambiguous, and deceptive information. The application of a Structured Analysis allows to break a problem into its component parts and specify which process can handle these parts. Furthermore, these techniques ensure that preconceptions and assumptions are not taken for granted.

SAT have the main objective of supporting the externalization of internal thought processes so that the results can be shared and analyzed also by other analysts. A classification of SAT is reported in the CIA Tradecraft Primer (2009) that organizes the techniques in Diagnostic, Contrarian, and Imaginative Thinking: "*diagnostic techniques are aimed at making analytic arguments, assumptions, or Intelligence gaps more transparent; contrarian techniques explicitly challenge current thinking; and imaginative thinking techniques aim at developing new insights, different perspectives and/or develop alternative outcomes*" (Primer 2009).

Figure 2.3 shows an overview of the SAT grouped by their categories in Diagnostic, Contrarian and Imaginative. These categories correspond to the functions that SAT must support:

- Diagnostic techniques have to instill rigor in confirming current beliefs. This can be done by making analytic argument, checking assumptions, comparing hypotheses.
- Contrarian techniques have to purpose to challenge and re-framing current mindset. This can be done, for instance, by using techniques such as Team A/Team B or the Devil's advocacy. These techniques essentially leverage on one or more analysts that provide alternative and contradicting viewpoints of stated and unstated assumptions and others analysts that defend the original viewpoints.
- Imaginative techniques are aimed at developing creative and alternative insight such as alternative scenarios and/or different perspectives. Usually, this can be done using structured processes (e.g., Brainstorming) to stimulate new thinking with members of the process that, first, generate new ideas, scenarios, hypotheses (including also non obvious ones) and, then, try to converge in ranking these ideas, scenarios, hypotheses and identifying the most important ones.

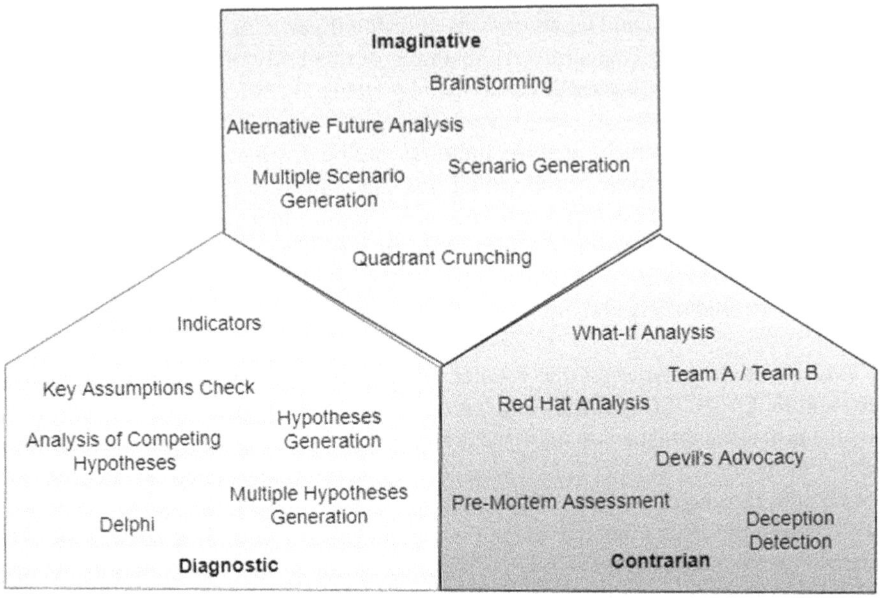

Fig. 2.3 An overview of SAT

2.5.1 *Families of SAT*

Heuer (1999) categorizes SAT into different families. In the following, families and the most adopted techniques in each family are summarized:

- Decomposition and Visualization. These techniques are devoted to simplify a complex problem by: *(i)* decomposing it into smaller parts that can be considered and analyzed separately and *(ii)* visualize these parts in an organized manner with some types of maps or graphs to facilitate the comprehension of how the parts are related among them. In this family several techniques fall: Network Analysis (used in counter-terrorism, protection of critical infrastructures, map and analyze relationships among people, groups, organizations), Mind and Concept Maps (that are graphic representations of how an individual or a group thinks about a topic of interest or a problem), Matrices (tools to sort and organize data in a way that allows their comparison and analysis), Timelines and GANTT (used to organize information on events or actions to understand the sequence of events and to identify key events) and several checklists that, usually, are evaluated at the beginning of an Intelligence analysis project (e.g., Initial Checklist, Customer Checklist, Issue Redefinition).
- Idea Generation. This family of techniques aims at facilitating the emergence of new and non-obvious ideas with the support of collaborative tools. The most adopted techniques of this family are Brainstorming (and its variants, such as Structured Brainstorming), Starbursting (that is focused on generating questions,

rather than eliciting ideas or answers, and visualizing the Who? What? When? Where? Why? And How? in a six points star) and Quadrant Crunching (that aims at listing the key assumptions of a project and compare with their opposites to generate a complete list of alternative outcomes).

- Scenarios and Indicators. These techniques allow analysts to identify and monitor scenarios in order to understand which scenario is developing. The techniques include Scenario Analysis (a method that forces the analysts at identifying multiple and alternative ways in which a situation might evolve and helping in reducing uncertainty), Indicators (that are observable phenomena or events associated to the scenarios with the purpose of seeking early warning signals of undesirable events and measure change toward an undesirable condition) and Indicators Validation (to assess the diagnostic power of an indicator. Usually, an indicator is diagnostic when it clearly point to a scenario).
- Hypotheses Generation and Testing. The purpose of these techniques is to support analysts in a core function of the Intelligence Analysis: the generation and testing of hypotheses. Hypotheses generation is the primary technique of this family that support analysts with the types of generation: simple hypotheses, multiple hypotheses and quadrant hypotheses. Simple hypotheses refer to the generation of a individual hypotheses. In general, a good hypothesis has some features such as: it is written as a definite statement not as a question, it is based on observations and knowledge, it must be testable and falsifiable, it must include a depended variable (i.e., the phenomenon to explain) and an independent one (i.e., the variable that explains). Multiple hypotheses generation differs from simple generation in that it is focused on generating mutually exclusive lists of hypotheses and their possible permutations and Quadrant hypothesis generation is a more sophisticated approach to generate four potential scenarios that represent the extreme conditions of two major drivers. The Analysis of Competing Hypotheses (ACH) is an important technique of this family. ACH allows to identify a set of mutually exclusive explanations of a phenomenon (i.e., the hypotheses), assessing the consistency or inconsistency of each item of evidence with each hypothesis, and selecting the hypothesis that best fits the evidence. The basic idea is, however, to refuse the hypotheses that are less consistent with the evidence rather than confirm the hypotheses that are more consistent with the evidence. Lastly, Deception Detection is a technique belonging to this family that allows analyst to assess the possibility of deception by an adversary. This technique is based on a step-by-step process allowing the analyst to avoid over-reliance on a single source of information, to look for material and concrete evidence, identify situations where on sources initially appears correct but later turns out to be wrong, and other steps that are devoted to assess potential deceiver. In this process, the analyst can be supported by several checklists.
- Assessment of Cause and Effect. These techniques have the objective of assessing the cause of current events and forecast effects that might happen in the future. Key Assumptions Check is an important technique of this family. This technique enforces analytical judgments by forcing the analyst to systematically question the assumptions that guide an interpretation of evidence or the reasoning about a

problem. Structured Analogies is a reasoning technique based on analogy allowing to compare a situation with multiple potential analogies and selecting the one for which the circumstances are most similar. Red Hat Analysis is focused on perceive threats and opportunities by using a different hat (i.e., as other persons can see them) and Outside-in-Thinking forces the analyst to identify what can be outside an area of interest (e.g., political, economic, technological, social forces and trends) but can have impact and affect the issue under analysis.

- Challenge Analysis. This family refers to a set of techniques devoted to challenge current mind-set with three types of challenges: Self Critique, Critique of others, Critique by others. In this family, most adopted techniques are: Pre-mortem Analysis that supports an analyst in reducing the risk of analytic failure by identifying and analyzing a potential failure before it occurs; What-I? Analysis to informs analysts on event that could happen, if some conditions change or develop, even if the event seems unlikely; High Impact/Low Probability Analysis that is used analyze low-probability events and situations that could have, if developed, high-impact; Devil's Advocacy that is a contrarian technique by which a different analyst takes the role of the Devil's Advocate and makes the best possible case against a proposed analytic judgment; Red Team Analysis that is a type of analysis devoted to challenge conventional wisdom about how an adversary or competitor thinking about an issue; Delphi Method that is a traditional process to generate ideas and opinions from a geographically dispersed panel of experts.
- Conflict Management. The objective is to encourage, manage and govern conflicts of opinions. With these techniques, conflicts can be a learning experience. Adversarial Collaboration is a set techniques belonging to this family. They seek to find an agreement between opposing parties on how they have to work in teams to resolve their differences and to gain a better understanding of how and why they differ. Structured Debate in a type of debate that forces debaters in refusing the opposing argument rather than supporting their own.
- Decision Support. As the name of this family suggests, these techniques support decision making. They are necessary since human cognitive processes (e.g., short-term memory) presents limitations that do not allow to keep trace of all the pros and cons of multiple options at the same time. So, decision support procedures such as Decision matrices, the development of complex computer models and simulations, and SWOT (Strengths, Weaknesses, Opportunities, Threats) Analysis to develop a plan or strategy for achieving a specified goal can support the analyst. Decision support techniques, in general, can support several techniques of the above described families. In fact, decision support techniques help overcome the short-term memory cognitive limitation by laying out all the options and interrelationships in graphic form to test alternative options. In this respect, they are closely related with all the techniques mentioned above.

SAT provide a range of systematic approaches to consider and assess alternative assumptions in Intelligence Analysis so that analysts can overcome limitation from perceptual and cognitive biases. SAT may also support analysts in making sense from big volumes of data that can be ambiguous, contradictory, and misleading. A question, however, can be: what type of SAT to use and when?

2.5.2 *Adoption of SAT in the Intelligence Analysis Process*

An experienced Analyst has the ability to use the correct technique at the most appropriate stage of the analysis process. As example, Clark (2019) suggests the adoption of Key Assumption Check and Brainstorming in the first phases of a process, when issues have to be comprehended and decomposed. In Primer (2009), it is reported a similar suggestion for the adoption of these two techniques at the beginning of an Intelligence project. Key Assumptions Check belongs to the diagnostic techniques and is devoted to list and revise the key working assumptions on which fundamental judgments rest. Brainstorming, instead, is considered as an imaginative thinking technique and is a group process designed to generate new ideas and concepts. Their combination helps an analyst make sure that important factors and key assumptions are not overlooked or taken for granted, and that new assumptions can be properly challenged and evaluated.

An important phase of the analysis process is the evaluation of evidence and hypotheses. To this purpose, SAT provide large number of methodologies. The Analysis of Competing Hypotheses is a good method that can be used along all the analysis process to systematically evaluate evidence that are consistent or not consistent with a set of hypotheses, and discard those hypotheses that contains more inconsistent data. Hypotheses testing can be done also with the support of contrarian technique to challenge the conventional line that is developed.

Denial and deception are key issues to be managed during the analysis process. The first term refers to activities devoted to deny access to information sources or, in general, to accurate information. The second term refers to activities devoted to deceive causing someone to accept as true (or valid) something that is false (or wrong). In evaluating evidence, thus, the analyst must consider the fact that this data and information may be deliberative provided by an opponent with misleading or harmful purposes. Clark (2019) proposes defensive strategies against denial and deception that involves the protection of sources of Intelligence such as OSINT and HUMINT. Techniques and methods to detect possible deception and denial strategies by an adversary are part of SAT. It is the case, for instance, of the Quality of Information Check that is a diagnostic technique used to evaluates completeness and soundness of available information sources.

The timeline proposed in Primer (2009) is shown in Fig. 2.4. From Fig. 2.4, it can be observed that an Intelligence Analysis project usually starts with creative thinking based on Contrarian Techniques (Brainstorming) since are useful at the beginning to analyze the problem statement and assumptions that are checked with

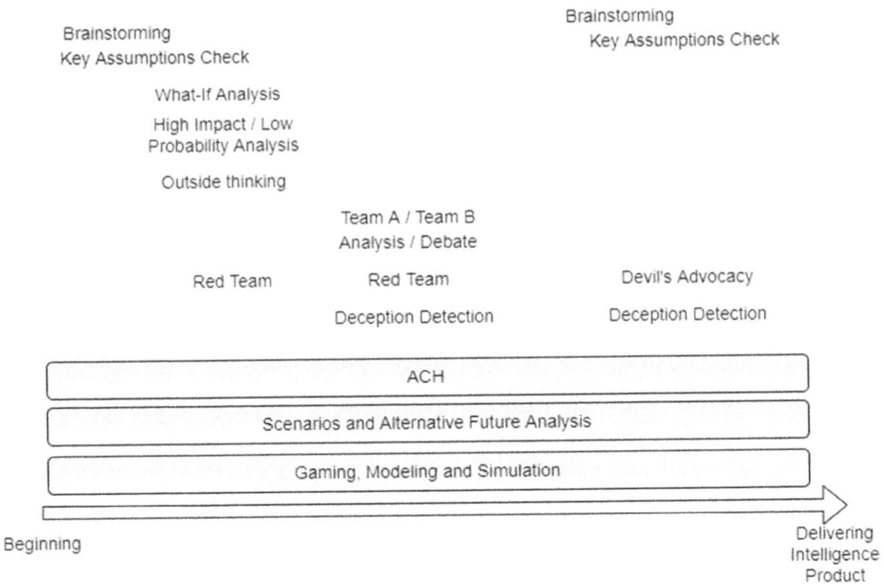

Fig. 2.4 A timeline of SAT [(our elaboration from Primer (2009)]

Key Assumptions check. The Analysis of Competing Hypotheses can be used in all the phases of the project to highlight evidence that is most "discriminating" in making an analytic argument. As the analysis process is being to be finalized, in Primer (2009) is suggested to re-use Key Assumptions Check and Brainstorming as a final check on the underlying logic of the analysis, and to challenge the final products with contrarian techniques. SAT can be complemented with more sophisticated techniques such as Gaming, Modeling, and Simulation.

The Analytic Tradecraft has been the subject of discussion, also in consideration of the failure of Intelligence after the attacks of 9/11 (Marchio 2014) and SAT have been the subject of studies aimed at their restructuring (Chang et al. 2018). In general, the same concept of Intelligence Analysis has been revised for some time also in the light of new technological advances (Odom 2008). A discussion of this aspect is carried out in the Sect. 2.6 of this chapter. For now it is sufficient to highlight the one of the main advantages of using a sounded Analytic Tradecraft for Intelligence analysis consists in reducing the cognitive traps related to the analysis.

2.5.3 *Cognitive and Perceptual Biases*

Heuer (1999) emphasizes the pitfalls in Intelligence analysis due to the so-called cognitive traps that are cognitive and perceptual biases that can affect human judgment and decisions. Heuer argues that mental models (also called mindset) influence the way individuals assimilate and evaluate information and, also, what information the analyst is prone to accept. As clearly reported in Primer (2009), mental models have some risks such as expectations (i.e., the analysts perceive what they expect to perceive), resistance to change (i.e., a formed mental model is difficult to change), erroneous assimilation of new information in formed mental models, dismissing conflicting information.

Some cognitive traps resemble the demons of Situation Awareness (SA demons) discussed in Sect. 3.3.1. This is, for instance, the case of Target Fixation that presents analogy with the SA demon of Attention Tunneling. However, some cognitive traps are directly relates to Intelligence analysis activities. In the following, it is reported a brief overview of the main ones analyzed by Heuer (1999).

Perceptual Biases refer to systematic errors that disrupt and distort the perceptual process leading, thus, to erroneous decision making. These biases includes Expectations (i.e., individuals tend to perceive what they expect to perceive), Resistance (i.e., perceptions are hard to change even in the light of new evidence) and Ambiguities (i.e., an exposure to ambiguous stimuli interferes with accurate perception).

Biases in Perceiving Causality refer to the order expected by a mental model. These biases include rationality that tends to exclude, from the explanation of an event, randomness, accidents and errors.

Biases in Estimating Probabilities that include Availability (i.e., a wrong estimation of probabilities for similar events), Anchoring (i.e., a wrong estimation of probabilities influenced by a reference point or anchor) and Overconfidence (i.e., a wring estimation of probabilities due to overconfidence in a particular situation).

Biases in Evaluating Evidence that include Consistency (i.e., a wrong evaluation of evidence due to the fact that conclusions are drawn from a small body of consistent data rather than from a larger body of less consistent data) and Discredited Evidence (i.e., even if the evidence satisfying a perception are proved to be wrong, the perception is resistant to change).

Intelligence analysts question their mind-sets by applying analytic techniques to make explicit and expose their assumptions so that cognitive traps can be avoided.

2.6 Some Challenges of Intelligence Analysis

Modern Intelligence Analysis is characterized by a combination of traditional and innovative aspects. As Weinbaum and Shanahan (2018) state: "*the best Intelligence analysis derives from the right combination of art and science. The art of Intelligence may be the same today as it was 2000 years ago. What is different now, however, is the necessity of getting much better much faster at the science of the tradecraft, which is centered on data. Analysts must have the tools they need to deal with massive amounts of information that enable them to close Intelligence gaps and enable better operational outcomes at the speed of data.*" From this it can be deduced that Intelligence analysis, today, is aimed at innovating art (that is, traditional methods and techniques) with recent technological advancements such as data-driven technologies. It must be considered that, if this combination is not well balanced, Intelligence analysis can lead to failures. In fact, one of the typical problems of current data-driven technologies consists of information overload that is not always able to reduce the information gap, i.e., the distance that exists between the gathered information and the analysts needs..

Weinbaum and Shanahan (2018) report an example of failure due to information overload and emphasize how "*in a more data-oriented era, it is increasingly possible to draw Intelligence of value from the data in aggregate (temporal and geospatial behavior patterns, for example). This can result in an ironic dilemma in which there is too much data for humans to search effectively for needles, yet not enough accessible data from which to draw and validate useful Intelligence*".

Information overload can cause the activation of some cognitive traps described above. For this reason, modern Intelligence analysis requires new types of models, techniques and tools to minimize the risks associated with decision biases and cognitive traps.

Furthermore, as Clark (2019) reports, there can be several sources of failure for Intelligence analysis such as failure to share information, to analyze collected material objectively and of the customer to act on Intelligence. While the failure of analyzing collected material in a correct way and objectively may be due to cognitive biases or wrong mindset and mental models, the other sources of failure are connected to a poor situational awareness of the actors involved in the Intelligence Analysis process. In the case of failure to share information, there is a poor situational awareness among the members of a team while in the case of failure of the customer to act on Intelligence it appears clear that the decision-makers has not acquired a correct comprehension of the situation.

SAT are valid techniques for Intelligence analysis. However, as noted by Haines and Leggett (2003), single minded attention to these techniques runs the risk of reducing the Intelligence analysis to a mechanical processes focused on gathering and processing right data to satisfy customers' needs. So it emerges the need to contextualize data into a more comprehensive model for Intelligence analysis. This is also the effort done by Clark (2019) in the definition of his target-centric approach.

The author of this book found this model in the Situational Awareness model defined by Endsley (1995b). In other words, the idea underlying this book is to use the Endsley's model to guide the whole process and to methodologically rule the integration of the computational techniques, and their execution, to support the Intelligence Analysis.

The computational techniques, which are reported in Chaps. 5, 6, 7, 8, make use of the Granular Computing paradigm and formal methods for decision making in conditions of uncertain and imprecise information. On the basis of these methods, which are described in the following Chap. 3, some analysis techniques will be implemented such as, for example, What-If analysis and Scenario analysis and applied in case studies related to Intelligence Analysis.

Chapter 3
Foundations of the Computational Techniques

The chapter aims at providing the foundational concepts and information to understand the computational techniques and the main paradigms adopted by the approaches described in the book. The common factor to these techniques is the increase in the situational awareness of the operators during the intelligence analysis cycle in order to improve the quality of decision-making. For this reason, this chapter begins with the description of the concept of Situation Awareness (SA) and the Mica Endlsey model of Situation Awareness (Endsley 1995b) and then continues with the description of Granular Computing (Zadeh 1997; Bargiela and Pedrycz 2016; Yao 2005) which enables information processing and approximate reasoning mechanisms to make rapid decision making in operational situations. The chapter continues with the description of the formal methods for Granular Computing, mainly those related to the treatment of uncertain and imprecise information, and then concludes with a hands-on section that allows readers to practice with tutorials.

3.1 Learning Objectives of the Chapter

This is key chapter of this book. In this chapter, the reader will understand the core concepts and methods that represent the foundations of the methodology (in Chap. 4) and of the computational techniques (in Chaps. 5, 6, 7 and 8) of this book.

Four pillars form the foundation of what follows in this book and they are: (1) Situation Awareness, (2) Granular Computing, (3) Rough and Fuzzy sets theories and (4) Three-Way decisions models.

The specific Learning Objectives of this chapter are:

- Describe and discuss the main concepts of Situation Awareness.
- Using the Goal-Directed Task Analysis to develop Situation Awareness requirements.

V. Loia et al., *Computational Techniques for Intelligence Analysis*,
https://doi.org/10.1007/978-3-031-20851-5_3

- Describe the main features of the Granular Computing.
- Describe and discuss the main concepts of Rough and Fuzzy sets theories.
- Select the proper theory to deal with a specific type of information uncertainty.
- Describe and discuss the main concepts of Three-Way decisions models.
- Execute python code for granulation operations with equivalence classes.
- Execute python code for fuzzy set operations such as fuzzyfication and evaluation of fuzzy relations.
- Use and Implement Three-Way decisions models with Rough Sets and Probabilistic Rough Sets.
- Experiment different implementation for Three-Way decisions models based on Rough Sets and Probabilistic rough Sets models and analyze different outcomes.

The first six points refers to level 2 (Understand) of the revised taxonomy of bloom (see Fig. 1.2), the last point to the level 4 (Analyze) and the others to the level 3 (Apply).

3.2 Topic Map of the Chapter

The topic map of this chapter is shown in Fig. 3.1. The chapter mainly focuses on three topics: Situation Awareness, Granular Computing and methodologies to deal with imprecise and uncertain information. With respect to the first topic, the chapter describes the Endsley's model of SA, the Goal-Directed Task Analysis method to derive SA requirements and introduces the so-called SA demons which, as can be seen from the link highlighted by the dotted line of the map, have links with the cognitive and perceptual biases described in Chap. 2. With respect to Granular Computing, the chapter introduces the fundamental concepts of this paradigm and then focuses on the triarchic description of Granular Computing to show its relationship with the SAT families described in Chap. 2. Finally, the third topic concerning the methodologies for the treatment of imprecise and uncertain information presents the Rough and Fuzzy sets theories. Also this topic is, in some way, related to Granular Computing as Fuzzy and Rough sets can be seen as formal settings for the creation of information granules.

3.3 Situation Awareness

Situation Awareness or Situational Awareness (SA) is defined by Endsley (1995b) as "*the perception of elements in the environment within a volume of time and space, the comprehension of their meaning, and the projection of their status in the near future*" and is recognized as a key factor to make decisions in operational situations within heterogeneous contexts like, for instance, civil and military sectors. The above definition of SA is divided into three parts: perception of elements in the environment,

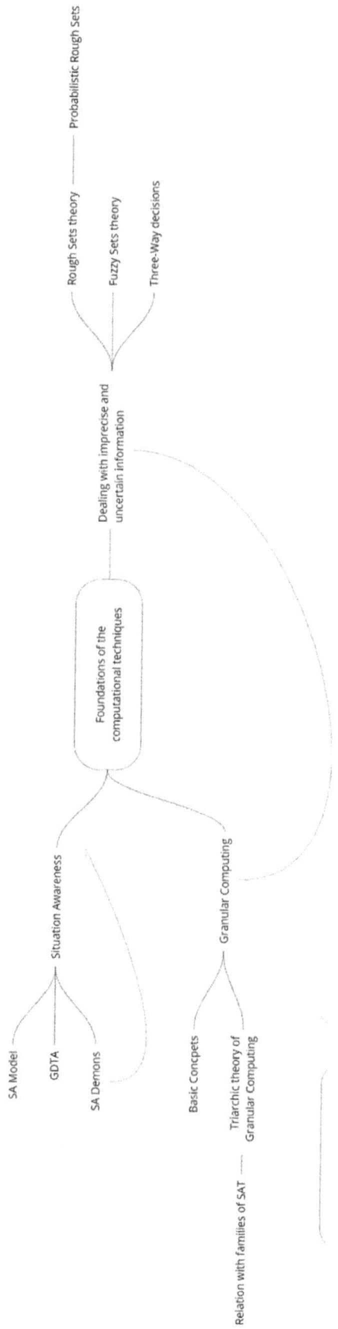

Fig. 3.1 Topic map of the chapter

their understanding in the context of a concept called "*situation*", and their projection into the near future. Endsley, in her SA model (Endsley, Bolte, and Jones 2003), systematizes these three parts and introduces three levels of SA:

- (i) Level 1, also referred to as "Perception", that relates to the immediate perception of the elements of the environment,
- (ii) Level 2, also referred to as "Comprehension", in which a human operator comprehends the current situation in relation to her goals and objectives,
- (iii) Level 3, also referred to as "Projection", in which the operator has the capacity to forecast the evolution of the current situation.

These three levels contribute to the incremental growth of the operators' SA: in order to have SA at level 2 it is necessary to have a good degree of awareness at level 1 and, similarly, SA at level 3 requires correct awareness at level 2. In other words, to comprehend a situation it is required a correct perception of the elements of an environment, and to predict the evolution of a situation it is required a correct comprehension. The process by which SA is created relies on cognitive capabilities of analysis and synthesis. At level 1 the elements of the environment are perceived by themselves, in an isolated way, to then be aggregated and related to the goals of an operator so as to result in an abstraction called situation. Typically, the human operator's goals are related to the task (or tasks) she is executing. A situation (abstraction) is the core of level 2 and, if the operator has knowledge of the phenomena that comprise it, predictions can be made at level 3.

The terms "operator" and "human operator" are used indistinguishably in this section. However, it is interesting to note that in the context of SA such terms are used in reference to human operators executing complex tasks like, for instance, piloting a military aircraft. This is due to the historical roots of the studies on SA. Although it is important to consider such roots, it is also fundamental to remember that the tasks in which SA is crucial are also daily (and apparently) simple tasks like, for instance, crossing a road: i) perception of simple elements like cars or other vehicles which are relevant for achieving the goal, road signs, etc., ii) comprehension of the current situation related to the possibility to cross the road safety by assigning the correct meaning to the perceived elements, and iii) projecting the current situation in the future in order to understand if during the estimating crossing time the road will be safe by predicting the vehicle positions along the considered time interval. As the reader has observed, although crossing the road is a common tasks for people, it foresees complex cognitive activities.

In some cases, as reported by Endsley (1995b), shortcuts are possible for which an operator can, for instance, directly acquire SA at level 2 or simplify the cognitive work at all the three levels of SA. This is due to the role played by external and internal factors of the Endsley model such as mental models, expectations, automaticity. Mental models are useful to guide the attention to relevant aspects of the situation, to integrate and assign meaning to the perceived information and to project the current state of affairs to future states. Mental models simplify the formation of SA and allows to execute numerous common tasks by spending a very low cognitive effort. Expectations, due to mental models, prior experiences, instructions, etc., influence the formation of SA by guiding the attention of people to see what they expect to see. Thus, expectations simplify the formation of SA when the employed mental models are correct but they could have a negative effect when incorrect mental models have been activated. Automaticity is another mechanism developed with experience that can influence situation awareness. This mechanism allows good performance in achieving SA with low levels of attention in well understood (typically known) environments. Automaticity can negatively impact SA when novel (with respect to the known environments) stimuli or information become fundamental for SA.

As anticipated before, the human operator's task (or goal) guide the formation of SA. Moreover, is could also characterize the type of SA to deal with. For instance, if the operator is a pilot, the different categories of SA could be:

- Geographical SA, e.g., location of own aircraft, path to desired locations;
- Spatial/Temporal SA, e.g., altitude, flight path, projected flight path, projected landing time;
- System SA, e.g., system status, system functioning and settings;
- Environmental SA, e.g., weather conditions, projected weather conditions, flight safety;
- Tactical SA, e.g., location and flight dynamics of other aircraft, threat prioritization, mission timing and status.

The above examples are in the military domain but could be easily moved to different domains. In general, such categorization is particularly important to understand that SA is typically represented as a process but it is also described as a product used to help decision-making activities.

In such activities, SA is fundamental to make qualitative decisions and it is interesting to note that decision-making should be considered a separate phase from the three levels of SA. This vision is motivated by the fact that a suitable level of SA does not necessarily lead to a good decision. Someone could achieve very high levels of SA and make poor quality decisions. Such considerations are useful to design coherent architectures for decision support systems based on SA. For example, a military aircraft pilot could achieve optimal levels of SA but she could execute an erroneous maneuver or a man who wants to cross a road could correctly understand the dangerous situation and still try to carry out the action.

3.3.1 SA Demons

As already discussed in the above sections, SA is recognized as a key successful factor for decision making. Decision making, mainly under risk, suffers of cognitive biases (Tversky and Kahneman 1974) and this is even more true for what concerns the application sector analyzed in this book, namely intelligence analysis (Odom 2008). In addition to cognitive biases, SA suffers of its specific enemies: the so-called SA demons (Endsley et al. 2003):

- *Attentional tunneling* refers to the fact that human operators typically lock in on certain aspects or features of the environment they are trying to process and will either intentionally or inadvertently drop their scanning behavior. Achieving a good level of SA may be very good on the part of environment they are concentrating on, but will quickly become outdated on the aspects they have stopped attending to.
- *Requisite memory trap* is the SA demon of the working memory. Working memory is a short-term memory that act as a central repository where features of the current situation are brought together and processed into a meaningful picture of what is happening. However, this memory has some limits in terms of the maximum number of piece of information that is capable to store and process. Given the complexity and sheer volume of information required for SA in many systems, it is no wonder that memory limits create a significant SA bottleneck.
- *Workload, anxiety, fatigue, and other stressors* are factors that can significantly strain SA. Definitely, these factors undermine SA by making the entire process of taking in information less systematic and more error prone. So, it is important to design systems to support effective, efficient intake of needed information to maintain high level of SA.
- *Data overload* is a significant problem in many domains. The rapid rate at which data changes creates a need for information intake that quickly outpaces the ability of person's sensory and cognitive system to supply that need. In this case, human brain is a bottleneck but by designing systems to enhance SA, significant problems with data overload can be reduced.
- *Misplaced salience* refers to the compellingness of certain forms of information that can be, in some cases, directed just and only to the main goal. Misplaced salience may be difficult to control and, with respect to SA systems, information filtering and properties such as movement or color can be used to draw attention to critical and highly important information.
- *Complexity creep* is directly depended from data overload and refers to the availability of numerous and heterogeneous devices and sensors to take into account. Complexity can slow down the ability of people to take in information. This demon works to undermine human ability to correctly interpret the information presented and to project what is likely to happen (i.e., levels 2 and 3 of SA).
- *Errant mental models* result, as the previous demon, in poor comprehension at level 2 and projection at level 3. Mental models are shortcuts for SA that tell to a person how to combine disparate pieces of information, and how to develop reasonable projections of what will happen in the future. However, if mental models are wrong, operators may misunderstand information because they believe that the system is in one mode when it is really in another.
- *Out-of-the-loop syndrome* is a SA demon related to automation. Automation can undermine SA by taking people out-of-the-loop. In this state they develop poor SA on both how the automation is performing and the state of the elements the automation is supposed to be controlling.

The SA demons can be reduced by designing software systems that follows the SA principles (Endsley et al. 2003). Among other things, the computational techniques that are described in the latter chapters of the book aim at reducing some of the SA demons.

3.3.2 Information Processing for SA

Once understood the importance of SA for both simple and complex human tasks, the focus is on the possibility to design and develop information processing approaches to support SA. In other words, the idea is to implement systems able to sustain the formation of SA at the three levels of the Endsley's Model and, consequently, to provide outcomes able to support decision-making processes. Such support is required, for instance, when it is needed to consider large and complex environments producing huge amount of heterogeneous data with different velocity and different degrees of veracity. In such a scenario, all the three levels of SA need to be sustained by technologies. For example, sensors can be employed to gather raw data from the environment of interest and help human operators at the Perception level. Classification or clustering algorithms could be useful to assign the correct meaning to such data at the Comprehension level. Lastly, predictive analytics could be employed to support the Projection level. Additional techniques could be requested to clean raw data, to organize it and to deal with streams. Definitely, non-trivial data pipelines have to be architected for helping people to achieve suitable levels of SA. Furthermore, such pipelines should consider one of the main challenges related to data (but also to SA): uncertainty. Uncertainty is recognizable at different levels:

- **Data uncertainty**. At this level, sensors measurements could have some errors associated with them. These errors contribute to the degree of uncertainty of perceived data. In particular, it is possible to recognize several types of uncertainty: missing information, reliability/credibility of data, incongruent/conflicting data, timeliness of data and ambiguous or noisy data. Missing data, for instance, is common in military scenarios where the enemy hides or denies relevant information. But missing data is also a problem in the healthcare domain where the lack of patients' past medical history is commonly experienced. Sensors or persons sometimes are not 100% reliable. In fact, some sensors could function poorly in specific conditions (e.g., cloud cover or high humidity levels). A related aspect is the accuracy that is a characteristic of the specific sensor. For instance, GPS (Global Positioning Systems report an object location within 50ft. Reliability and accuracy are causes of incongruent and conflicting data. For example, two sensors with different levels of accuracy could provide different data when observing the same phenomenon. Moreover, low frequencies of observations could provide data when the observed phenomenon has already changed. Lastly, some contexts are noisy and ambiguous and, as a consequence, collected data are uncertain. Within

a battlefield, tanks and vehicles could be camouflaged and their detection could be obstructed.
- **Comprehension uncertainty**. At this level, perceived data are aggregated or classified in order to provide an interpretation of their meanings. Uncertainty in the results of such tasks, due to the quality of data or algorithms processing them, could be introduced.
- **Projection uncertainty**. At this level, uncertainty is introduced by the uncertainty of underlying data and operations but also by the ability to predict future behaviors and events. In some cases, good mental models can be useful to reduce the uncertainty.
- **Decision uncertainty**. At this level, the uncertainty is strictly related to the confidence that a specific course of actions will produce the desired outcome.

3.3.3 Goal-Directed Task Analysis

Design and implementation of information processing approaches to support SA and SA-oriented reasoning requires suitable analysis methodologies. Endsley et al. (2003) propose the Goal-Directed Task Analysis (GDTA) as a method to elicit information requirements for situational awareness. GDTA is a cognitive analysis which focuses on the goals an operator must achieve and the information requirements that are needed to make appropriate decisions. Information is, step-by-step, decomposed until reaching finer elements that cannot be further decomposed. GDTA focuses on dynamic information requirements rather than static system knowledge, i.e. it considers the information, needed to perform well a specific task, that has to be acquired and analyzed by the operator in a certain domain during the execution of such task. The needs for this information are called SA requirements. Figure 3.2 shows how the results of a GDTA analysis can be organized into a hierarchical structure that, following a top-down approach, allows to decompose a major goal into several sub-goal and to associate decisions to each sub-goal. For each decision to be made, SA information requirements are elicited.

The GDTA structure is, therefore, a necessary tool for supporting operational situations. It allows to understand what information to acquire to increase situation awareness at all levels of the Endsley's model and contextualize it to decisions and goals.

It is important to highlight an aspect relating to information processing. Indeed, it may seem that the top-down nature of the GDTA structure supports only this type of information processing, i.e. top-down or goal-driven. Nothing could be more wrong. The GDTA structure represents a snapshot of the links that exist between SA requirements, decisions and goals. This also supports a bottom-up or data-driven approach to information processing allowing, among other things, an operator to understand that a sub-goal is becoming more or less important as some elements of the environment change.

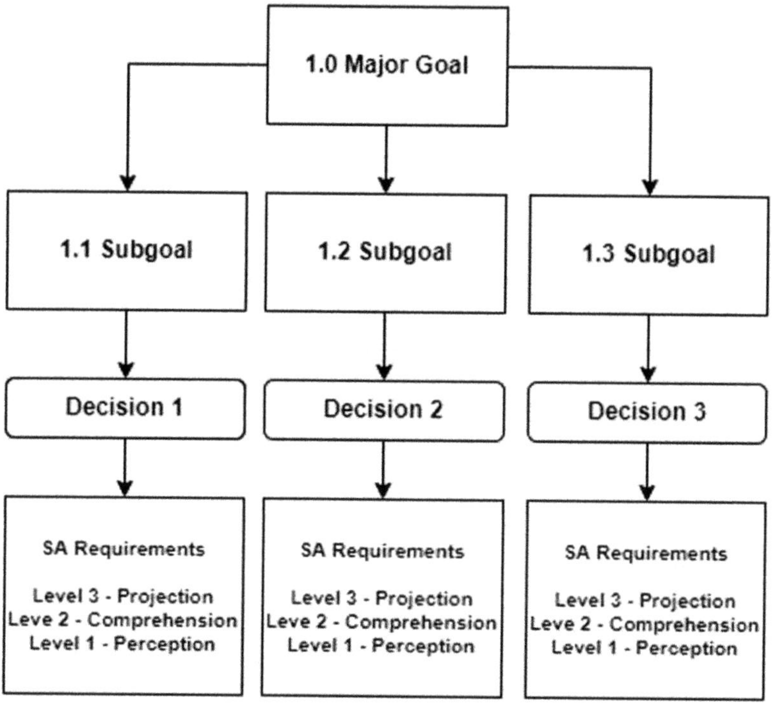

Fig. 3.2 GDTA

As will be clarified in later chapters of the book, computational techniques to support intelligence analyses leverage both of these types of information processing.

3.3.3.1 An Example of GDTA

It is possible now to describe how a GDTA can be created. Figure 3.3 shows the steps to create a GDTA.

Step 1 is devoted to create the Goal Structure. In this step, a group of domain experts identify the major goals and its sub-goals. A constrain for the creation of the GDTA goal structure is that there is not a goal sequencing or prioritization. The product of this step is a structure of goal and sub-goals.

Step 2 has the objective of determining decisions for each goal or sub-goal. Decisions can be framed as questions (e.g., for a goal related to assessing trajectory of a vessel), a decision can be framed as a question such as: Which trajectory requires minimum time to travel?

Step 3 requires to identify the information requirements associated to each decision and goal. The requirements are divided in perception (SA Level 1), comprehension (SA Level 2) and projection (SA Level 3). A practical way to classify the

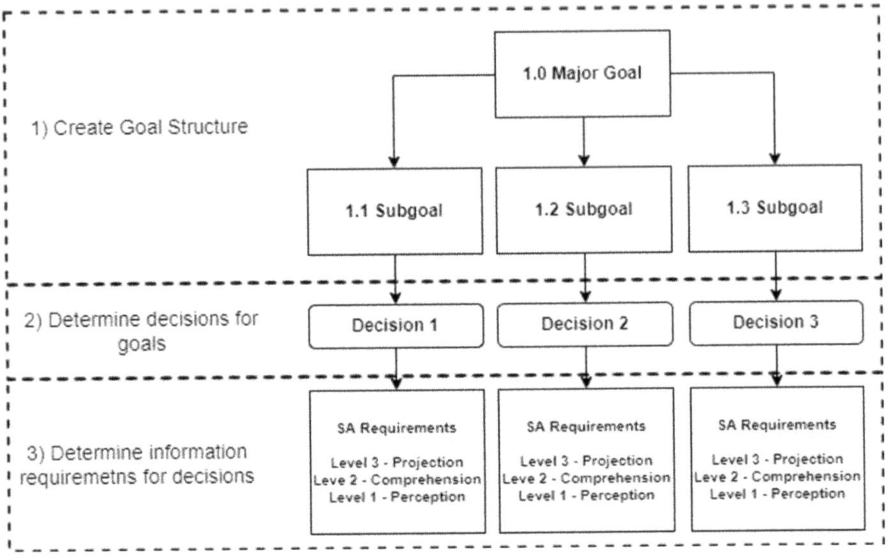

Fig. 3.3 Process to develop a GDTA

requirements is to remember that Level 1 requirements have to refer to isolated observation of the elements of an environment (e.g., the velocity of a vessel), while Levels 2 and 3 refer to fused information (e.g., a trajectory and its evolution) to make decisions. At the end of this step, SA requirements are organized to inform how the lower level of raw data feeds into the higher-level information needs for comprehensions and projection.

Let us consider a simple example of GDTA related to a vessel surveillance (see the case reported in Chap. 5). A major goal is to determine the best trajectory for a vessel. This goal, however, has to be decomposed in a number of sub-goals (refer to Fig. 3.4) such as: Assess the possible trajectories; Determine if a planned trajectory has to be changed; Adoption of a new trajectory. A sub-goal can be further decomposed. For example, the sub-goal related to the adoption of a new trajectory can be decomposed in: Assessing the impact on time schedule of the new trajectory; sharing the information on the changes of trajectory to interested parties.

Once a Goal Structure is created, decisions and SA requirements has to be associated to goals. Let us consider sub-goal 1.1.2 Assess Safety of Trajectories. One of the decision associated to this sub-goal is understanding if a vessel is drifting (refer to Fig. 3.5 where the decision has been depicted with a rhombus shape).To support decision making on this aspect, the SA requirements are associated to this decision as shown in the left-hand side of Fig. 3.5. The requirements are derived from expert knowledge (Willems et al. 2013) where a vessel is considered drifting if some conditions are met such as it is moving slowly, usually with a velocity between 3 and 5 knots, and its course and orientation have a significant difference, and so on.

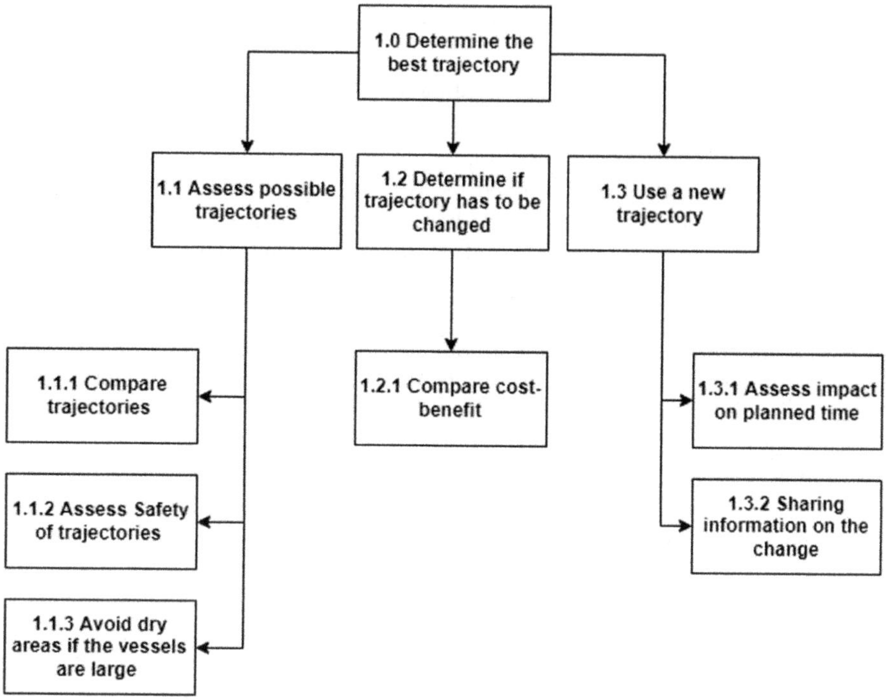

Fig. 3.4 An example of goal structure

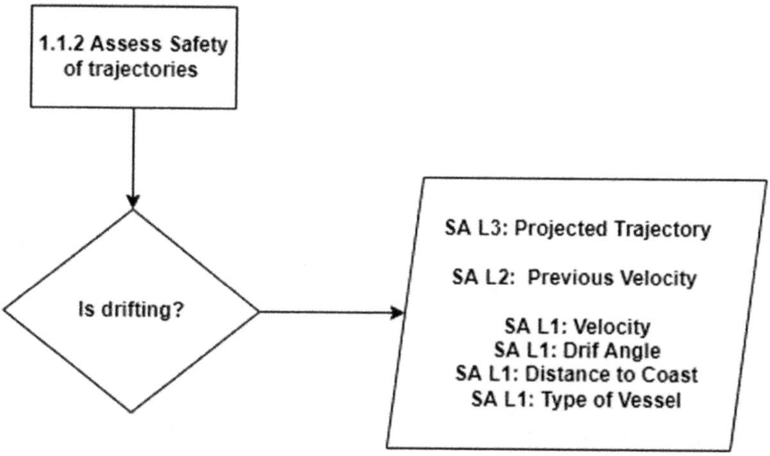

Fig. 3.5 An example of decision and requirements

3.3.4 Representing Operational Situations

Information processing approaches dealing with SA and SA-oriented reasoning need to consider how to represent and reason on situation. This represents a complex issue that has been investigated by several scholars. An overview of the main approaches is presented and discussed by Ye et al. (2012) that identify two main trends: specification-based and learning-based techniques. The former are based on techniques that allows to formally specify a situation through mathematical and formal models such as partition lattices, formal contexts, ontologies, etc. Specification-based techniques have the advantage of representing explicitly and formally a situation with the possibility of making inference on those representations but, usually, they are not so flexible as to adapt to changes without substantial modifications. The latter consist of approaches that are able to learn complex associations between situations and sensor data but, on the other side, do not provide a formal and explicit model of the situations with the risk of leaving operators out of the loop.

In concrete scenarios of operational situations it is often required a combination of both the techniques. The authors of this book have defined a methodology to support representation and reasoning on operational situation that is based on previous results in Gaeta et al. (2021). The methodology, which will be described later in Chap. 4, is based on two basic assumptions. The first relates to the need of computationally representing operational situations and, thus, demands a link between the different representations of a situation and the information available in a GDTA structure. The second assumption is related to the principle of maintaining the human in the loop and this requires the creation of formal and explicit structures that, however, must be flexible and adaptable to changes of the environment due to the actions of agents.

3.4 Granular Computing

Granular Computing (GrC) (Zadeh 1997; Bargiela and Pedrycz 2016; Yao 2005) is emerging as a sound approach for rapid decision making because of its capability of reasoning on *information granules*, which are defined by Zadeh as data or objects grouped together according to criteria such as similarity, proximity, functionality and indistinguishability.

GrC can be defined according to different perspectives. Yao (2005) defines a triarchic theory of GrC combining three perspectives: philosophy of structured thinking, methodology of structured problem solving, and mechanism of structured information processing.

As structured thinking, GrC allows discovering and reasoning on multi-level abstractions that exist in the real world, and supports analysts in achieving both an accurate and natural description, as well as in-depth understanding, of the inherent structures and complexity of the real world.

As a structured problem solving method, GrC is based on a divide and conquer strategy, which promotes the creation and adoption of hierarchical organizations and structures. With this strategy, a problem described with larger granules can be decomposed into a family of sub-problems (top-down) described with smaller granules, and the solution of the problem is obtained by combining the solutions of sub-problems (bottom-up).

With respect to the perspective of information processing, GrC offers a way to create and process information granules. The information granules are created through a process, called *information granulation*, which can be performed in different formal settings, such as the Rough and Fuzzy sets described in the following sections. Information granules can be considered as basic elements of knowledge. Granules may be built at different levels of abstraction and, by changing the size of the granules, it is possible to hide or reveal a certain amount of details. Granules can be organized in more complex Granular Structures and a wide set of relationships has been developed (Yao et al. 2013) to organize granules in hierarchies, trees, networks, and so on.

A challenge in GrC is how to design granules in an appropriate way, where the term "appropriate" refers to the creation of information suitable and representative of experiential evidence, a specific context or application domain. Pedrycz and Homenda (2013) have proposed the principle of justifiable granularity as a way to evaluate the performance of informative granules. This principle is based on a trade-off between two measures that do not strictly depend on the specific application: coverage and specificity. In general, coverage is related to the ability of covering data and specificity deals with the level of abstraction of the granule by considering its size.

GrC can be useful for Intelligence Analysis.

Figure 3.6 shows how the three perspectives of GrC are related to the families of SAT described in the previous chapter. The principle of Structured Problem Solving is the same of the Decomposition and Visualization family of SAT. In both the cases, in fact, the goal is to divide a complex problem into its parts so that the parts can be easily organized and processed to solve the problem. With GrC the parts can be organized in different structures, such as hierarchies, networks, lattices, and this support also the Visualization techniques. Structured Thinking is reflated to Structured Problem Solving and, in some sense, the latter enables the first. One a problem is decomposed into its parts and these parts are structurally organized, the analyst can reason in a structured way. This is what the majority of SAT requires to an analyst. Techniques such Idea Generation, Hypotheses Generation, Scenario Analysis are based on good capacity of Structured Thinking that GrC can enforce. Also more complex techniques, such as the Analysis of Competing Hypotheses, require is some important phases (e.g., identifying a set of mutually exclusive hypotheses). The perspective of Information Processing is related to SAT in two ways. First, as Information Processing paradigm, GrC allows to process information granules. With this information granules, several mechanisms of reasoning can be implemented (Liu and Liu 2002; Skowron et al. 2016; Yao 2010) to enable abduction, deduction and induction that are core for intelligence analysis. In a second way, GrC as Information Processing can support analysis on Granular Structures to evaluates analogies,

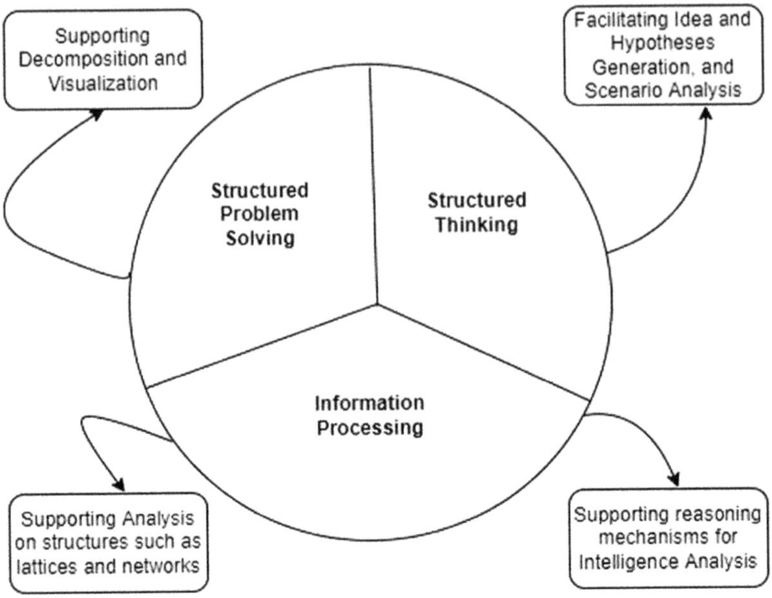

Fig. 3.6 Relations among the GrC perspectives and the families of SAT

similarities, oppositions and also to derive indexes and measures in structures such as lattices and networks. The adoption of some cases (i.e., analysis of structures of opposition, network analysis) are presented in the following chapters of this book.

It will be detailed later, in Chap. 4, how SA and GrC can be combined in the context of Intelligence Analysis cycle. For now, it is sufficient to observe that the GrC allows: (i) to granulate information according to different criteria and requirements that can provide a guide to the so-called intelligence cycles and (ii) to reason on situations and address problems at different levels of abstractions allowing analysts and decision makers to work on the most suitable one and use properties of GrC to obtain answers at the other levels (if a correlation exists).

3.5 Dealing with Imprecise and Uncertain Information

Real-world data is almost always incomplete, uncertain, vague, imprecise, inconsistent. Decisions must be made mostly by leveraging on imprecise and uncertain information, especially in the context of Intelligence Analysis, where the validation of sources and the gathering of data represent difficult tasks. Therefore, in order to construct data-driven tools to support the decision-making processes along the Intelligence Cycle, it is needed to consider mathematical theories able to deal with such characteristics of data. The main mathematical theories adopted in this book are: Rough (Pawlak 1982) and Fuzzy Set Theory (Zadeh 1965). In the next sections, very basic notions on the aforementioned theories will be introduced. These notions, opportunely integrated, extended and contextualized, are fundamental for understanding the methodologies described in Chaps. 5–8.

3.5.1 *Rough Set Theory*

Rough Set Theory is introduced, in early eighties, by Zdzislaw Pawlak as an extension of set theory for the study of intelligent systems characterized by imprecise (insufficient or incomplete) information (Yao et al. 1997). Rough Set Theory can be defined as a mathematical approach to data analysis able to support several data mining tasks (Pawlak et al. 2001) such as feature selection, feature extraction, data reduction, decision rule generation, and pattern extraction (templates, association rules). Rough Set Theory can be also employed for identifying partial or total dependencies in data, eliminating redundant data, giving solution to null values, missing data, dynamic data and so on. The main advantage of Rough Set Theory, with respect to Probability Theory or Dempster-Shafer Theory, is that it does not need any preliminary or additional information about data. Such benefit is demonstrated by the plethora of real-life problems which Rough Set Theory is applied to (medicine, pharmacology, engineering, banking, financial and market analysis, etc.). Rough Set Theory allows studying vague concepts starting from imprecise and uncertain data and, consequently, it is useful to deal with situation representation and reasoning in complex environments. Rough Set Theory expresses vagueness by employing a boundary region of a set and not by means of membership functions as in the case of Fuzzy Theory. A non-empty boundary region of a set means that our knowledge about the set is not sufficient to define the set precisely. More in detail, every object of the universe of discourse is associated to some information useful to describe it (represented as values for the object attributes). Objects characterized by the same information are said to be indiscernible. The indiscernibility relation, coming from the ideas of Leibniz (Ariew and Garber 1989), is the basis of the philosophy of rough sets. In particular, any set of indiscernible objects is called elementary set and forms an information granule (or granule of knowledge) of the universe. Any union of some granules is referred to as crisp (precise) concept, otherwise the concept is rough (imprecise, vague) (Pawlak and Skowron 2007) and has a non-empty boundary region. In Rough Set Theory, vague concepts (sets) are described by a couple of precise sets, called lower and upper approximations.

3.5.1.1 Indiscernibility Relation and Granulation

The indiscernibility relation is the starting point of the Rough Set Theory. It conceptually expresses the idea that in cases of insufficient information (or knowledge) it could be not possible to discern some objects of the universe of discourse. In general, in order to realize such discernment it is required to consider further information (or knowledge).Therefore, once fixed the available information (or knowledge) the analyst can observe the problem as a set of information granules, where each granule is composed of one or more indiscernible objects.

The indiscernibility among two or more objects can be defined starting from the definition of Information System, i.e., a formal representation of data.

An Information System is a pair $IS = (U, A)$ where the non-empty finite set U is the universe of discourse and A is the non-empty finite set of attributes describing the objects $x \in U$. An attribute $a \in A$ is a function $a : U \rightarrow V_a$, where V_a is a set of values of attribute a, called domain of a. Any Information System can be represented by a data table where rows describe individual objects and columns describe attributes. Any pair (x, a), with $x \in U$ and $a \in A$, define the table entry consisting of the value $a(x)$ (Pawlak and Skowron 2007).

An Indiscernibility Relation I_B on U, where $B \subseteq A$, is defined as it follows:

$$I_B = \{(x, y) : x, y \in U \wedge \forall b \in B, b(x) = b(y)\}. \tag{3.1}$$

Once defined I_B it is possible to create information granules starting from the available information (or knowledge) about the objects belonging to the universe of discourse. In particular, each granule is constructed as an equivalence class based on I_B:

$$[x]_B = \{y \in U : (x, y) \in I_B\}. \tag{3.2}$$

All the equivalence classes $[x]_B$ form the blocks of the partition U/B and are called *B-elementary granules* generating a granulation of U. Changes to B lead to changes in the composition of granules.

3.5.1.2 Approximation Operators

Starting from what has been introduced in the previous section, i.e., Information System, Indiscernibility Relation and B-elementary granules, it is possible to introduce the two following operators:

$$\underline{B}(X) = \{x \in U : [x]_B \subseteq X\}, \tag{3.3}$$

$$\overline{B}(X) = \{x \in U : [x]_B \cap X \neq \emptyset\}. \tag{3.4}$$

$\underline{B}(X)$ and $\overline{B}(X)$ are the *B-lower approximation* and the *B-upper approximation* of the set $X \subseteq U$. The *B-boundary region* characterizing the vagueness of the concept (set) X is:

$$BND_B(X) = \overline{B}(X) - \underline{B}(X). \quad (3.5)$$

More in detail, if $BND_B(X) \neq \emptyset$ concept X is vague, otherwise concept X is crisp.

3.5.1.3 Probabilistic Rough Sets

The main limitation of the traditional Rough Set Theory is that it does not allow (paradoxically) any uncertainty in the definition of both lower and upper approximations (Wang et al. 2009). In order to introduce such tolerance the probability approximation space was brought into the Rough Set Theory (Yao et al. 2015; Wong and Ziarko 1987). A widely adopted variant of Probabilistic Rough Sets is represented by the Decision-theoretic Rough Set Model (Yao 2007) based on the notions of rough membership and rough inclusion that can be interpreted in terms of conditional probabilities. In particular, it is considered $P(X|[x])$, i.e., the probability that an object belongs to the concept X given that such object belongs to the equivalence class $[x]$. The conditional probability can be calculated as $P(X|[x]) = \frac{|X \cap [x]|}{|[x]|}$. Thus, the approximation operators, in the Decision-theoretic Rough Set Model, are defined as it follows:

$$\underline{B}(X) = \{x \in U : P(X|[x]_B) \geq \alpha\}, \quad (3.6)$$

$$\overline{B}(X) = \{x \in U : P(X|[x]_B) > \beta\}, \quad (3.7)$$

where α and β $(0 \leq \beta < \alpha \leq 1)$ are probabilistic thresholds and establish the tolerance degree used to determine both lower and upper approximations. The previously introduce Eqs. (3.6) and (3.7) are defined by considering the Information System $IS = (U, A)$ and the Indiscernibility Relation I_B, where $B \subseteq A$.

3.5.2 *Fuzzy Set Theory*

Fuzzy Set Theory introduced by Zadeh (1965) provides an appropriate framework for dealing with uncertain data/information. The interpretation of a fuzzy set is formulated in contrast to that of crisp set where an element is either a member or not a member of such set within a universe of discourse. On the other hand, fuzzy set theory allows partial membership of an element to a set, i.e., a fuzzy set. To give a practical example, assume that the set X is the universe of numbers of killed people during terrorist attacks and the idea is to define the concept/set of middle-seriousness terrorist attacks (between 10 and 30 killed people). Such concept/set should be useful when it is needed to classify or not a new attack as a middle-seriousness attack. In the case of a crisp concept/set definition it is possible to define the set $A = \{x \in X : 10 \leq x \leq 30\}$ and using the following function to classify new data: $\chi_A(x) : X \rightarrow \{0, 1\}$. $\chi_A(x)$ returns 1 if $10 \leq x \leq 30$ (therefore $x \in A$) or 0 otherwise (therefore $x \notin A$).

3.5.2.1 Fuzzy Sets

Fuzzy concepts/sets (Zadeh 1965; Klir and Yuan 1995; Zimmermann 2011) extend the concept of crisp concepts/sets by allowing gradual degrees of membership between 0 and 1 for elements into a set. For instance, the middle-seriousness concept represented as a fuzzy set it is:

$$B = \{(x, \mu_B(x)) : 10 \leq x \leq 30\}. \tag{3.8}$$

Thus the middle-seriousness membership degree of a new terrorist attack (where x is the number of killed people for such attack) is expressed mathematically by means of the function $\mu_B(x) : X \rightarrow [0, 1]$ and, of course, such degree depends on the shape (e.g., triangular, trapezoidal, gaussian) of the function associated to B. Figure 3.7 shows a triangular membership function that can be used for characterizing the fuzzy concept/set middle-seriousness.

For instance, the membership degree of an attack a_1 produced a number of killed people $x_{a1} = 20$ is $\mu_B(x_{a1}) = 1$. Moreover the membership degree of a_2 with $x_{a2} = 15$ is $\mu_B(x_{a2}) = 0.5$. In general terms, the triangular membership function is calculated by using the following equation:

$$\mu_x = \begin{cases} \frac{x-l}{m-l}, & l \leq x \leq m \\ \frac{u-x}{u-m}, & m \leq x \leq u \\ 0, & otherwise \end{cases} \tag{3.9}$$

In the example above, $l = 10$, $u = 30$ and $m = 20$. An additional way to represent a fuzzy set as it follows:

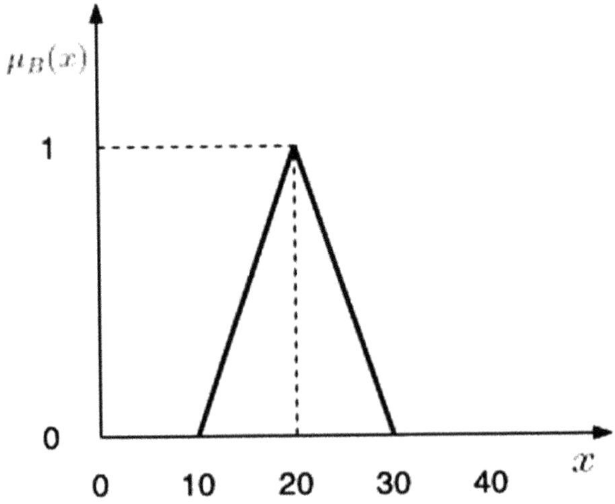

Fig. 3.7 Triangular membership function

$$B = \{\frac{x_1}{\mu_B(x_1)}, \frac{x_2}{\mu_B(x_2)}, \ldots\} \tag{3.10}$$

for all the elements $x_i \in X$.

3.5.2.2 Fuzzy Relations

A Fuzzy Relation on sets (Zadeh 1965; Klir and Yuan 1995; Zimmermann 2011) is a fuzzy set defined on the Cartesian product of two or more crisp sets. Let X, Y be universal sets, then

$$R = \{((x, y), \mu_R(x, y)) : (x, y) \in X \times Y\} \tag{3.11}$$

is called a fuzzy relation on $X \times Y$.

Furthermore, let A a fuzzy set on the universe X with the membership function μ_A and B a fuzzy set on the universe Y. Then $R = \{((x, y), \mu_R(x, y)) : (x, y) \in X \times Y\}$ is a fuzzy relation on A and B if:

$$\mu_R(x, y) \leq \mu_A(x), \forall (x, y) \in X \times Y \tag{3.12}$$

and

$$\mu_R(x, y) \leq \mu_B(y), \forall (x, y) \in X \times Y \tag{3.13}$$

Choosing $\mu_R(x, y) \leq min\{\mu_A(x), \mu_B(y)\}$ will satisfy Eqs. (3.12) and (3.13).

Fuzzy signatures, which are fundamental to model individuals' and groups' behaviors (as explained in the next sections), are based on fuzzy relations.

3.6 Three-Way Decisions

Three-Way Decisions (3WD) theory (Yao 2016) models a particular class of human ways of problem solving and information processing. The basic idea of such theory is to divide a universal set (of objects) into three pair-wise disjoint regions, or more generally a whole into three distinctive parts, to handle complexity, and to act upon each region or part by developing an appropriate strategy.

Figure 3.8 depicts the trisecting-and-acting model adopted by the 3WD. In such a model, as asserted above, the Universe of discourse (`U`) is partitioned into three regions (`Region I`), `Region II` and `Region III` respecting the following constraints:

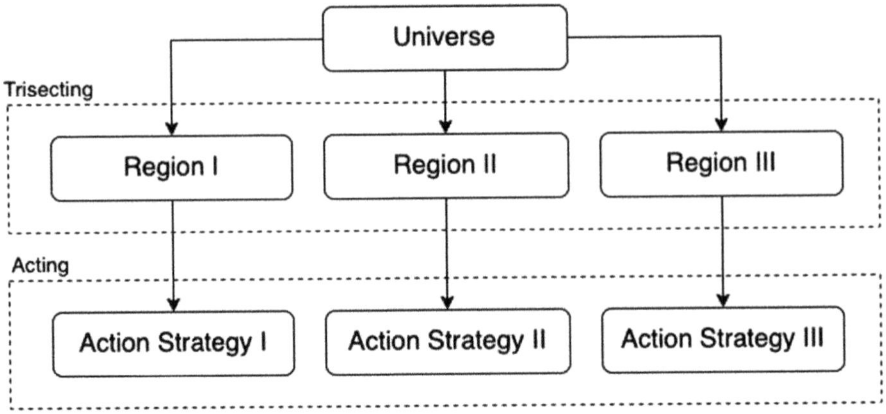

Fig. 3.8 Trisecting-and-acting model [elaborated from Yao (2016)]

$$
\begin{aligned}
(Region I) \cap (Region II) &= \emptyset, \\
(Region I) \cap (Region III) &= \emptyset, \\
(Region II) \cap (Region III) &= \emptyset, \\
(Region I) \cup (Region II) \cup (Region III) &= U.
\end{aligned}
\tag{3.14}
$$

On one side, 3WD is borrowed from the way human brain tends to represent and solve problems. On the other side, 3WD can be adopted to support human decision making when the problem is represented by a universe of objects. The aforementioned support is particularly useful for handling complexity due to the huge number of involved data.

Therefore, 3WD provides an overall approach able to sustain human cognitive processes, in general, when dealing with data and, in particular, when data must be processed to represent situations and reason on them in the context of tasks requiring good levels of situation awareness.

Evaluation-based Three-Way Decisions (Yao 2016) and Three-Way Decisions based on Rough Sets (Yao 2009) are two of the main classes of concrete models to implement 3WD.

The first class is based on the definition[1] of an evaluation function $v : U \rightarrow [0, 1]$, where U is the universe of discourse, and a pair of thresholds (β, α), with $0 \leq \beta < \alpha \leq 1$. Function v is used to partition U into three sets representing the three regions of 3WD:

[1] Take care that the definition reported in this book is a special case of the general definition provided in the paper (Yao 2016).

$$
\begin{aligned}
POS &= \{x \in U : v(x) \geq \alpha\}, \\
BND &= \{x \in U : \beta < v(x) < \alpha\}, \\
NEG &= \{x \in U : v(x) \leq \beta\}.
\end{aligned}
\tag{3.15}
$$

The second well-known class of models for 3WD is based on Rough Set Theory. In particular, Yao proposes the application of both Pawlak Rough Set Theory and Probabilistic Rough Set Theory (with a pair of thresholds). More in detail, the three regions can be calculated as it follows:

$$
\begin{aligned}
POS(C) &= \underline{B}(C), \\
BND(C) &= \overline{B}(C) - \underline{B}(C), \\
NEG(C) &= U - \overline{B}(C).
\end{aligned}
\tag{3.16}
$$

In the previous equations, $C \subseteq U$ is a concept defined as a subset of the universe of discourse U and (U, A) is an information table/system where A is a set of attributes describing the objects $x \in U$. More in detail, three regions $POS(C)$, $BND(C)$ and $NEG(C)$ respectively represent the sets of i) objects that certainly belong to C, ii) objects for which it is not possible to affirm that they belong to C nor that they do not belong to C, and iii) objects that certainly do not belong to C. The three regions can be computed by using Pawlak Rough Sets, i.e., Eqs. 3.3 and 3.4, or Probabilistic Rough Sets, i.e., Eqs. 3.6 and 3.7.

3WD is particularly suited for representing context in which observed entities (objects) are classified with respect to their occurring situation (e.g., safe or unsafe).

Non-trivial tasks are the definition of the evaluation function and the selection of the pair of thresholds. Typically, such tasks are domain-dependent although general approaches are available in the scientific literature. In particular, the evaluation function is typically defined by considering the descriptions of the objects once they have been represented through an information table/system. Moreover, the selection of the pair of thresholds is often realized by considering the overall risk of the partitioning defined by adding the risk of the three regions:

$$
R(\alpha, \beta) = R_{POS}(\alpha, \beta) + R_{BND}(\alpha, \beta) + R_{NEG}(\alpha, \beta). \tag{3.17}
$$

The idea is to select the pair (α, β) that minimizes the overall risk.

3.6.1 Setting Thresholds in 3WD

There are several approaches to find values for the thresholds in 3WD model. This sections outlines the three important approaches based on Bayesian decision theory, Information theoretic measures (i.e., Shannon entropy) and Game theory.

Yao (2011) discusses the adoption of Bayesian decision theory to set α and β. According to Yao (2011), to approximate a concept $C \subseteq U$ there are two states $\Omega = \{C, C^c\}$ and three actions $A = \{a_p, a_b, a_n\}$ related to acceptance, deferment and rejection of an object x, i.e. the three actions correspond to deciding $x \in POS(C)$, $x \in BND(C)$, and $x \in NEG(C)$. The loss function regarding the risk or cost of actions in different states is given by a 3×2 matrix such as Table 3.1.

The risk of assigning an object into the boundary region is between a correct classification and an incorrect classification: $\lambda_{pp} < \lambda_{bp} < \lambda_{np}$, $\lambda_{nn} < \lambda_{bn} < \lambda_{pn}$.

On the basis of Bayesian decision theory, it is possible to interpret Ω as a finite set of states, A as a finite set of 3 possible actions and $\lambda(a_i|C_j)$ the loss, or cost, for taking action a_i when the state is C_j. Let be x and object where an action is taken. It is possible to calculate the conditional risk or cost as: $R(a_i|x) = \sum_j Pr(C_j|x)\lambda(a_i|C_j)$. On the basis of the evaluation of the conditional risks of the three actions given an equivalence class $[x]$, Yao (2011) derives the thresholds α and β in terms of the values of the lost function matrix as follows:

$$\alpha = \frac{\lambda_{pn} - \lambda_{bn}}{(\lambda_{pn} - \lambda_{bn}) + (\lambda_{bp} - \lambda_{pp})} \tag{3.18}$$

$$\beta = \frac{\lambda_{bn} - \lambda_{nn}}{(\lambda_{bn} - \lambda_{nn}) + (\lambda_{np} - \lambda_{bp})} \tag{3.19}$$

Another approach to evaluate the two thresholds is based on information theoretic measures such as entropy. Deng and Yao (2012) propose the adoption of Shannon entropy as a measure of uncertainty to develop an information-theoretic approach to the interpretation and determination of thresholds. The approach can be summarized as follows. Given a concept to approximate, T, and the pair (β, α) s.t. $0 \leq \beta < 0.5 \leq \alpha \leq 1$, the problem of finding an optimal pair of thresholds is formulated as follows:

$$arg\ min_{(\beta,\alpha)} H(\pi_T \mid \pi_{(\beta,\alpha)}), \tag{3.20}$$

where

Table 3.1 Loss function matrix

	C	C^c
a_p accept	$\lambda_{pp} = \lambda(a_p\|C)$	$\lambda_{pn} = \lambda(a_p\|C^c)$
a_b defer	$\lambda_{bp} = \lambda(a_b\|C)$	$\lambda_{bn} = \lambda(a_b\|C^c)$
a_n reject	$\lambda_{np} = \lambda(a_n\|C)$	$\lambda_{nn} = \lambda(a_n\|C^c)$

Table 3.2 Strategy matrix

Action (strategy)	Method	Outcome
$\alpha_1(\downarrow \alpha)$	Decrease α by c_1	Larger POS
$\alpha_2(\downarrow \alpha)$	decrease α by c_2	
$\alpha_3(\downarrow \alpha)$	decrease α by c_3	
$\beta_1(\uparrow \beta)$	Increase β by c_1	Larger NEG
$\beta_2(\uparrow \beta)$	increase β by c_2	
$\beta_3(\uparrow \beta)$	increase β by c_3	

$$\begin{aligned} H(\pi_T \mid \pi_{(\beta,\alpha)}) =& Pr(POS_{(\beta,\alpha)}(T))\ H(\pi_T \mid POS_{(\beta,\alpha)}(T)) + \\ & Pr(BND_{(\beta,\alpha)}(T))\ H(\pi_T \mid BND_{(\beta,\alpha)}(T)) + \\ & Pr(NEG_{(\beta,\alpha)}(T))\ H(\pi_T \mid NEG_{(\beta,\alpha)}(T)), \end{aligned} \tag{3.21}$$

with

$$\begin{aligned} H(\pi_T \mid POS_{(\beta,\alpha)}(T)) =& -Pr(T\ |POS_{(\beta,\alpha)}(T)))\ log Pr(T\ |POS_{(\beta,\alpha)}(T))) - \\ & Pr(T^c\ |POS_{(\beta,\alpha)}(T)))\ log Pr(T^c\ |POS_{(\beta,\alpha)}(T))). \end{aligned} \tag{3.22}$$

Formulas similar to Eq. (3.22) can be used to evaluate $H(\pi_T \mid BND_{(\beta,\alpha)}(T))$ and $H(\pi_T \mid NEG_{(\beta,\alpha)}(T))$.

Herbert and Yao (2011) leverage on game theory and propose a game-theoretic rough set (GTRS) model. The determination of the thresholds is formulated as a game consisting of two players (i.e., α and β) competing for classification measures such as accuracy and precision. By gradually modifying various decision costs, the GTRS model searches for a cost function that defines the thresholds. The approach is summarized in the following. A game is defined as: $G = \{O, S, F\}$, where $O = \{\alpha, \beta\}$ is a set of players, $S = \{S_\alpha, S_\beta\}$ is the set of strategies used by the players and F is a set of payoff functions. The goal of each player is to reduce the size of the boundary region, thus competition between the players exposes their strategies for decreasing the boundary region.

The actions for the two players consists in small decrements (for the α player) and small increments (for the β player). These actions have the effect of moving equivalence classes from the boundary region to either the positive region (decrease of α) or negative region (increase of β). Decreases and increases can be done using a set of constants $C = \{c_1, c_2, ...\}$. For a classical winner-take-all scenario, the strategy matrix is reported in Table 3.2.

The payoff functions for actions α_i and β_i are as follows:

$$\mu(\alpha_i) = \frac{|POS|' - |POS|}{\alpha - \alpha \times c_i} \tag{3.23}$$

$$\mu(\beta_i) = \frac{|NEG|' - |NEG|}{\beta \times c_i - \beta} \tag{3.24}$$

where $|POS|$ and $|NEG|$ are the cardinality values of the current positive and negative regions, $|POS|'$ and $|NEG|'$ are the ones of the new positive and negative regions. As it can be seen from Eqs. 3.23 and 3.24, the payoff functions are formulated in a way that the magnitude in parameter change is indicative of the number of equivalence classes that are moved from the BND region. In their work, Herbert and Yao (2011) define also other payoff functions for more complex scenarios such as coalition and contextualize the actions for competition based on accuracy and precision. For instance, in this case, a suitable action to increase approximation accuracy for the α player to obtain a larger POS region is the decrease of λ_{pp} or λ_{pn}, where λ_{pp} and λ_{pn} are that ones of the loss matrix of Table 3.1.

3.7 Hands-on Lab

This section consists of three tutorials aiming at demonstrating how to apply the background knowledge offered by this chapter by using Python, its third-party libraries and the library provided by the authors. In particular, the first tutorial will drive the reader in writing the source code to prepare a decision table and calculate lower and upper approximations by using Probabilistic Rough Sets (PRST) and Traditional Rough Sets (RST). The second tutorial will focus on the source code for tri-partitioning a universe of discourse by using Three-Way Decisions Theory (3WD) based on PRST and RST. Lastly, the third tutor is about the use basic manipulations of Fuzzy Sets and Relations in Python. The processing task implemented by using the Python source code can be also executed manually by the reader in order to better fix the concepts underlying the adopted theories. The sample data used by both the two tutorials is extracted from the Global Terrorism Database[2](GTD). GTD contains information on terrorist attacks from 1970 to 2016. Data and notebooks are published on https://github.com/ctiabook/firstedition-tutorials. In particular, the notebook for this section is `CTIA02_background.ipynb`. Readers can download such file and open it into Colab either copy and paste the code into Colab and after running it.

3.7.1 Basic Source Code

In order to execute the tutorials it is needed to firstly execute the definitions related to three basic classes (provided by the authors of this book). Therefore, once created a new notebook in Colab, it is requested to run the following class definitions: `RoughSets` (for calculating approximations through traditional Pawlak rough sets

[2] https://www.start.umd.edu/research-projects/global-terrorism-database-gtd.

or probability-based rough sets and applying Three-Way Decisions based on the above rough sets), `RoughSetsUtility` (for manipulating condition attributes and generating equivalence classes from them) and `ThreeWayVisualization` (for generating a graphical representation of the result of a tri-partitioning through Three-Way Decisions). Let show the source code for the `RoughSets` class:

```
import numpy as np

class RoughSets:

    '''
    "itable" is a list of lists containing the
        values into a decision table.
    "features" is a list of column indices.
    '''
    def __init__(self, itable, features):
        self._itable = np.array(itable)
        self._features = np.array(features)
        self._roughness = -1

    '''
    It checks if two values are equals (a part of
        indiscernibility)
    '''
    def __overlap(self, xvalue, yvalue):
        if (xvalue == yvalue):
            return 0
        else:
            return 1

    '''
    Indiscernibility relation.
    '''
    def __IND(self, xvector, yvector):
        count = 0
        for index in self._features:
            count += 1
            if self.__overlap(xvector[index], yvector[
                index]) == 1:
                count-=1
                break
        if count == len(self._features):
            return 1
        return 0

    '''
    Function able to calculate the equivalence class
        of the row xindex.
    '''
    def __equivalence(self, xindex):
        eq_x = np.array([], dtype=int)
        for yindex in range(len(self._itable)):
```

```
                if self.__IND(self._itable[xindex], self.
                    _itable[yindex]) == 1:
                    eq_x = np.append(eq_x, [yindex])
        return eq_x

    '''
    Approximations calculated by means of the
        indiscernibility function.
    '''
    def approximations(self, concept):
        _lower = np.array([], dtype=int)
        _upper = np.array([], dtype=int)
        for x in range(len(self._itable)):
            N = self.__equivalence(x)
            if set(N).issubset(set(concept)):
                _lower = np.append(_lower, N)
            den = len(set(N).intersection(set(concept)
                ))
            if den != 0:
                _upper = np.append(_upper, N)
        if len(_upper) > 0:
            self._roughness = len(_lower)/len(_upper)
        return set(_lower), set(_upper)

    '''
    Approximations calculated by means of the
        indiscernibility function and
    conditional probability.

    "concept" is a list of indices defining the
        concept to study as a subset
    of the Universe.
    "beta" and "alpha" are two thresholds to build
        the approximations.
    '''
    def papproximations(self, concept, beta, alpha):
        _lower = np.array([], dtype=int)
        _upper = np.array([], dtype=int)
        for x in range(len(self._itable)):
            N = self.__equivalence(x)
            membership = len(set(N).intersection(set(
                concept)))/len(set(N))
            if membership >= alpha:
                _lower = np.append(_lower, N)
            if membership > beta:
                _upper = np.append(_upper, N)
        if len(_upper) > 0:
            self._roughness = len(_lower)/len(_upper)
        return (set(_lower), set(_upper))

    '''
    Three-Way Decisions.
```

```
    "concept" is a list of indices defining the
        concept to study as a subset
    of the Universe.
    "beta" and "alpha" are two thresholds to execute
        the tri-partitioning.
    "probability" is a boolean value indicating if
        probility-based rough sets
    must be calculated.
    "l" and "u" are default approximations (if None
        they will be calculated).
'''
def calculate3WD(self, concept, l=None, u=None,
    probability=False, beta=0.3, alpha=0.6):
    if (l==None) or (u==None):
        if not probability:
            l, u = self.approximations(concept)
        else:
            l, u = self.papproximations(concept,
                beta, alpha)
    POS = l
    NEG = set([i for i in range(len(self._itable))
        ]).difference(u)
    BND = u.difference(l)
    return (POS, BND, NEG)

'''
    Roughness measure by Pawlak.
'''
def roughness(self):
    return self._roughness

'''
    Accuracy of approximation based on roughness.
'''
def accuracy(self):
    if self._roughness != -1:
        return 1-self._roughness
    else:
        return -1
```

The class provides a method to calculate lower and upper approximations through traditional Pawlak rough sets (`RoughSets.approximations()`), a method to calculate the above approximations by using probability-based rough sets (RoughSets.papproximations()) and a method that uses the aforementioned ones for tri-partitioning the universe through Three-Way Decisions (`RoughSets.calculate3WD()`).

Note that the above implementation of rough sets is not optimized, partial and not bug free. It is provided only for didactic objectives. Many insights for high-performance and qualitative implementations of rough sets will be provided in the Appendix A of this book. The `RoughSetsUtility` class is a simple class supporting the tasks executed by `RoughSets`. The source code is:

```
class RoughSetsUtility:

    '''
      "data" is a Pandas DataFrame.
      "names" is a list of strings (column names).
    '''
    def __init__(self, data, names):
        self._data = data
        self._names = names

        if names != None:
            self._columns = data.columns

    '''
      Returns numerical indices in the place of
          feature names.
    '''
    def columns_index(self):
        columns = self._columns
        l=list()
        for n in self._names:
            l.append(list(columns).index(n))
        return l

    '''
        Checks for equivalent values.
    '''
    def _sameValues(self, vals1, vals2):
        for i in range(len(vals1)):
            if vals1[i] != vals2[i]:
                return False
        return True

    '''
        Builds the equivalence classes (information
            granules).
    '''
    def granules(self):
        data = self._data[self._names]
        d = dict()
        d1 = dict()

        for k in list(data.index):
            d[k] = 0
            d1[k] = {}

        for i in range(len(data.index)):
            k0 = list(data.index)[i]
            if d.get(k0) == 0:
                d[k0] = 1
                d1[k0] = {k0}
                for j in range(len(data.index)):
                    k = list(data.index)[j]
```

```
                    if d.get(k) == 0 and self.
                        _sameValues(list(data.values)[i
                        ], list(data.values)[j]):
                        d[k] = 1
                        d1[k0] = d1[k0].union({k})

        for k in list(data.index):
            if len(d1[k]) == 0:
                del d[k]
                del d1[k]

        return list(d1.values())
```

In particular, the method `RoughSetsUtility.columns_index()` takes a list with names of columns (in a Pandas DataFrame) representing the condition attributes and returns a list of numerical indexes for such attributes. Moreover, `RoughSetsUtility.granules()` builds and returns the equivalence classes by exploiting an equivalence relation based on the selected condition attributes. Also in this case, the reader has to be informed that the implementation has a didactic objective and could be redundant in some aspects. The last class is `ThreeWayVisualization` that is useful to generate graphical representations of a tri-partitioning. The main method of this class is `ThreeWayVisualization.show()` The source code is the following one:

```
import matplotlib.pyplot as plt

class ThreeWayVisualization:

    '''
     "regions" is a tuple of three sets.
    '''
    def __init__(self, regions):
        self._regions = regions

    '''
     Visualize data for a tri-partitioning result.
    '''
    def show(self):

        regions = list(self._regions)

        regions[0] = list(regions[0])
        regions[1] = list(regions[1])
        regions[2] = list(regions[2])

        for i in range(len(regions[0])):
            regions[0][i] = str(regions[0][i])
        for i in range(len(regions[1])):
            regions[1][i] = str(regions[1][i])
        for i in range(len(regions[2])):
            regions[2][i] = str(regions[2][i])
```

```
sPOS = "POS: "+ ", ".join(regions[0])
sBND = "BND: " + ", ".join(regions[1])
sNEG = "NEG: " + ", ".join(regions[2])

fig, ax = plt.subplots()

size = 0.3

cmap = plt.get_cmap("tab20c")
outer_colors = cmap(np.arange(3) * 4)
inner_colors = cmap(np.array([1, 2, 5, 6, 9,
    10]))

ax.pie([len(regions[0]), len(regions[1]), len(
    regions[2])], radius=1, colors=outer_colors
    , labels=[sPOS, sBND, sNEG], wedgeprops =
    dict(width=size, edgecolor='w'))
plt.show()
```

In order to prepare the environment for running the following tutorials, it is needed to copy the source code for the three aforementioned classes and paste it into the Colab cells (it is possible to use one cell for the three classes or once cell for each class indifferently) and run such cells by using the play button. If the class definitions have been correctly provided, the green sign will appear on the left of the used cells as shown in Fig. 3.9.

How to use the three above defined classes will be explained in the context of the tutorials described in the next sections.

3.7.2 *Probabilistic and Traditional Rough Sets*

As explained before, the following decision table has been extracted from the whole GTD:

Table 3.3 reports 11 terrorism episodes described by means of attack type (`attack`), target type (`target`), country in which the attack was perpetrated (`country`) and name of the perpetrator (`gname`). Such episodes are the objects belonging to the universe of discourse. The condition attributes are `attack`, `target` and `country`. The decision attribute is `gname`. The idea is to study the concept of `attack behaviour of Boko Haram` by calculating lower and upper approximations by means of PRST and RST.

First of all, it is needed to load data and create the decision table:

```
import pandas as pd
from google.colab import files

uploaded = files.upload()

df = pd.read_csv("dfsample_4p.csv")
```

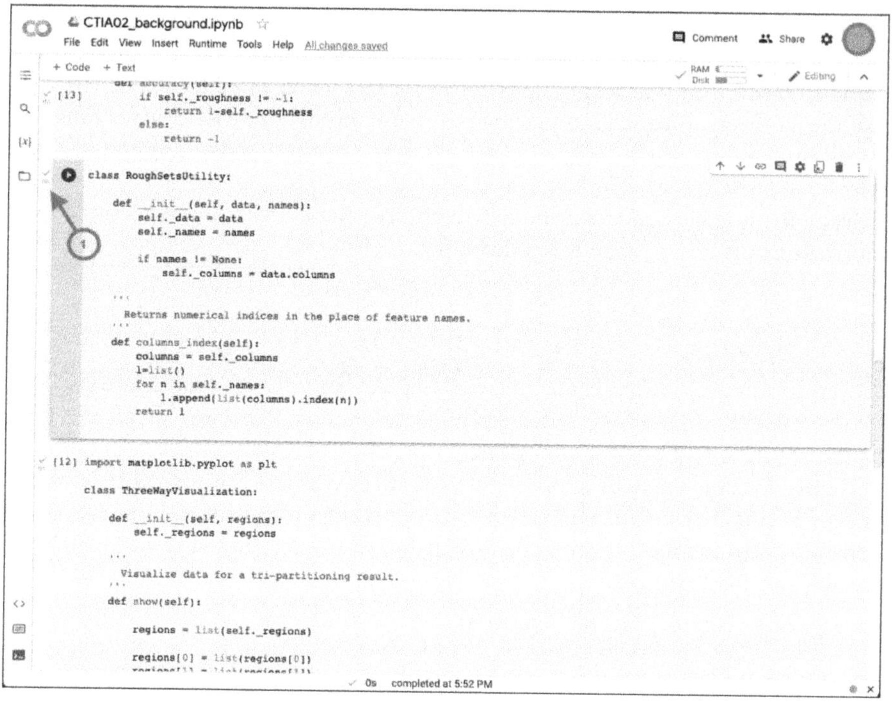

Fig. 3.9 Running class definitions

Table 3.3 GTD fragment

ID	Attack	Target	Country	gname
0	Armed assault	Military	Somalia	Al-Shabaab
1	Bombing/explosion	Military	Somalia	Al-Shabaab
2	Bombing/explosion	Police	Nigeria	Boko Haram
3	Armed assault	Educational institution	Nigeria	Boko Haram
4	Bombing/explosion	Business	Kenya	Al-Shabaab
5	Armed assault	Military	Nigeria	Boko Haram
6	Armed assault	Private citizens and property	Nigeria	Boko Haram
7	Bombing/explosion	Police	Somalia	Al-Shabaab
8	Armed assault	Government (general)	Nigeria	Boko Haram
9	Assassination	Journalists and media	Somalia	Al-Shabaab
10	Armed assault	Private citizens and property	Nigeria	Boko Haram

The previous code fragment imports Pandas and the module `files` from google.colab. The function `files.upload()` is invoked to allow the Colab user to upload a file from the local computer to the notebook in cloud. Once the right CSV file has been uploaded it is possible to read it through the `read_csv` function, offered by Pandas, which returns a `DataFrame` instance containing the decision table.

Secondly, it is needed to set the indiscerbility relation by using the simple class `RoughSetsUtility`. See the code below:

```
B1 = ["attack", "target", "country"]

B1_granules = RoughSetsUtility(df, B1)
B1_index = B1_granules.columns_index()
```

Such code configures the indiscernibility relation on the basis of all the three condition attribute of the decision table.

Thirdly, the concept to be approximated has to be defined. The idea is to define the concept of `attack behaviour of Boko Haram` by using the objects of the universe related to attacks perpetrated by `Boko Haram`. The source code to define the such concept is simply:

```
decisions_d1 = df[df.gname == "Boko Haram"]
decisions_d1 = decisions_d1.index
```

The fourth and last step is calculating lower and upper approximations by using the class `RoughSets` and its method `RoughSets.papproximations()` provided by the book authors:

```
infoTable = df.values

nrs = RoughSets(infoTable, B1_index)
l, u = nrs.papproximations(decisions_d1, beta=0.2,
    alpha=0.7)

print("LowA:", l)
print("UppA:", u)
```

In the previous source code, the variable `infoTable` contains data about the information system[3] included into the whole decision table. The class `RoughSets` is instantiated (`nrs`) with the aforementioned data and the indirscendibility function definition represented in `B1_index`. The method `papproximations()` is then applied on the instance `nrs` to calculate lower and upper approximations by using the PRST approach. The aforementioned method needs to receive, as arguments, the definition of the concept to be approximated (`decisions_d1`) and the thresholds values (`beta` and `alpha`). The lower approximation and the upper approximations are then stored into variables `l` and `u`. Once executed, the previous code produces the following result:

[3] The information system is a view of the whole decision table obtained by eliminating only the column related to the decision attribute.

```
LowA: {2, 3, 5, 6, 8, 10}
UppA: {2, 3, 5, 6, 8, 10}
```

where lower and upper approximations are the same, i.e., the concept under analysis is not rough with respect to the adopted indiscernibility function but crisp.

An additional class provided by the authors, namely `Granulation`, allows to evaluate the equivalence classes defined by the adopted indiscernibility function. The following source code can be used for the aforementioned aim:

```
eclasses=B1_granules.granules()

print("EQ. CLASSES:", eclasses)
```

In the case of `B1=["attack", "target", "country"]`, the equivalence classes are:

```
EQ. CLASSES: [{0}, {1}, {2}, {3}, {4}, {5}, {10, 6},
{7}, {8}, {9}]
```

where attacks `10` and `6` are indiscernible (see Table 3.3 to interpret such indexes) and included in the same equivalence class.

Furthermore, if the indiscernibility function changes its definition by considering only the condition attributes `attack` and `target`:

```
B1 = ["attack", "target"]
```

the results change as well. In particular, the new values for lower and upper approximations are:

```
LowA: {8, 10, 3, 6}
UppA: {0, 2, 3, 5, 6, 7, 8, 10}
```

where, this time, roughness is 0.4 and the equivalence classes obtained by means of the new indiscernibility relation are:

```
EQ. CLASSES: [{0, 5}, {1}, {2, 7}, {3}, {4}, {10, 6},
{8}, {9}]
```

It is possible to observe that considering only two attributes (`attack` and `target`) also the terrorism events 0 and 5 are indiscernible as well as 2 and 7. The interpretation of the above result is that if less details, about the phenomenon to analyse, are available also the capability to distinguish different objects is less precise.

Lastly, an interesting experiment is to compare PRST and RST against the same data. Consider the concept (to be approximated) `attack behaviour of`

`Al-Shabaab` and an indiscernibility relation based only on the attribute `attack` and execute the source code:

```
df = pd.read_csv("dfsample_4p.csv")

B1 = ["attack"]

B1_granules = RoughSetsUtility(df, B1)
B1_index = B1_granules.columns_index()

decisions_d1 = df[df.gname == "Al-Shabaab"]
decisions_d1 = decisions_d1.index

infoTable = df.values
nrs = RoughSets(infoTable, B1_index)

# traditional rough sets
l, u = nrs.approximations(decisions_d1)
# probabilistic rough sets
pl, pu = nrs.papproximations(decisions_d1, beta=0.2,
    alpha=0.7)

print("Trad. LowA:", l)
print("Prob. LowA:", pl)
print("Trad. UppA:", u)
print("Prob. UppA:", pu)
```

The result is the following one:

```
Trad. LowA: {9}
Prob. LowA: {1, 2, 4, 7, 9}
Trad. UppA: {0, 1, 2, 3, 4, 5, 6, 7, 8, 9, 10}
Prob. UppA: {1, 2, 4, 7, 9}
```

where it is evident that both the lower and upper approximations are different in the case of RST with respect to PRST. More in detail, with PRST it is introduced a tolerance allowing more objects (terrorist attacks) to be included in the lower approximation. Moreover, the upper approximation, calculated by means of RST, contains a greater number of objects than the one produced by means of PRST. This is due to the tolerance introduced by the probabilistic approach also for the set of objects that do not belong to the defined concept certainly and that, subsequently, do not belong to its upper approximation. Such intuition will be clearer in the next section where the application of Three-Way Decisions Theory is explained.

3.7.3 Three-Way Decisions

As explained in the sections above, Three-Way Decisions theory (3WD) is applied to a universe of discourse in order to provide a tri-partitioning of such universe. 3WD supports decision-making processes by mimicking the way human brain make some kind of decisions. Typically, it is needed to focus on a given concept (that is also a subset of the universe) for classifying the objects of such universe into three regions: positive (the objects for which it is possible to affirm that they belong to the concept certainly), boundary (the objects for which it is not possible to affirm that they belong to the concept certainly nor that they do not belong to it) and negative (the objects for which it is possible to affirm that they do not belong to the concept certainly). 3WD approach can be implemented by using several methods.

The following script is applied on the dataset in Table 3.3 and provides a tri-partitioning of the universe by using PRST with thresholds `beta=0.2` and `alpha=0.7`:

```
df = pd.read_csv("dfsample_4p.csv")
B1 = ["attack"]
B2 = ["attack", "target"]

B1_granules = RoughSetsUtility(df, B1)
B2_granules = RoughSetsUtility(df, B2)

B1_index = B1_granules.columns_index()
B2_index = B2_granules.columns_index()

infoTable = df.values

decisions_d1 = df[df.gname == "Boko Haram"]
decisions_d1 = decisions_d1.index

nrs_B1 = RoughSets(infoTable, B1_index)
regions_B1 = nrs_B1.calculate3WD(decisions_d1,\
     probability=True, beta=0.2, alpha=0.7)

nrs_B2 = RoughSets(infoTable, B2_index)
regions_B2 = nrs_B2.calculate3WD(decisions_d1,\
     probability=True, beta=0.2, alpha=0.7)

twview_B1 = ThreeWayVisualization(regions_B1)
twview_B1.show()

twview_B2 = ThreeWayVisualization(regions_B2)
twview_B2.show()
```

The analysis performed by executing the previous script is sequential and simulates the arrival of new information about the objects in the universe. Such simulation is realized by considering two indiscernibility relations, the first one based on the set of attributes `{attack}` and the second one based on the set of attributes `{attack, target}`. Note that the first is a subset of the second in order to mimic the increas-

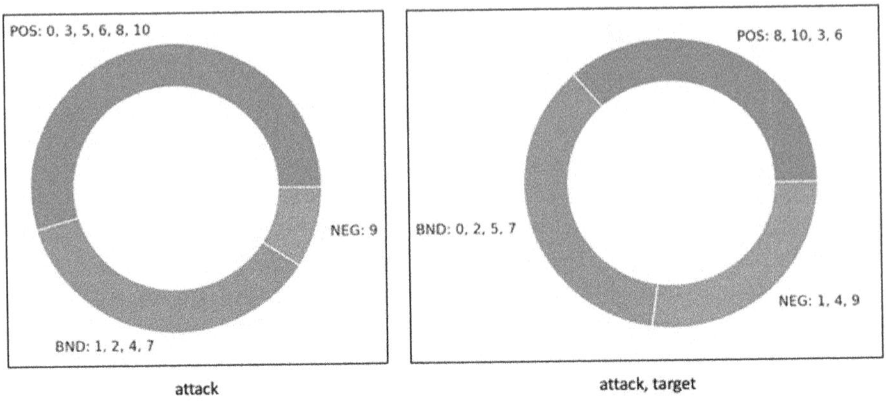

Fig. 3.10 Result of the application of three-way decisions (probabilistic rough sets)

ing knowledge. In the script, the method `calculate3WD` is used to create the three regions: positive, boundary and negative. The returned value is a tuple of three sets. Note that the method receives the concept to be studied and (in this case) three parameters: `probability` used to specify if the PRST-based implementation is requested (`True`) and `beta` and `alpha` to set the known thresholds.

The provided result, generated by means of the use of the library `Matplotlib`, is reported in Fig. 3.10 where it emerges that the three regions change as the indirsceni-bility relation changes. The calls to `Matplotlib` are embedded into the class `ThreeWay Visualization` included in the authors' library.

Furthermore, two additional cases can be considered. The first one considers two different operations of tri-partitioning, both based on PRST, with two different couples of thresholds.

The second case considers two different operations of tri-partitioning. The first operation based on RST and the second operation based on PRST.

The first case is realized by the following script:

```
'''
    please insert the code lines to load the dataset,
    set the indiscernibility function based only on
    the attribute "attack", prepare the information
        table
    and set the concept to study as "Boko Haram"
'''
regions_P1 = nrs.calculate3WD(decisions_d1,\
    probability=True, beta=0.1, alpha=0.9)

regions_P2 = nrs.calculate3WD(decisions_d1,\
     probability=True, beta=0.2, alpha=0.7)

twview_P1 = rst.ThreeWayVisualization(regions_P1)
twview_P1.show()
```

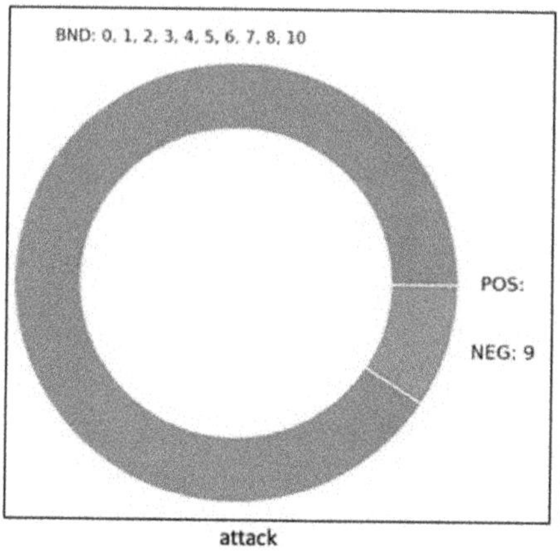

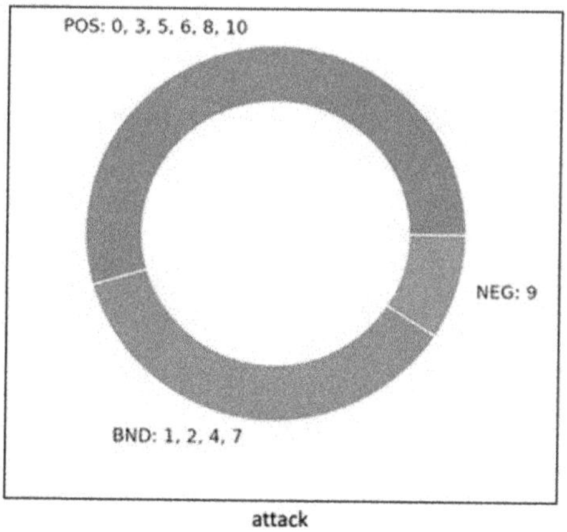

Fig. 3.11 Result of the application of three-way decisions (probabilistic approach) along two couples of thresholds

```
twview_P2 = rst.ThreeWayVisualization(regions_P2)
twview_P2.show()
```

Note that the indiscernibility relation is based only on the attribute `attack`. The result of the above script is reported in Fig. 3.11 where the first triple of regions is calculated by using `beta=0.1` and `alpha=0.9`. Moreover, the second triple of region is obtained by setting the thresholds with `beta=0.2` and `alpha=0.7`. Intuitively, the boundary region of the first triple is greater than the same region in the second triple because the tolerance used in the second tri-partitioning is greater than the tolerance in the first tri-partitioning. Therefore, also the number of objects belonging to the first boundary region must be greater or equal than the number of objects belonging to the second boundary region.

Lastly, the script for the second case is:

```
'''
    please insert the code lines to load the dataset,
    set the indiscernibility function based only on
    the attribute "attack", prepare the information
        table
    and set the concept to study as "Al-Shabaab"
'''

regions_T = nrs.calculate3WD(decisions_d1,\
    probability=False)

regions_P = nrs.calculate3WD(decisions_d1,\
    probability=True, beta=0.3, alpha=0.8)

twview_T = ThreeWayVisualization(regions_T)
twview_T.show()
```

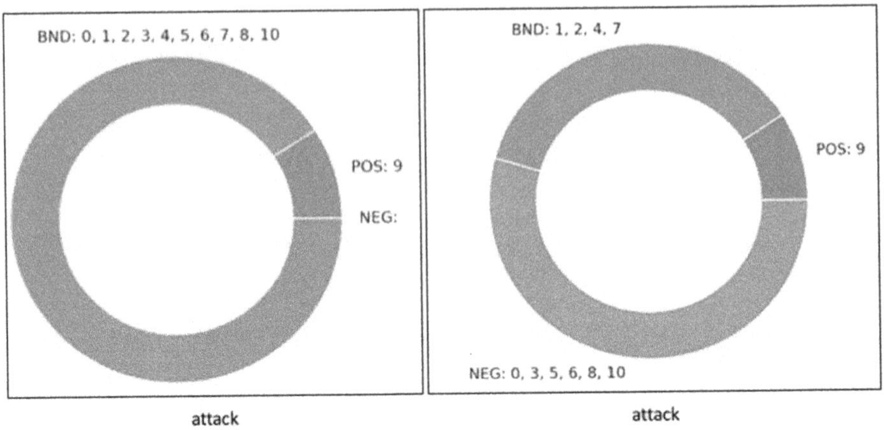

Fig. 3.12 Result of the application of three-way decisions with traditional and probabilistic rough sets

```
twview_P = ThreeWayVisualization(regions_P)
twview_P.show()
```

As clear from the script, the method `calculate3WD` is invoked twice with different arguments. The first invocation is for the RST-based implementation. The second one is for the PRST-based implementation.

The result of the above script is reported in Fig. 3.12.

In particular, it is possible to observe the differences between the regions obtained through the traditional approach and those produced by the probabilistic approach. In the second case, the boundary region is smaller, due to the tolerance introduced for positive and negative regions.

3.7.4 Fuzzy Sets and Fuzzy Relations

The libraries needed for this simple tutorial are SciKit-Fuzzy, NumPy and Pandas. The last two are pre-installed in the Colab environment. Moreover, SciKit-Fuzzy, as already announced before, must be installed by using the following instruction and running it in a Colab cell:

```
!pip install scikit-fuzzy
```

In the first part of the tutorial the objective is to model imprecise information as fuzzy sets. Let start from a fragment of the GTD:

Table 3.4 reports 8 episodes regarding terrorism events described by `id` (the identifier of the attack), `iyear` (the year in which the attack has been perpetrated), `gname` (the abbreviated name of the perpetrator), `country` (the country in which

Table 3.4 A further GTD fragment

ID	iyear	gname	Country	Attack	nkill	nwound
0	2014	NDFB	India	Armed assault	7.0	2.0
1	2013	UALA	India	Armed assault	8.0	3.0
2	2015	CPI-Maoist	India	Armed assault	42.0	25.0
3	2015	CPI-Maoist	India	Bombing/ explosion	4.0	7.0
4	2014	Maoists	India	Armed assault	10.0	8.0
5	2015	LeT	India	Armed assault	9.0	7.0
6	2016	Maoists	India	Armed assault	4.0	0.0
7	2016	LeT	India	Armed assault	24.0	17.0

the attack has been perpetrated), `attack` (the attack type), `nkill` (the number of people killed) and `nwound` (the number of wounds). Starting from this data it is possible to define the concept of middle-seriousness as a fuzzy set by using Python and further library along few steps.

Firstly, it is needed to import useful libraries:

```
import skfuzzy.membership as sm
import pandas as pd
```

Secondly, data (Table 3.4) must be loaded as a Pandas `DataFrame` and extracted into a NumPy `ndarray`. In order to accomplish this task you need to upload the dataset file into the Colab environment by means of the following code:

```
uploaded = files.upload()
```

Subsequently, the NumPy array must be created starting from a Pandas dataframe:

```
df = pd.read_csv("dfsample_7a.csv")
nkills = df["nkill"].values
```

When executed, the previous source code puts the following `ndarray` into the variable `nkills`

```
[7.0, 8.0, 42.0, 4.0, 10.0, 9.0, 4.0, 24.0].
```

Such values are the numbers of people killed by the attacks in Table 3.4.

Thirdly, in order to define and apply a membership function associated to the fuzzy set middle-seriousness it is needed to execute the following code:

```
midser = sm.trimf(nkills, [5, 20, 35])
print(midser)
```

The function `trimf` is able to apply a triangular membership function (as indicated by Eq. (3.9) with $l = 5$, $m = 20$ and $u = 35$). The result is a `ndarray` representing the membership degrees of all the considered attacks:

`[0.13333333, 0.2,0.,0.,0.33333333,0.26666667,0.0.733 33333].`

Thus, the obtained fuzzy set is the following one:

$$\left\{\frac{0}{0.13}, \frac{1}{0.2}, \frac{2}{0.0}, \frac{3}{0.0}, \frac{4}{0.33}, \frac{5}{0.27}, \frac{6}{0.0}, \frac{7}{0.73}\right\}. \tag{3.25}$$

The second part of this tutorial aims at explaining how to define a fuzzy relation by using Python. Let A and B two fuzzy sets representing respectively `attractiveness of target types` and `popularity of attack types` in the context of terrorism attacks. Such fuzzy sets are defined in this way:

$$A = \left\{\frac{AA}{0.0}, \frac{BU}{0.5}, \frac{EI}{0.3}, \frac{GO}{0.5}, \frac{MI}{0.5}, \frac{PO}{0.8}, \frac{TO}{0.0}, \frac{PC}{1.0}, \frac{RE}{0.1}\right\} \tag{3.26}$$

and

$$B = \left\{\frac{AR}{0.5}, \frac{BO}{1.0}, \frac{HT}{0.3}, \frac{AS}{0.1}, \frac{UA}{0.0}\right\}. \tag{3.27}$$

Acronyms have been used to specify the elements in the fuzzy sets A and B. In particular, the universe of A includes `AA=Airports & Aircraft`, `BU=Business`, `EI=Educational Institution`, `GO=Government (General)`, `MI=Military`, `PO=Police`, `TO=Tourists`, `PC= Private Citizens & Property` and `RE=Religious Figures/Institutions`. Moreover, the universe of B includes `AR=Armed Assault`, `BE=Bombing/Explosion`, `HT=Hostage Taking (Kidnapping)`, `AS=Assassination` and `UA=Unarmed Assault`.

Let define a fuzzy relation R on A and B by using Eq. (3.11) and considering $\mu_R(x, y) = min\{\mu_A(x), \mu_B(y)\}$.

The following source code, that mainly exploits the function `cartprod` provided by SciKit-Fuzzy, produces a matrix (stored in the variable `mR`) containing the membership values $min\{\mu_A(x), \mu_B(y)\}$ for all (x, y) belonging to the Cartesian product $X \times Y$ where X is the universe of A and Y is the universe of B:

```
import skfuzzy as sf
import numpy as np
import itertools

# defining the universes
targets = ["AA", "BU", "EI", "GO", "MI", "PO", "TO", "
    PC", "RE"]
attacks = ["AR", "BO", "HT", "AS", "UA"]

# defining the membership degrees
mTargetAttr = np.array([0.0, 0.5, 0.3, 0.5, 0.5, 0.8,
    0.0, 1.0, 0.1])
mAttackPopu = np.array([0.5, 1.0, 0.3, 0.1, 0.0])

# processing of the membership degrees for the fuzzy
    relation into a matrix
mR = sf.cartprod(mTargetAttr, mAttackPopu)
```

If it is needed to print each pair (x, y), $x \in X$ and $y \in Y$, together with the corresponding $\mu_R(x, y)$ it is possible to execute the following code:

```
# reshaping the matrix into a 1D array
mRflat = np.array(mR).reshape(len(targets)*len(attacks
    ),1)

# printing the results
count=0
for pair in itertools.product(targets, attacks):
    print(pair, mRflat[count][0])
    count+=1
```

More in detail, the above matrix (2D array) is reshaped into a 1D array by using the method `np.ndarray.reshape`. Then, all the pairs $X \times Y$ are created by using the function `product` of the Itertools library. In other words it is executed a cartesian product of the universes. Lastly, the iterator of the pairs is explored contextually to the 1D array containing the membership degrees. The last script result is reported below on more columns:

```
('AA', 'AR') 0.0
('AA', 'BO') 0.0
('AA', 'HT') 0.0
('AA', 'AS') 0.0
('AA', 'UA') 0.0
('BU', 'AR') 0.5
('BU', 'BO') 0.5
('BU', 'HT') 0.3
('BU', 'AS') 0.1
('BU', 'UA') 0.0
('EI', 'AR') 0.3
('EI', 'BO') 0.3
```

```
('EI', 'HT') 0.3
('EI', 'AS') 0.1
('EI', 'UA') 0.0
('GO', 'AR') 0.5
('GO', 'BO') 0.5
('GO', 'HT') 0.3
('GO', 'AS') 0.1
('GO', 'UA') 0.0
('MI', 'AR') 0.5
('MI', 'BO') 0.5
('MI', 'HT') 0.3
('MI', 'AS') 0.1
('MI', 'UA') 0.0
('PO', 'AR') 0.5
('PO', 'BO') 0.8
('PO', 'HT') 0.3
('PO', 'AS') 0.1
('PO', 'UA') 0.0
('TO', 'AR') 0.0
('TO', 'BO') 0.0
('TO', 'HT') 0.0
('TO', 'AS') 0.0
('TO', 'UA') 0.0
('PC', 'AR') 0.5
('PC', 'BO') 1.0
('PC', 'HT') 0.3
('PC', 'AS') 0.1
('PC', 'UA') 0.0
('RE', 'AR') 0.1
('RE', 'BO') 0.1
('RE', 'HT') 0.1
('RE', 'AS') 0.1
('RE', 'UA') 0.0
```

3.7.5 Useful Resources

- Pandas, https://pandas.pydata.org/. This is the official Web Site of Pandas.
- Pandas: get started (I), https://pandas.pydata.org/docs/getting_started/index.html#getting-started. This Site provides a simple introduction to get start with Pandas. https://pandas.pydata.org/docs/user_guide/index.html#user-guide. Go here to find a simple guide to learn Pandas basics for data analysis and management.

- Pandas: get started (II), https://pandas.pydata.org/docs/user_guide/index.html#user-guide. This Site provides a simple guide to learn Pandas basics for data analysis and management.
- Matplotlib: Visualization with Python, https://matplotlib.org/. This is the official Web Site of Matplotlib.
- SciKit-Fuzzy: user guide, https://pythonhosted.org/scikit-fuzzy/user_guide.html. Go here to learn how to use the SciKit-Fuzzy library for defining and process fuzzy sets and more.
- NumPy, https://numpy.org/. This Site is the official Web Site of NumPy.
- Itertools (API docs), https://docs.python.org/3/library/itertools.html. Go here to learn how to use itertools to create combinatoric iterators.
- Using Pandas and Python to Explore Your Dataset, https://realpython.com/pandas-python-explore-dataset/. This Site offers a good tutorial to learn data science basics in Pandas.
- How to use Numpy reshape, https://www.sharpsightlabs.com/blog/numpy-reshape-python/. This Site provides a tutorial to learn basic notions of reshaping operations in NumPy.

Chapter 4
Applying Situation Awareness to Intelligence Analysis

Situation Awareness helps human operators to make qualitative decisions and, consequently, to select a suitable course of action. As such, it is a model that can support Intelligence Analysis and the specific phases of an Intelligence Cycle.

In particular, as discussed in the previous chapter, the Endsley's model of SA Endsley (1995b) proposes three SA levels: perception, comprehension and projection of a situation of interest. From a data perspective, at the first level (perception), relevant data are perceived and gathered by sensors from the environment of interest. At the second level (comprehension), perceived data are interpreted to assign meanings to them with respect to the current situation occurring within the environment. Lastly, at the third level (projection), interpreted data are projected in the future to predict the possible evolution scenarios of the situation.

All the three SA levels can be enforced by computational methods and techniques allowing: (i) gathering, cleansing and pre-processing raw sensor data, (ii) fusing and processing such data to learn more abstract concepts called situations, and (iii) integrating learned concepts with further data and also with existing knowledge to analyze the evolution of the aforementioned "situations".

This chapter briefly introduces the overall information processing framework (Sect. 4.3) putting all together the elements already discussed in the previous chapters, contextualizes it to its application to the Intelligence Cycle (Sect. 4.4) and, lastly, describes how such framework is instantiated along different workflows (methodologies) that can be applied to a class of problems (Sect. 4.5). In the next chapters, a sample scenario will be discussed for each instantiated methodology.

4.1 Learning Objectives of this Chapter

This chapter systematizes the concepts learned in the previous chapters in an SA-Driven analysis methodology. The only didactic objective present in this chapter therefore refers to level 3 (Apply) of the taxonomy shown in Fig. 1.2. The reader will learn to:

V. Loia et al., *Computational Techniques for Intelligence Analysis*,
https://doi.org/10.1007/978-3-031-20851-5_4

- Use the concepts learned in Chaps. 2 and 3 to execute an SA-Driven Intelligence Analysis process.

4.2 Topic Map of the Chapter

The topic map of this chapter is shown in Fig. 4.1. This chapter essentially deals with a main topic: the revision of Intelligence Cycle with SA and GrC. The results of this revision is a new methodology for SA-Driven Intelligence Analysis.

4.3 Information Processing: Overall Framework

According to the above vision, the idea of enforcement that drives this book is strongly related to the uncertainty underlying the data-driven decision-making processes. In other words, the authors propose an overall information processing framework defined to support SA and based on Granular Computing paradigm. Subsequently, such framework is instantiated in concrete methodologies (workflow) in order to provide suitable solutions taking into account the peculiarities of different classes of problems.

More in detail, the framework instantiation is represented by the integration, according to the Granular Computing paradigm, of a set of methods and techniques (see Chap. 3) within concrete workflows of information processing.

Granular Computing makes it possible to meet the technological requirements of each of the phases of SA and enhance these phases. At the Perception level, Granular Computing allows to group data according to different requirements (i.e., similarity, proximity, functionality, indiscernibility) and increase their level of abstraction making them more understandable. This is the result of the granulation process allowing to create information granules. At the Comprehension level, these information granules are related to each other to build granular structures, that are collections of information granules. These structures can be created on the basis of different relationships that can offer different perspectives of a situation. Furthermore, the information granules can be classified to increase the level of comprehension of certain aspects of the situation. At the Projection level, the evolution of a situation can be supported by projecting in the near future the granular structures created with the

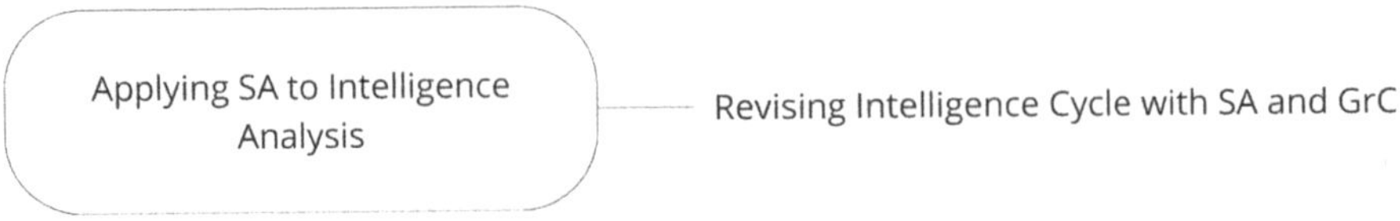

Fig. 4.1 Topic map of the chapter

adoption of granular time series analysis or by creating additional granular structures on the basis of the SA Level 3 requirements of the GDTA.

With this support, it is possible to reduce some SA errors. A taxonomy of SA errors has been defined by Endsley (1995a) and includes errors at Perception, Comprehension and Projection levels. The first type of errors (Perception Level) refers to difficulty in perceiving data. These failures to observe data can be reduced with a proper granulation process that creates granules according to the GDTA requirements. When granulated and properly organized in structures, data becomes more easy to be perceived and understood. At the Comprehension Level, errors arise because information is correctly perceived but its meaning is not comprehended. At this level, an important role is played by mental models. A poor mental model, in fact, does not support human operators in understanding data and information. Mental models can be supported with granular structures able to present situations according to different perspectives and by the capability of zooming in-out granules allowing to have different views (more fine or more abstract) of the same information. At the Projection level, usually, an operator is able to comprehend the current situation but has a poor mental model to project the situation in the near future. With Granular Computing it is possible to use evolvable granular structures. Different granular structures, furthermore, can be compared to reason on both the current situation and its possible evolution.

A further challenge to consider, as anticipated in Sect. 3.3.2, is related to uncertainty. Uncertainty is a significant factor in human decision-making and action (Endsley et al. 2003). Therefore, computational techniques aiming at supporting the formation of suitable levels of SA under the umbrella of Granular Computing need to consider and to deal with uncertainty and the correlated concept of confidence level of information. More in detail, uncertainty plays a role throughout the whole decision process. In fact, there is certain level of uncertainty associated with (i) basic data perceived from the environment, (ii) the comprehension of such data, (iii) the ability to project the current situation in the future, and (iv) the ability to produce desired outcomes from decisions.

It is clear that uncertainty must be managed when dealing especially when dealing with decision-making and situation awareness. In particular, if the objective is to provide computational techniques to support intelligence analysis, specific formal methods are needed. The techniques provided in this book adopt, for instance, set approximation operators, indiscernibility relations, non-crisp set definitions, etc. Strategies to manage uncertainty, by reducing it, are numerous. For instance, it is possible to search for more information when the level of uncertainty is too low to make qualitative decisions with a suitable confidence. Another plausible strategy is to fill in missing data by using default values (coming from mental models). This strategy allows experienced operators to make decisions in difficult contexts (missing data). The uncertainty of course will continue to exist. Conflicting data need to be resolved. Simple mathematical averages, in general, do not work. Sensor data fusion as well as consensus assessment algorithms needs to be considered to handle situations in which more sensors provide conflicting outcomes related to the same phenomena. Moreover, in some scenarios it is not needed to completely resolve uncertainties.

Hence, in these cases thresholding could be enacted. It allows to make decisions in uncertainty conditions when enough certainty levels have been achieved. Probability theory is largely adopted in the methodologies described in this book in order to provide tolerance when dealing with classification or partitioning tasks. A further strategy to consider is well-known as contingency planning. In particular, in such a case what-if analysis could be employed to plan for the worst case of possible future events.

The following sections of the chapter help the reader to understand the methodologies described in the next chapters. In particular, Sect. 4.4 presents a mapping between the Intelligence Cycle phases and the SA levels. Lastly, Sect. 4.5 summarizes the used computational techniques and contextualizes them to the specific SA level in which such techniques will be adopted.

4.4 Mapping into Intelligence Cycles

To support Intelligence Analysis through the enforcement of Situation Awareness, the authors propose a methodology whose backbone is defined by connecting the Intelligence Cycle to the aspects of the Endsley's Model (of Situation Awareness) and, consequently, to concrete practices, methods and techniques.

More in detail, the **Planning/Direction** phase is carried out by conceptual effort provided by experts and consumer of the intelligence products. From a methodological point of view, the outcome of such phase should be a structured document describing needs and requirements. In the proposed methodology, the aforementioned analysis tasks can be executed by means of GDTA (Goal-Directed Task Analysis) the method described in Sect. 3.3.3. The result of the Planning/Direction phase will guide all the subsequent cycle phases. In particular, the **Collection** phase mainly concerns source selection, data gathering, and data cleansing. Moreover, the Collection phase contributes to perceive the relevant aspects (objects of interest and their features) of the monitored environment also through the organization of such data by using suitable (with respect to the objectives) structures.

A further contribution to Perception (Endsley's Model) is provided by the **Processing** phase, in which the cleaned relevant and organized data can be evaluated and granulated according to the the requirements specified by the GDTA as well as for the Collection phase. The Processing phase also supports the Comprehension (Endsley's Model) of situations occurring in the environment by means of the learning of specific concepts and their approximations in cases of uncertainty.

Comprehension is also supported by the **Analysis/Production** phase where learned concepts and approximations are analysed by using existing knowledge. The aim of such phase is also generating Projection (Endsley's Model) of situations in the next future and to employ decision models able to support human operators reasoning on the analysis result with respect to the goals depicted in the GDTA.

The schema of Fig. 4.2 is exploited in the next chapters in order to depict methodologies applied in specific case studies.

4.5 Selection and Adoption of Concrete Techniques

With reference to Fig. 4.2, the computational techniques that can be adopted in the various phases of the proposed methodology are described. The major part of such techniques have been selected to exploit their capabilities to deal with uncertainty underlying information processing and be easily integrated into an approach based on Granular Computing.

At the Perception level, raw data are collected, organized in useful structures and granulated. For this purpose, this level leverages on the adoption of computational techniques to construct information granules and evaluate their quality.

First, data are collected and organized into meaningful data structure. It is the case, for example, of Information and Decision systems of Rough Set Theory (see Sect. 3.5.1). These systems organize data in tables whose columns are labeled by attributes, rows are labeled by objects of interest and entries of the table are attribute values. Attributes set include condition and decision attributes. These table provides a *descriptive* perspective of the environment to be perceived. Other perspectives are, however, important to perceive: a *relational* perspective for which graph structures can be employed and a *behavioral* perspective allowing to represent in multi-dimensional structure the actions of the objects of the environment.

The granulation process starts from these data structures. The granulation criteria (e.g., similarity, proximity) are derived from the GDTA level 1 requirements that, as mentioned in the previous section, guides the collection phase. Concrete examples of information granules are the equivalence classes constructed in Sect. 3.7 with Rough Sets and Probabilistic Rough Sets intrinsically dealing with uncertainties in data. These theories are also able to be integrated with approaches for the processing of

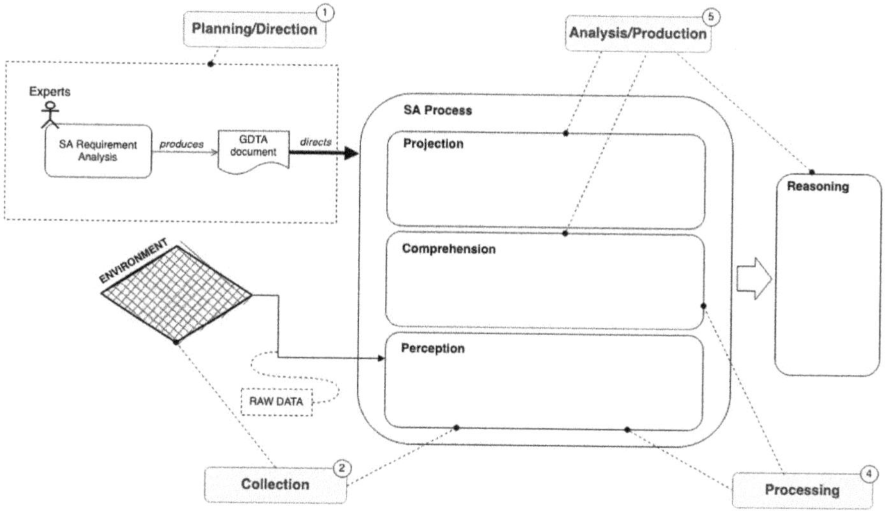

Fig. 4.2 The methodology template with respect to the intelligence cycle phases

missing data. Another example reported in Sect. 3.7 is to the adoption of fuzzy sets and fuzzy relation to construct information granules that relate two sets. In general, however, any computational technique that is such to partition data according to the criteria of a GDTA can be adopted for granulation purposes.

At the Comprehension phase, the information is processed and analyzed to support situation comprehension. This means that the information granules are organized in meaningful granular structures that can have different levels or hierarchies. An example is the derivation of the three regions with the Three-Way Decisions (see Sect. 3.6 for basic notions) as reported in Sect. 3.7. The three regions represent, de-facto, a second level of granulation contextualized to a particular objective. With this multilevel granular structure an analyst can reason only with the support of the first granular structure, on both the two granular structures or only on the second granular structure to have an improved comprehension of the elements of a situation. Another example of granular structure is the partition lattice (see Hands-on Lab section of the Chap. 5). In this phase, approaches like Three-Way Decisions are employed to allow thresholding and, consequently, admitting a certain level of tolerance in classification or other data analysis tasks.

In the Projection phase, information is analyzed to produce new information. New information is produced by projecting in the near future a comprehended situation. This can be done reasoning on a family of granular structures created at different time instants and/or for different Situation Awareness requirements. An example of how to reason on different granules structures for projection (and how this can support production of new information) is reported in the Hands-on Lab section of the Chap. 5. In this phase, approaches like what-if analysis are used to sustain decision processes in presence of uncertainty.

Table 4.1 Overview of the analysis and methods

Analysis	Methods	Scenario	Chapters
Decision-making through what-if analysis	Creation and comparison of granular structures three-way decisions	Vessel surveillance	5
Resilience analysis with network analysis	Three-way decisions on graphs	Intentional attacks towards critical infrastructures	6
Counter-terrorism analysis	Behavioral modeling with fuzzy signatures similarity measures	Attribution of attack hypotheses to terrorist groups	7
Analysis of contradictory or contrasting assumptions and opinions	Creation and comparison of structures of opposition based on rough set theory and three-way decisions	Influence of fake news on people's opinions	8

Reasoning refers to the adoption of analytic techniques, such as that one of the Analytic Tradecraft described in Sect. 2.3, to take decisions. In this phase, the granular structures of comprehension and projection phases are used to perform different intelligence analysis activities such as what-if (see Chap. 5), analysis of phenomena in large scale systems (see Chap. 6), counter-terrorism analysis (see Chap. 7), analysis of contradictory or contrasting assumptions and opinions (see Chap. 8) helping to deal with uncertainty during the reasoning tasks.

Lastly, before starting to deal with specific workflows (methodologies), Table 4.1 synthetically reports few information for each one of them.

Part II
Computational Techniques

Chapter 5
Decision Making Through What-If Analysis

According to CIA—Center for the Study of Intelligence—report on Structured Analytic Techniques (Primer 2009), what-if analysis is a *contrarian technique for challenging a strong mind-set that an event will not happen or that a confidently made forecast may not be entirely justified.* What-if analysis allows shifting the focus from the fact that an event could occur to how it could happen. With this techniques, analysts suspend the judgment on the probability of occurrence of an event by focusing on possible evolution and developments of a scenario, even unlikely. This analysis can complement a difficult judgment reached and help decision makers consider events and situations that may develop in light of changes in data and information.

From a computational perspective, what-if analysis is a simulation technique useful to understand what can happen if some changes occur in the scenario or situation of interest. The starting point of this analysis is the assumption that an event or a situation has occurred. Then, some triggering events or factors are identified and new scenarios are created and evaluated to understand what happens on the basis of such variations.

What-if analysis can be used to enforce SA of human operators. This type of analysis can be applied to situation recognition and projection with the objective of supporting decision makers in understanding which are the factors that can lead to a change in a recognized situation. So, specifically, what are the conditions under which a situation classified in a certain way, such as safe, can evolve toward situations classified differently, such as unsafe.

5.1 Learning Objectives of the Chapter

This chapter contextualizes the analysis method of Chap. 4 to a what-if analysis. The Learning Objectives of this chapter refer to the levels 2 (Apply) and 3 (Analyze) of the taxonomy shown in Fig. 1.2).

V. Loia et al., *Computational Techniques for Intelligence Analysis*,
https://doi.org/10.1007/978-3-031-20851-5_5

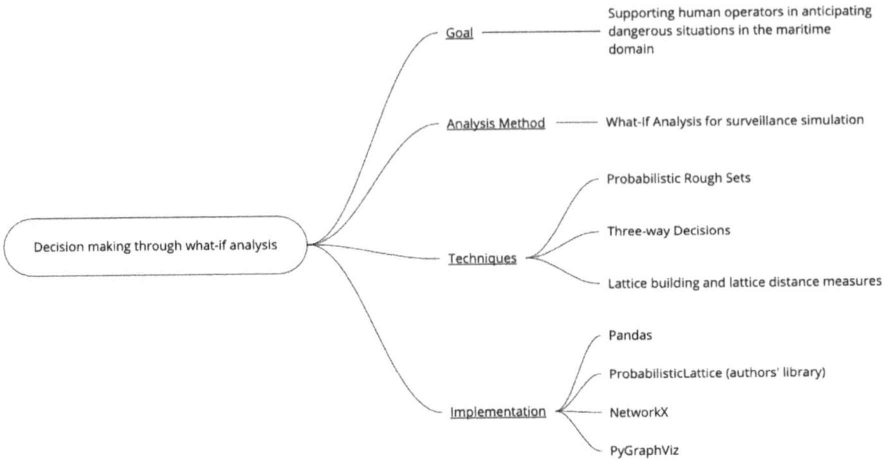

Fig. 5.1 Topic Map of the chapter

The Learning Objectives of this chapter are:

- Implementation and Execution of the methodology of Chap. 4 for a what-if analysis.
- Use of Probabilistic Rough Sets to build a granular structure in the form of a lattice of partitions.
- Use of a Three-Way decisions model to improve the comprehension of a lattice of partitions.
- Use of distance measures to evaluate similarity and difference in lattices of partitions.
- Examine distances between lattices of partitions to assess situation evolution.
- Experimenting the methodology with hands-on lab.

5.2 Topic Map of the Chapter

As shown by the topic map in Fig. 5.1, this chapter introduces a methodology aiming at supporting human operators to anticipate dangerous situations in the maritime domain. Such methodology is based on a well known analysis method, namely What-If Analysis (mainly used for simulation-based decision support systems), and is realized by means of Three-Way Decisions supported by Probabilistic Rough Sets. The results of the analysis are represented by time-related intelligible structures called lattices that enforce human reasoning.

The techniques on which the methodology is realized can be implemented by means of a set of Python-based tools and libraries indicated by the topic map.

5.3 Case Introduction: Vessel Surveillance

A case of intelligence analysis in which what-if can be applied is the analysis of anomalous maneuvers such as the split maneuvers of commercial aircraft or vessels. These anomalous maneuvers, in some cases, can be indicators of terrorist attacks, e.g., hijacking.

More in detail, this case study focuses on anticipating anomalous situations in which vessels drift and generate possible dangers within the monitored environment. The what-if analysis is used to help operators in issuing early warning for unsafe situations (such as a vessel near to harbors) by identifying potential drifting vessels while they are docking. Typically, a vessel is said to be drifting when it has a velocity between 3 and 5 knots and an angle between its course and orientation greater than 30°C (see Fig. 5.2a). This is a decision heuristic which, however, is subject to cognitive biases such as the anchoring that typically occurs when individual's decisions are influenced by a particular reference point or 'anchor' (Tversky and Kahneman 1974). In this case, for example, anchoring can occur when an operator is influenced by the reference values of a "normal" trajectory for a particular type of vessel and incorrectly estimates the differences between these values and those of another type of vessel. In these situations, what-if analysis is able to undermine this mind-set.

Figure 5.2b shows a sample scenario that can be analyzed. In such a scenario, there are a number of different vessels whose trajectory is monitored. As long as the vessels follow a normal path to the harbor, the general situation is classified as safe. When one or more vessels perform anomalous maneuvers (such as drift), the situation could change and be classified as unsafe.

The what-if analysis allows to anticipate any anomalous development of a situation by carrying out simulations that involve the variations of one or more surveillance parameters. For example, when a situation is uncertain, difficult to classify, its evolution is simulated to better understand what happens when, for instance, velocities and drifting angles of the vessels change.

Considering a vessel surveillance scenario, what-if analysis can be performed through the following steps:

- assumes the normal trajectory of a vessel as an expected event during vessel surveillance. This situation is classified as safe;
- assumes that some events may allow the situation to evolve in a different and anomalous way. For example, one can postulate the sudden approach of a vessel to the coast and/or the abrupt variation of a drift angle. Such developments are classified as unsafe;
- identifies one or more plausible scenarios for anomalous situations;
- develops arguments and reasoning to explain how those scenarios can happen.

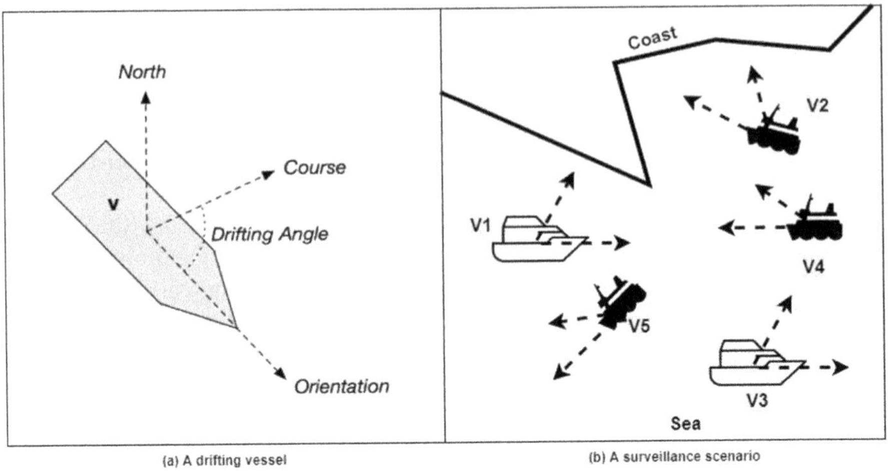

Fig. 5.2 Vessel Surveillance (Elaborated from Gaeta et al. 2021).

5.4 Methodology

The methodology is shown in Fig. 5.3. The first step is a requirements analysis that produces a GDTA document. The document informs the operator on the data and information requirements to gather at SA levels 1, 2 and 3 and, thus, directs intelligence cycles to this purpose. This step resembles the Planning and Direction phase of an intelligence cycle.

For the specific case study, at SA level 1, it is executed the Collection phase of an Intelligence cycle. For the case study under analysis, this phase is aimed at acquiring information relating to the type and number of vessels in the harbor area, and data from sensors such as velocity, drift angle and distance from the coast.

At level 2, the situation must be understood by a surveillance operator and, therefore, level 1 information must be fused and abstracted. To this end, the GDTA document informs on how level 1 information is processed. For the specific case study, the information must be granulated with respect to the attributes of interest of the situation and classified. The criterion to granulate information is the equivalence, i.e. objects that are indistinguishable with regards to the values of attributes that are of interest to the situation

Finally, at level 3, the GDTA document informs the operator about the triggering factors and events in order to understand how situations could evolve. This may require changes of the values of the attributes of interest underlying the granulation of information.

The GDTA document is used in combination with the environmental raw data to perform the Processing, Analysis and Production phases of an Intelligence Cycle, according to the SA Endsley model.

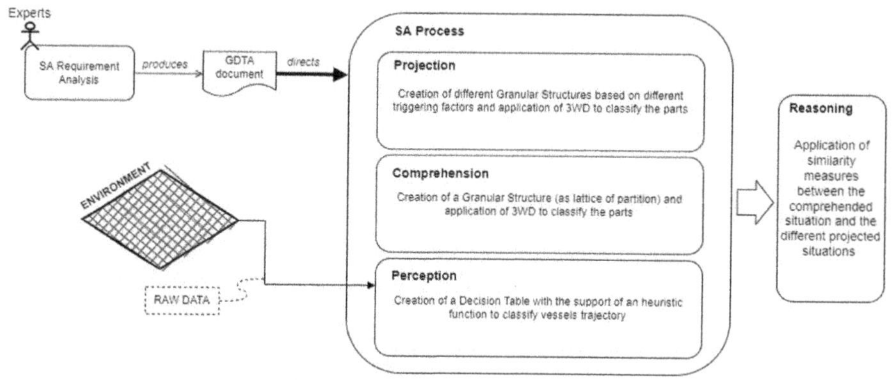

Fig. 5.3 The methodology for what-if analysis.

At the Perception level, a Decision Table is created like the one shown in Table 5.1. The Decision Table obviously refers to the objects (vessels) and descriptive attributes of level 1 of the GDTA and, to evaluate the decision attribute, domain decision heuristics are used. From a computational point of view, heuristics can be used to evaluated data coming from distributed sensors but, obviously, the results of the evaluation are characterized by uncertainty. The presence of uncertain and imprecise information therefore motivates the granulation approach, based on the upper and lower approximations of the rough sets described in the Sect. 3.5.1, adopted for the Comprehension level.

In fact, to recognize a situation at the Comprehension level, the information is abstracted through a granulation process. This involves the creation of a granular structure which is a collection of information granules that can be graphically represented as a partitions lattice. The information granules report more abstract information that can be classified, with respect to a desired situation (such as the safe one), with decision-making heuristics such as 3WD.

To evaluate how a recognized situation can evolve, the creation of different lattices is carried out in the Projection level in accordance with the requirements of level 3 of the GDTA. The what-if analysis takes place, therefore, by comparing the situation recognized at the Comprehension level with the possible developments constructed

Table 5.1 Example of decision table

	Velocity	Drifting Angle	Distance from coast	Type	Decision (safe or unsafe)
v1	Low	Low	Far	Cargo	Safe
v2	Low	Mid	Near	Ferry	Unsafe
v3	Mid	Low	Mid	Cargo	Safe
v4	Mid	Mid	Mid	Research	Safe
v5	Mid	Low	Far	Research	Safe

at the Projection level. The reasoning behind these evaluations relies on distance (or similarity) measures between granular structures. As this distance increases, an evolution tend to differentiate from a recognized situation.

5.5 Computational Techniques

This section discusses the computational techniques that can be used to execute the methodology above presented. In the following, U is an universal set consisting of all the objects (vessels) under consideration and A is the set of attributes of the objects. $A = C \cup D$ where C is a set of conditional attributes such as `Velocity, Drifting Angle, Type of vessel` and D consists of a decision attribute related to the single object. $d \in D$ is the decision attribute that is used to classify objects (i.e., vessels) with respect to their states. Values for `d` (i.e., `Safe or Unsafe`) are calculated by means of heuristics and human operators' knowledge. An example of heuristic to evaluate d has been reported in Sect. 5.3. F, lastly, is an information function providing values to the attributes of A.

5.5.1 Lattice Derivation with Probabilistic Rough Sets

Starting from the SA level 1 requirements, a decision system $DS = \langle U, A, F \rangle$ is constructed. A concrete artifact of a DS is the so-called Decision Table. An example of Decision Table is Table 5.1 that shows the classification of objects considering a scenario with five different types of vessels and data coming from vessels sensors such as velocity, drift angle and distance from coast. The values of the attributes, evaluated with the information function F, have been discretized.

From DS, in accordance with the SA level 2 requirements, equivalence classes are created and organized in a lattice.

Let C be the set of conditional attributes and E a subset of attributes belonging to the sequence of subsets $e : E_1 \subset E_2 \subset \cdots \subset E_m \subseteq C$. A partition lattice, L_{E_i}, where $i = 1, 2, ..., m$, can be constructed by using the equivalence classes $[x]_{E_i}$

Let $E_1 = \{DriftingAngle\}$ be the subset of attributes. Then, starting from Table 5.1, there are two equivalence classes that can be organized as L_{E_1} of Fig. 5.4. L_{E_1} gives a snapshot of the current situation that, however, can be hard to comprehend. The comprehension can be improved using the capability of zooming-in (adding more information to obtain finer granules). Let $E_2 = \{DriftingAngle, Velocity\}$ be another subset of attributes. It is evident that $E_1 \subset E_2$ and, thus, the equivalence classes created with E_2 provide finer information, i.e., are less abstract, and the lattice created with these equivalence classes, L_{E_2} of Fig. 5.4, simplifies the comprehension of a situation. In this last case, in fact, the equivalence class $\{V1, V3, V5\}$ of L_{E_1} has been divided into $\{V1\}$ and $\{V3, V5\}$ to clarify that the vessels have different velocity. A similar argument is applied to the equivalence class $\{V2, V4\}$ of L_{E_2}.

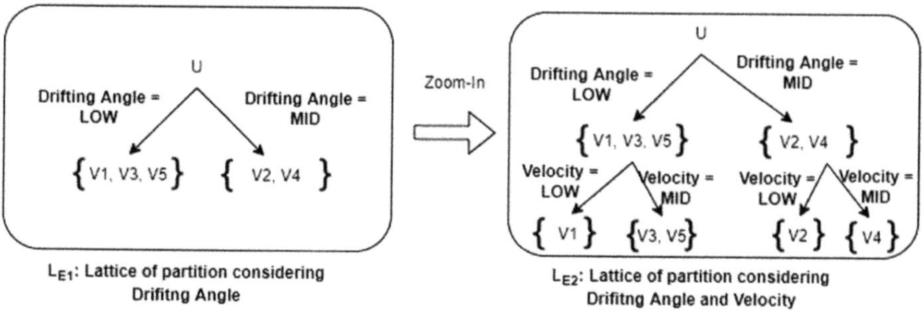

Fig. 5.4 Lattice of partition created with different subsets of attributes.

L_{E_1} and L_{E_2} do not show, however, how the objects are classified with respect to the objective of analysis. To enforce the comprehension of the situation, 3WD is applied. Let $H \subseteq U$ be a target concept, consisting of all the objects that are in a desired situation, e.g. Safe. Through the execution of 3WD based on probabilistic rough sets (see Sect. 3.6), it is possible to determine POS, NEG and BND regions for H at each level of the sequence e. Le be $P(H|[x]_E) = \frac{|H \cap [x]_E|}{|[x]_E|}$, the application of 3WD to the subset E is as reported in eq. (3.16).

Let $H = \{V1, V3, V4, V5\}$ be the concept of `Safe` situations, $\alpha = 0.63$ and $\beta = 0.25$ are the values used for the 3WD thresholds. Applying 3WD to the granulation represented with L_{E_1} (where the only available knowledge is that related to `DriftingAngle`), $P(H|\{V1, V3, V5\}) = 1$ and $P(H|\{V2, V4\}) = 0.5$, thus $POS(H) = \{V1, V3, V5\}$, $NEG(H) = \emptyset$ and $BND(H) = \{V2, V4\}$. The classification of the parts shows that the objects V1, V3 and V5 can be considered in a `Safe` situation while the objects V2 and V4 require additional analysis.

When an additional attribute is considered (i.e., `Velocity`), it is possible to calculate $P(H|\{V1\} = 1$, $P(H|\{V3, V5\} = 1$, $P(H|\{V2\} = 0$, $P(H|\{V4\} = 1$, thus $POS(H) = \{V1, V3, V4, V5\}$, $BND(H) = \emptyset$ and $NEG(H) = \{V2\}$. Now, the situation is cleared with object V2 that appears to be in a `Unsafe` situation because of an anomalous combination of `Drifting Angle` and `Velocity`. Figure 5.5 shows L_{E_1} and L_{E_2} with the enrichment of 3WD classification.

The situation comprehension ends with the construction of a lattice whose levels are built by considering the partitioning of U induced by the subsets of C. In order to support the projection phase, it is needed to apply situation comprehension to an updated decision table of our DS. For the sake of simplicity, assume that DT_0 is the decision table at time instant 0, DT_1 will be the decision table at time instant 1 and the two decision tables share the same universe U and the same set of attributes A. Once applied the above described approach to DT_1, a new lattice can be constructed. Such lattice represents the situation projected to time instant 1 and it can be compared with the previous one.

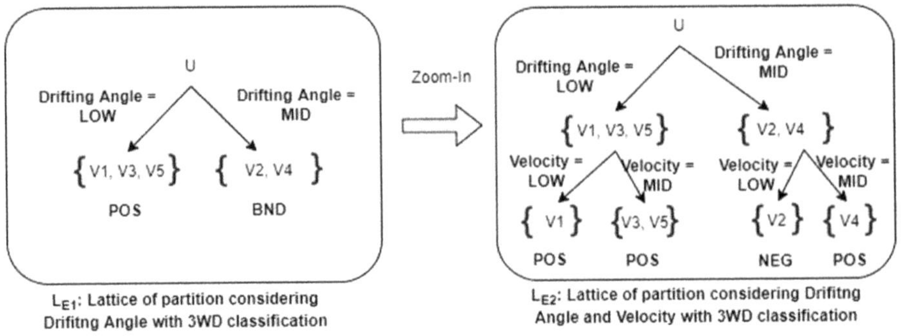

Fig. 5.5 Lattice of partition enriched with 3WD Classification.

5.5.2 *Measures for Situation Evolution*

Let L_E^0 and L_E^1 be two lattices created at time instants 0 and 1 over the same subset of attributes E. To evaluate how far a projected situation is from a current situation, it can be used a distance measure between partition lattices such as the one defined by Liang (2011):

$$Dis(L_E^0, L_E^1) = \frac{1}{|U|} \sum_{i=1}^{|U|} \frac{|L_E^0(x_i) \triangle L_E^1(x_i)|}{|U|} \tag{5.1}$$

where $|L_E^0(x_i) \triangle L_E^1(x_i)|$ is the cardinality of a symmetric difference between the the two families of partitions included in L_E^0 and L_E^1. The result of such measure is a qualitative indicator related to the situation evolution, i.e. high values indicate a change in the situation while low values indicate that the situation projected at time instant 1 is not very different from the recognized one at time instant 0.

5.5.3 *Reasoning with 3WD on Temporal Structures*

Once created the lattices for the recognized situation and the projected ones, what-if analysis can be executed as follows. Figure 5.6 shows how what-if analysis can be executed with lattices and distance measures. In Fig. 5.6, as in the following, when pointing out to lattices, the superscript indicates the time instant to which they refer.

L_{E1}^0 and L_{E2}^0 have been constructed to comprehend the situation at time instant 0.

To execute what-if analysis, L_{E3}^1 and L_{E4}^1 are constructed at time instant 1 using the same sequence of attributes subsets, i.e. $E_2 = \{DriftingAngle, Velocity\} \supset E_1 = \{DriftingAngle\}$, assuming variations in attribute values. Therefore both L_{E3}^1 and L_{E4}^1 of Fig. 5.6 represent possible developments of the situation recognized at time instant 0.

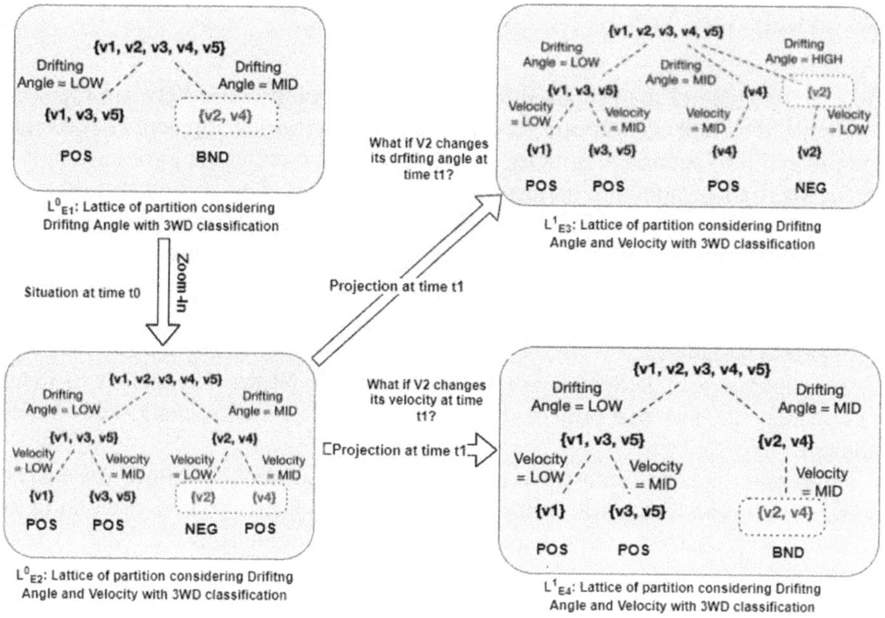

Fig. 5.6 Situation comprehension and projection for drifting vessels (Elaborated from Gaeta et al. 2021)

In creating the lattices for the projected situation, the decision heuristic to classify the objects is not evaluated since the objective of what-if analysis is to understand what may happen starting from the current classification of the situation. Thus, the concept of `Safe` situation does not change even if the attributes values of some objects are supposed to change.

In the first scenario, lattice L^1_{E3} of Fig. 5.6, the operator wants to project a situation in which the `Drifting Angle` of V2 is assumed to change its value to `HIGH` (increase). Using the distance measure of Eq. (5.1), it is possible to quantify the differences between the two lattices and the related situations: $Dis(L^0_{E2}, L^1_{E3}) = 0.2$. The operator evaluates the new situation and can easily understand that the vessel V2 can become a drifter as the drifting angle will be higher. Considering that the new projected situation differs from the previous one, the operator can perform some actions in order to avoid a worsening of the situation such as, for example, alerting the captain of the vessel and/or requesting more information on the reason for the anomalous maneuver.

A second possible projection scenario is the one of L^1_{E4} of Fig. 5.6 developed by increasing the `Velocity` of V2 from `LOW` to `MID`. If comparing L^0_{E2} and L^1_{E4} of Fig. 5.6, it is possible to conclude that the situation of V2 is safer when its velocity increases, i.e., it can not be a drifting vessel.

5.6 Analytical Value

The analytic value of the proposed method is in the compromise between the need to generate different and various scenarios relating to the development of a current scenario and the required simplicity of analysis of such scenarios in order to allow the analyst to focus attention on just one or two of them.

The What-If Analysis technique is useful for refocusing attention operationally on potential dangerous scenarios, e.g., anomalous trajectory of a vessel. The adoption of What-If analysis in the context of SA and 3WD based on Probabilistic Rough Sets allow the generation of different analysis scenarios related to different projection of a recognized situation.

The generation of lattices annotated as in Fig. 5.6 allows the analyst to focus the attention not just one projected scenario, but on several scenarios developed simultaneously.

The distance measure defined to compare the different scenarios allows the analyst to understand which scenario is the most deserving of attention by evaluating its difference with respect to the safe or normal scenarios of analysis.

5.7 Hands-on Lab

In this section the reader will face the lattice building task throw a sequence of attribute subsets and evaluate the situation evolution as explained in the methodological Sect. 5.5.1. For executing the tutorials in this section, the reader will use the library made available by the authors. Such library, with respect to the lattice building and drawing tasks, exploits respectively `NetworkX` and `PyGraphViz`, two Python third-party libraries. Thus, you need to install them into the Colab environment by using the following instructions:

```
!pip install -q pydot
!apt install libgraphviz-dev
!pip install pygraphviz
!pip install networkx
```

After the package installation it is needed to execute the authors' classes `RoughSets`, `RoughSetsUtility` and `ThreeWayVisualization` as in Sect. 3.7. Take care you must add the following method to the class `RoughSets`:

```
def find_regions(self, eclasses, regions):
    POS=regions[0]
    BND=regions[1]
    NEG=regions[2]
    l=list()
    for g in eclasses:
```

```
            if g <= POS:
                l.append("POS")
            elif g <= BND:
                l.append("BND")
            else:
                l.append("NEG")
        return l
```

Moreover, the source code of this section requires the following definitions (provided by the authors):

```
'''
  Class used to build and draw lattice structures.
'''
class Lattice:

    def __init__(self, data, attr):
        self._attr = attr
        self._data = data
        self._granules = []
        self._lattice = None
        self._d = None

        for i in range(len(attr)):
            l = attr[0:i+1]
            self._granules.append(RoughSetsUtility(
                data, l))

        self._granules.insert(0, RoughSetsUtility(data
            , []))

    def set_regions(self, regions):
        self._regions=regions

    def _set_connections(self, lattice, pnodes,
        parents, sons, count, d, labels):
        snodes = list()
        for p, np in zip(parents, pnodes):
            for (s,i) in zip(sons, range(len(sons))):
                if s <= p:
                    snodes.append(lattice.add_node(str
                        (s)+"_"+str(count+1), granule=s
                        ))
                    lattice.add_edges_from([(str(p)+"_
                        "+str(count), str(s)+"_"+str(
                        count+1))])
                    d[str(s) + "_" + str(count+1)] =
                        labels[i]
        return snodes

    '''
      Construction of the graph representing the
         lattice defined by granules and partitions
```

```
        obtained through RoughSets and
        ThreeWayDecisions.
    '''
    def build(self, decision, filename="lattice"):
        d=dict()
        self._d=d
        parents = self._granules[0].granules()
        lattice = nx.Graph()
        stri = str(parents[0])+"_"+str(0)
        pnode = lattice.add_node(stri, granule=parents
            [0])
        pnodes = [pnode]
        count=0

        regions, nrs =self._three_way(decision, self.
            _granules[0].columns_index())
        labels = nrs.find_regions(parents,regions)
        d[str(parents[0]) + "_" + str(0)] = labels[0]

        for g in self._granules[1:]:
            sons=g.granules()
            regions, nrs = self._three_way(decision, g
                .columns_index())
            labels = nrs.find_regions(sons, regions)
            snodes = self._set_connections(lattice,
                pnodes, parents, sons, count, d, labels
                )
            parents = sons
            pnodes = snodes
            count+=1
        self._lattice = lattice
        for n in lattice.nodes(data=True):
            n[1]["granule"] = str(n[1]["granule"])

        nx.write_gexf(lattice, filename+".gexf")


    def _three_way(self, decision, b_index):
        nrs = RoughSets(self._data.values, b_index)
        regs = nrs.calculate3WD(decision)
        return regs, nrs

    '''
      Drawing the lattice on the screen.
    '''
    def show(self):
        G = self._lattice
        fig = plt.figure(figsize=(15, 8))
        ax1 = plt.subplot(111)
        pos = nx.nx_agraph.graphviz_layout(G, prog="
            dot")
```

```
        nx.draw(G, pos, ax=ax1, with_labels=False,
            node_size=400, node_color="lightblue")

        d=dict(G.nodes())
        for k in d:
            d[k] = k +'\n'+self._d[k]
        nx.draw_networkx_labels(G, pos, labels=d,
            font_size=10, font_family='sans-serif')

        plt.show()

'''
   Extension of class Lattice to build a probability-
       based lattice.
'''
class ProbabilisticLattice(Lattice):


    def __init__(self, data, attr, beta, alpha):
        self._beta=beta
        self._alpha=alpha
        super().__init__(data, attr)


    def _three_way(self, decision, b_index):
        nrs = RoughSets(self._data.values, b_index)
        regs = nrs.calculate3WD(decision, probability=
            True, alpha=self._alpha, beta=self._beta)
        return regs, nrs
```

5.7.1 Lattice Building

The scenario case is related to the dataset fragment reported in the Table 5.1 except the vessel IDs, i.e., `V1` is replaced by `0`, `V2` is replaced by `1`, and so on. Firstly, the source code to build the lattice at time `0`:

```
import pandas as pd
import networkx as nx

df = pd.read_csv("dfsample_5.csv")

lattice = ProbabilisticLattice(df, \
    ["Drifting Angle", "Velocity"], 0.25, 0.63)

decisions_d1 = df[df.Decision == "Safe"]
decisions_d1 = decisions_d1.index

lattice.build(decisions_d1)
lattice.show()
```

In particular, the solution makes use of the class `ProbabilisticLattice` whose constructor (`__init__()` method in Python) takes as arguments the decision table (`df`) loaded from a CSV file through the support of Pandas, the sequence of condition attributes to analyse (`Drifting Angle` and `Velocity`), and the values for thresholds beta (`0.25`) and alpha (`0.63`). The idea underlying the lattice construction is that the first level of the lattice is represented by the granule containing all the objects. The second level is composed of the granules generated by using the first attribute of the above sequence, the third level is composed of the granules generated by using the first two attributes of the sequence. And so on. In order to activate the lattice building function it is needed to determine the concept to study (`Decision = Safe`) and to invoke methods `build()` (for generating the lattice) and `show()` to draw the lattice over a new window. Libraries Graphviz and PyGraphviz are often difficult to install. This difficulty is often due to numerous pre-requisites required by the installation procedure. Such libraries are needed to graphically depict the lattice but, in general, they can be used to visualize graphs and networks. A good alternative to these tools is represented by Gephi[1] that is a desktop application. Therefore, the idea is to use NetworkX to convert the built lattice into a suitable representation for Gephi. In such a case, the instruction `lattice.build()` must be replaced by the instruction `nx.write_gexf(lattice, "lattice.gexf")`.

Before executing the previous source code it is needed to upload the dataset `dfsample_5 .csv` into the Colab environment by using the usual code:

```
uploaded = files.upload()
```

The run of this tutorial main code produces the result reported in Fig. 5.7, where the first level contains only one granule containing all the vessels (no attribute is used to granulate). Moreover, the second level contains two granules obtained by granulating along the attribute `Drifting Angle`, the first one classified into the positive region (safe) and the second one classified into the boundary region (uncertainty). Lastly, the third level provides new knowledge about the granule previously belonging to the boundary region. In particular, such granule has been decomposed in two finer granules by using the attributes `Drifting Angle` and `Velocity`, vessel `1` and vessel `3`, respectively belonging to the negative (unsafe) and the positive (safe) regions.

5.7.2 *Assessing the Situation Evolution*

In order to execute the what-if analysis explained in the previous sections, it is needed to update the decision table used at time `0` in order to produce a decision table at time `1`.

[1] https://gephi.org/.

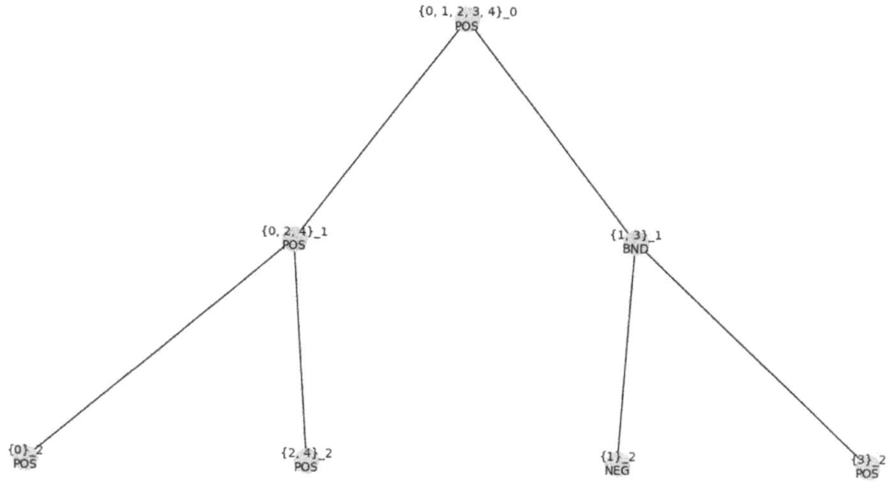

Fig. 5.7 Lattice generated and visualized by using the authors' library

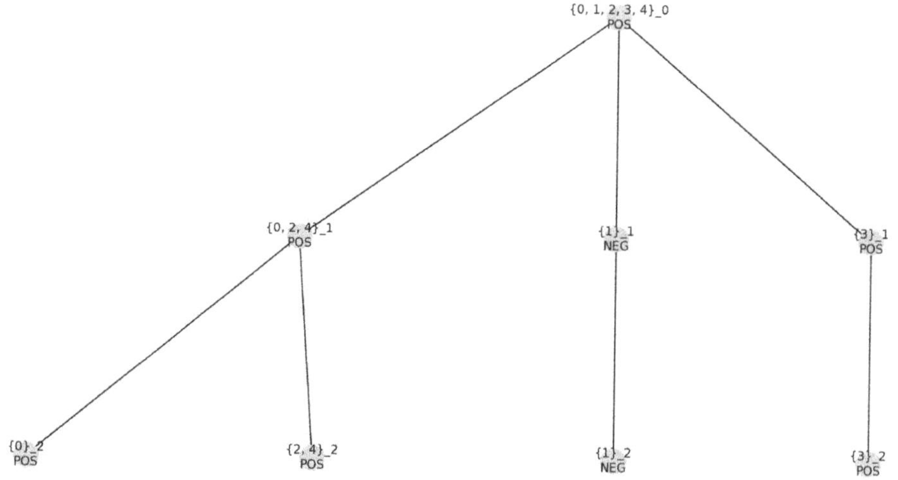

Fig. 5.8 Lattice for first future scenario: vessel `1` increases the drifting angle

In particular, assume that the decision maker needs to evaluate two future scenarios: (i) vessel `1` increases its drifting angle (`Drifting Angle = MID` is replaced by `Drifting Angle = HIGH`), and (ii) vessel `1` increases its velocity (`Velocity = LOW` is replaced by `Velocity = MID`). The source code described in Sect. 5.7.1 must be executed twice for simulating the two future scenarios. Note that in both the scenarios, at time `1`, the value for the decision attribute remains the same with respect to time `0`. Each execution must load the correct updated dataset. The results provided by the two executions are reported in Figs. 5.8 and 5.9. The analysis of the situation evolution is the same done in Sect. 5.5.1.

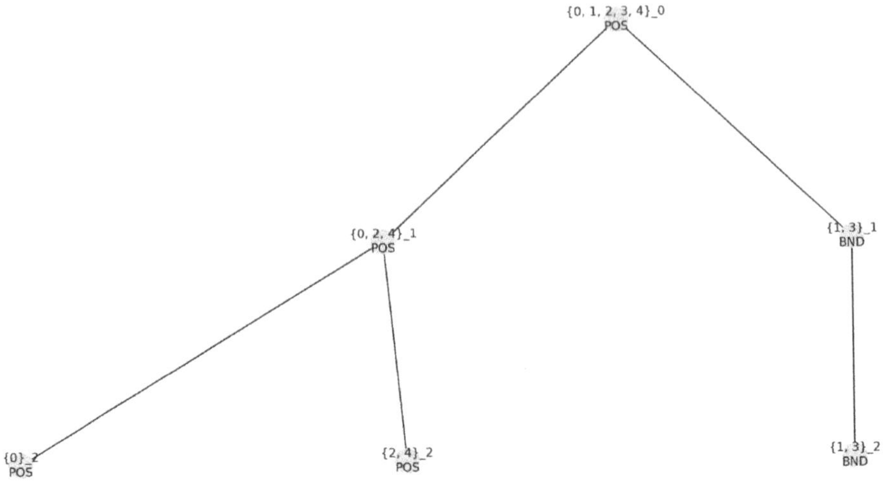

Fig. 5.9 Lattice for second future scenario: vessel 1 increases the velocity

5.8 Useful Resources

- NetworkX, https://networkx.org/. This is the official Web Site of NwtworkX. The Site provides the reference documentation, some tutorials and an installation guide.
- Graph Data Science With Python/NetworkX, https://www.toptal.com/data-science/graph-data-science-python-networkx. This Site provides a good tutorial on NetworkX for Data Science.
- PyGraphViz, https://pygraphviz.github.io/. This is the official Web Site of PyGraphViz. The Site provides a comprehensive documentation to generate graphical representation of graphs constructed by means of the NetworkX library.

Chapter 6
System Modelling with Graphs

A graph is a mathematical structure consisting of two sets called its vertex set and its edge set (Trudeau 1993). In a graph, each pair of vertices are related by edges. From a formal point of view, a graph is defined as a pair $G = (V, E)$, where V is the vertex set and $E = \{(x, y)|(x, y) \in V^2 \ and \ x \neq y\}$ is the edge set.

Graph-based technologies are tools used in Intelligence Analysis for several purposes. Two main complementary trends can be observed. As analysis tools, graphs provide methods for obtaining insights from connected data. For example, algorithms from graph theory and the analysis of social networks can be used to identify communities, highly connected individuals, or to understand information flows across complex networks. As visualization tools, graphs can be used to represent and analyze complex models, systems and networks. In intelligence analysis, these features are used to derive terrorist networks and identify potential threats (Krebs 2002) or improve pattern analysis (Coffman et al. 2004).

In this chapter, Graph theory and social network analysis are combined with evaluation based three-way decisions to support analysts in the identification of the critical nodes of a complex network. A node is *critical* if its removal or corruption seriously compromises the functionality of the network. Depending on the nature of the network, critical nodes can be components of a critical infrastructure, organizations of a complex network of analysts, a particular information source in an intelligence network.

6.1 Learning Objectives of the Chapter

This chapter contextualizes the analysis method of Chap. 4 to a network analysis. The Learning Objectives of this chapter refer to the levels 2 (Understand) and 3 (Apply) of the taxonomy shown in Fig. 1.2).

V. Loia et al., *Computational Techniques for Intelligence Analysis*,
https://doi.org/10.1007/978-3-031-20851-5_6

The Learning Objectives of this chapter are:

- Implementation and Execution of the methodology of Chap. 4 for a network analysis.
- Execution of python code to build a network.
- Use of Probabilistic Rough Sets to classify network nodes.
- Use of a Three-Way decisions model to evaluate the criticality of network nodes.
- Implementation and Execution of resilience measures to evaluate network resilience to hypotheses of intentional attacks.
- Experimenting the methodology with hands-on lab.

6.2 Topic Map of the Chapter

As shown by the topic map in Fig. 6.1, this chapter introduces a methodology aiming at supporting analysts to maintain a proper level of performance of a critical infrastructure in case of attacks (cyber-physics). Such methodology is mainly based on Resilience Network Analysis and is defined by means of Evaluation-based Three-Way Decisions supported by Graph Theory (structures and measures). Moreover, new measures for estimating the performance degree of critical functionalities are introduced.

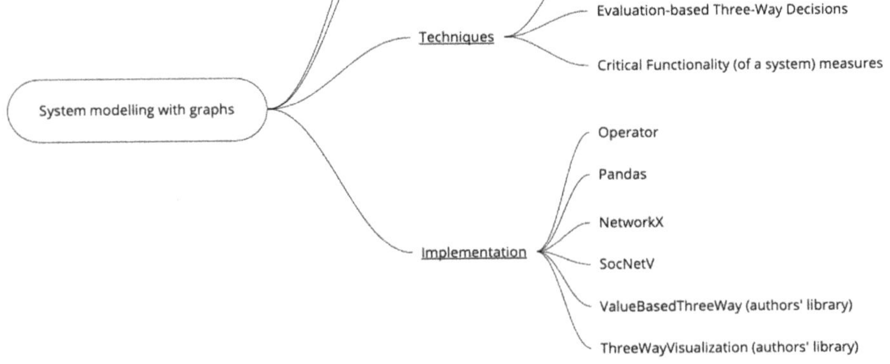

Fig. 6.1 Topic Map of the chapter

The techniques on which the methodology is based can be implemented by means of a set of Python-based tools and libraries indicated by the topic map. The hands-on lab section of this chapter shows also how to use the software SocNetV to visualize and process networks (graphs).

6.3 Case Introduction: Evaluation of Critical Nodes in a Critical Infrastructure

The case refers to the analysis of a large scale network that models a Critical Infrastructure (CI). As part of activities devoted to risk and threat assessment, an analyst may be interested in understanding the parts of the CI that are more vulnerable and critical in case of attack. Using heuristics based on trisection, such as the evaluation based 3WD, the analysis may identify three ordered regions of different importance and associate appropriate strategies to deal with the nodes belonging to these regions (see Fig. 6.2 where $RegionIII \succ RegionII \succ RegionI$ and *Resistance*, *Redirection* and *Reconstruction* refers to protection strategies to apply).

The overall objective of the analyst is to maintain a proper level of performance in case of attack and, to this purpose, executes a resilience analysis of the CI. Attacks events are simulated to assess the effects of the strategies associated to the regions.

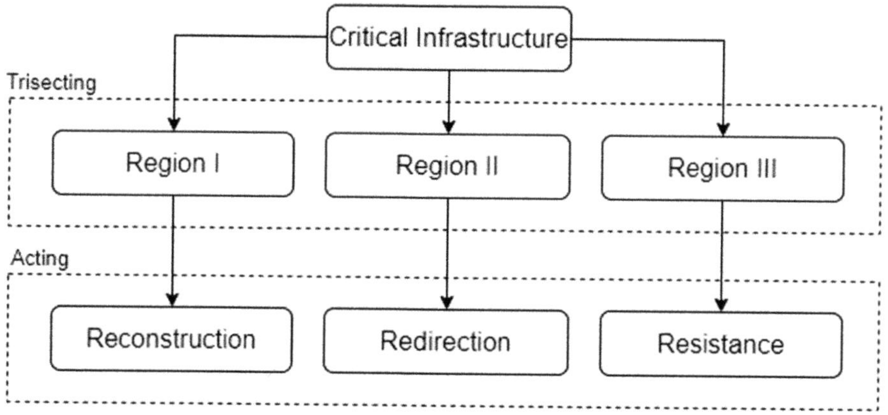

Fig. 6.2 Identification of parts and strategies.

6.4 Methodology

The case described in the previous section can be executed following the methodology shown in Fig. 6.3. The starting point is the GDTA reporting the SA requirements.

At the perception level, the requirements refers to functional and topological information on the network. Specifically, these requirements can include raw data such as performance data of the nodes and the adjacency matrix of the network. With the support of social network analysis measure, the data of the adjacency matrix can be elaborated to produce indexes of interests such as out-degree or in-degree. The output of this Perception phase is an Information Table such as Table 6.1) where each rows is a component of the CI described with a set of performance attributes (*p1*, *p2*, *p3*) and network indexes (*t1*, *t2*, *t3*).

At the comprehension level, the requirements give information on how to derive the three ordered regions in order to apply the strategies. So, in this phase, a partition based on 3WD is executed to derive a Decision Table is produced that reports also a classification of each node in a region. In this phase, however, depending on the specific SA level 2 requirements, a fusion of the performance attributes and social network indexes can be executed in order to enhance the comprehensions. An example of Decision Table resulting as output of this phase is reported in Table 6.2 where the decision attribute d presents the classification and is evaluated with the support of an evaluation function. This function should consider both the functional and topological importance of a node in the CI. The specific form, however, depends on the SA level 2 requirements.

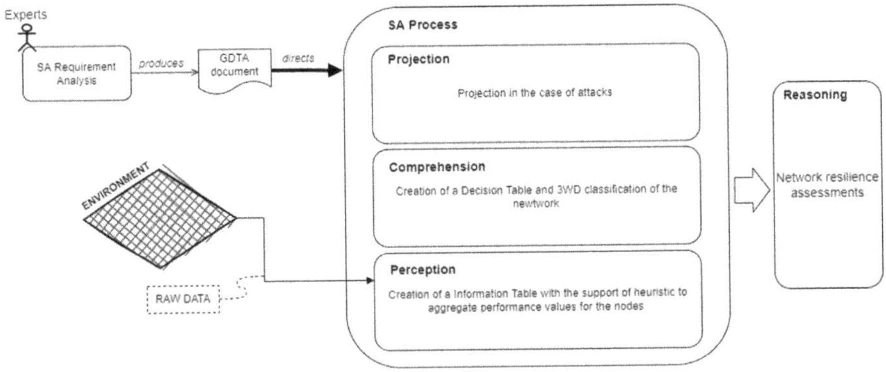

Fig. 6.3 The methodology for graph analysis with three-way decisions

Table 6.1 Sample information table

Node	p1	p1	p3	t1	t2	t3
1	0.4	0.4	0.6	0.34	0.54	0.1
2	0.34	0.14	0.46	0.4	0.4	0.3
...	...	...	...	...	...	...

Table 6.2 Sample decision table

Node	F	T	d
1	0.23	0.4	3
2	0.44	0.6	1
...	...	...	...

At the projection level, the requirements refer to changes in case of intentional attacks or natural disasters[1]. This phase is supported by the adoption of tools, such as Attack Trees or other graph models (Lallie et al. 2020), that are developed taking into account the projection requirements in the GDTA. In the context of this book, attack trees are modeled with Granular Computing.

6.5 Computational Techniques

This section discusses the computational techniques that can be used to execute the methodology above presented.

Let $G = (V, E)$ be a graph modeling a CI. A vertex $v \in V$ is a component of the CI and an edge $e \in E$ is a link between two components of the CI. Let us define $U = V \times E$ the universe consisting of all the components and links of the CI.

6.5.1 3WD Supported by Network Analysis

To classify the components of the CI in the three regions and associate proper resilience strategies to protect the most critical component, a trisecting-acting-outcome model of 3WD is adopted. Yao (2020) defines a trisecting acting outcome (TAO) model as a three-way decision models involving trisecting a whole into three parts and acting on the three parts, in order to produce an optimal outcome. With this approach, it is possible to associate actions to the regions (see Fig. 6.2) and evaluate the outcome the actions to adapt the tri-partition. This is, essentially, the purpose of the analysis method of this chapter: to associate protection strategies to parts of a CI and assess their effects under attack situation.

A discussion on the approaches to evaluate the most critical and influential components of a CI is reported by Latora and Marchiori (2005). In general, the criticality of a component is due to both its position in the network and services/functionalities/capabilities offered. On this basis, the method in this section is based on the definition of an evaluation function that combines two parts:

[1] In the following section, only intentional attacks are considered.

$$Ev(i) = \lambda T(i) + (1 - \lambda)F(i) \tag{6.1}$$

where $i \in V$ is a component of the CI (i.e., a vertex of the graph). Equation (6.1) takes into account topological ($T(i)$) and performance or functional ($F(i)$) aspects of a component to evaluate its criticality in the CI. The value of adopting this parameterized function is that an analyst, in deciding what are the components to better protect, can weight more or less their position in the network or their functionalities via the parameter $\lambda \in [0, 1]$. However, Eq. (6.1) has to be better contextualized case by case depending on the concrete CI under analysis.

$T(i)$ can be derived with network analysis measures or their combinations. Considering Table 6.1, $T(i)$ can be derived with combination of network indexes such as *t1*, *t2* and *t3*. For example, $T(i)$ may by a centrality measure, a combination of in-degree and out-degree and so on. The specific measures to be adopted can be derived from GDTA requirements.

$F(i)$ is evaluated by combining different performance values. In its general form, $F(i) = \nabla_{j=1}^{n} p_j$ where p_j $j = 1, 2, ..., n$ are the performance values of the components (see Table 6.1) and ∇ is an aggregation operator such as a mean, weighted mean, OWA and so on, that fuses the performance data of the components. Also in this case, the specific aggregator to adopt can be derived from GDTA requirements.

To comprehend that are the most critical parts of the CI, evaluation based 3WD is applied. The three regions are evaluated as as follows:

$$\begin{aligned} RegionI &= \{i \in U | Ev(i) \preceq \beta\} \\ RegionII &= \{i \in U | \beta \prec Ev(i) \prec \alpha\} \\ RegionIII &= \{i \in U | Ev(i) \succeq \alpha\} \end{aligned} \tag{6.2}$$

The three regions are ordered, so objects of Region III are preferable (i.e.: more critical) to objects of Region II, and these last ones are preferable to objects of Region I. The values of the two thresholds α and β can be estimated, at the beginning, with the approaches proposed by Yao (2011) based on the risk of mis-classification. The threshold values are, however, refined on the basis of the analysis of resilience in case of attacks (discussed in the following subsection).

After the application of Eq. (6.2), the result is a decision table such as Table 6.2 where each component is classified into a region.

6.5.2 *Reasoning on Graphs with GrC*

The analysis is interested in understanding if the strategies developed to protect the components belonging to the different regions are such to ensure a proper level of resilience.

In general, the analyst can reason using the what-if analysis described in the previous Chap. 5. However, the analyst should be aware of the type of attacks to

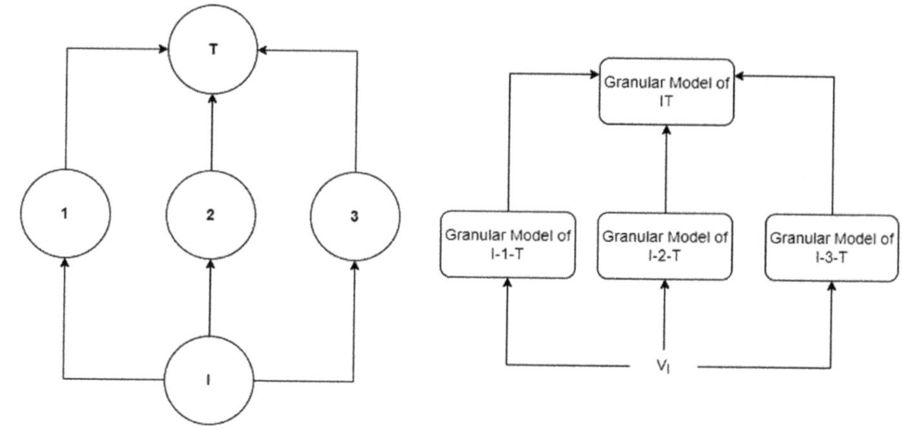

Fig. 6.4 Granular models of attacks

analyze. This information is reported in the GDTA Level 3 requirements and on the basis of this information Hierarchical Granular Models of attacks can be developed following the approach proposed by Pedrycz and Al-Hmouz (2015). Let us explain the core of this method with the support of Fig. 6.4 where the left-hand side shows a part of CI with a component labeled as I that indicates the the starting point of an attack and a component labeled T indicating a potential target of the attack. Between I and T, some paths are available.

The basic idea behind the creation of Granular Models of attacks (shown in the right-hand side of Fig. 6.4) is to build granular descriptors of the variation of components performances when under a specific attack. Let us describe their construction with a simple example and refer the interested reader to the details in (Fujita et al. 2018).

Let us suppose node I is the attack entry point of a CI such as a Smart Grid. This node can be infiltrated inside a trusted perimeter by humans with an USB stick exploiting, in this case, a vulnerability V_{I1}) or can have a poorly configured firewall allowing network based intrusion (this is another vulnerability V_{I2}). Let suppose that I controls the power load distribution to a transmission node (1) and a service provider (2), and communicates with a metering device (3). The target T is a customer of a smart grid. The first attack path, $I-1-T$, may result in a power shortage to the customer, in the second $I-2-T$ the power shortage to service provider node may result in a failure to delivery apps and services for smart home load balancing, with the third $I-3-T$ path an attacker may inject false information and meter data. All the attacks have influence on the normal energy consumption of the customer.

A Granular model of attack for this scenario can be defined by constructing granular descriptors, in terms of intervals, that report information on the loss of performance and level of activity of a node under attack. Numeric models can be built, in this case, in the form of bi-dimensional intervals reporting a range of values for the level of performance and activity of a node, e.g., $V_1 = [w_-, w_+][\pi_-, \pi_+]$ with w and

π are, respectively, performance and activity level values. Starting from these granular descriptions, fuzzy rules can be derived to represent the models. For instance, the three models shown in the right-hand side of Fig. 6.4) may be described by the if then rules: $if\ V_{I1}\ and\ V_1\ then\ V_{T1}$, $if\ V_{I2}\ and\ V_3\ then\ V_{T3}$, $if\ V_{I1}\ and\ V_2\ then\ V_{T2}$ where the first corresponds to $MI-1-T$, the second to $MI-2-T$ and the third to $MI-3_T$. The models can be fused in a more abstract granular model to represent the overall attack situation.

Now, if the goal is to protect the most critical components of a CI, i.e., the ones classified in Region III. Granular models of attacks including the possible paths to the target nodes (of region III) are constructed. Since the granular models are in the form of interval granules, they can be used to evaluate the resilience of the CI using system resilience measures such as the measure define by Cutter et al. 2013 based on the concept of Critical Functionality of a system:

$$K(t; N, L, C) = \frac{\Sigma_{i\in(N,L)} w_i(t; C)\pi_i(t; C)}{\Sigma_{i\in(N,L)} w_i(t; C)} \tag{6.3}$$

where $w_i(t; C)$ is a measure of the relative importance of node or link i at time t, and $\pi_i(t; C)$ represents the degree to which a node or a link is active in the presence of an adverse event. An alternative interpretation defines $\pi_i(t; C)$ as the probability that node or link i is fully functional. C is the set of temporal decision rules and/or strategies to be developed in order to improve the resilience of the system during its operation such as the ones shown in Fig. 6.2 . An object $c \in C$ represents a configuration of the system.

The critical functionality K of Eq. (6.3) is to be evaluated using augmented operations for addition $\oplus$ and multiplication $\otimes$ with intervals:

$$K = \frac{\sum_{\oplus_{i\in(N,L)}} [w_i^-, w_i^+] \otimes [\pi_i^-, \pi_i^+]}{\sum_{\oplus_{i\in(N,L)}} [w_i^-, w_i^+]} \tag{6.4}$$

6.6 Analytical Value

Graph and Network analysis belong to the Decomposition and Visualization family of Structured Analytic Techniques that support the analyst in decomposing a problem into its parts, organize and analyze the parts.

The use of evaluation based 3WD to analyze networks has some advantages from an analytical point of view:

- the possibility of defining an evaluation function of the nodes of a network that allows to balance topological and functional analysis of the network, and
- the cognitive simplicity linked to the three-partitions which helps the analyst in identifying the areas of the network that are more critical with respect to the analysis to be carried out.

6.7 Hands-on Lab

The objective of this tutorial is to guide the reader in applying evaluation-based three-way decisions to comprehend which are the critical aspects of a cyber-physical infrastructure and plan sustainable security-preserving maintenance operations. In other words, maintenance operations will be targeted only to the most critical components. Thus, the practical data-oriented task is the tri-partitioning of the infrastructure components. Such tri-partitioning, as affirmed before, must be realized by means of an evaluation function that will assess the criticalities of all the individual infrastructure components. Therefore, the first step is defining the adopted evaluation function. For the sake of simplicity, assume that such function is defined as it follows:

$$v(i) = \lambda T(i) + (1 - \lambda)F(i) \tag{6.5}$$

where i is the ith component of the infrastructure, $T(i)$ measures the importance of i within the infrastructure with respect to its connections with the other components, $F(i)$ measures the importance of i with respect to its function within the infrastructure, and λ is a balance factor. Assume that F values are provided as input and T values must be calculated starting from topological information. Lastly, λ is a configuration parameter.

6.7.1 *Dataset*

The sample dataset contains topological and functional information of all the infrastructure components. Consider the following data:

In particular, the rows represent the components of the cyber-physical infrastructure, column `node` reports the identifier of each component, at the ith row the `adjs` column reports the components reachable from i and the `func` column reports a value (in the scale [0, 1]) representing the importance of the functionalities of i (see function F in Eq. 6.5). For instance, the component 2 allows the access to the component 3 and the component 7, and has an importance of 0.4 with respect to its functionalities within the critical infrastructure.

6.7.2 *Building the Graph*

In order to build the graph representing the infrastructure of Table 6.3 it is possible to use the package `NetworkX`[2]. Let provide the needed source code into a sequence of fragments, which can be executed in the same Colab cell obviously.

[2] Note that the instructions for the installation of this library have been provided in the Sect. 5.7.

Table 6.3 Sample data for a critical infrastructure

Node	Adjs	Funcs
1	2;3	0.1
2	3;7	0.4
3	4	0.2
4	5;6	0.3
5	6	1
6	8	0.7
7	5;8	0.6
8		1

First of all, you need to upload the dataset `ci.csv` into the Colab environment, then it is requested to import `networkx` and `pandas` modules to exploit their functionalities. In particular, `Pandas` is needed to deal with the CSV file containing the adjacency lists representing the sample critical infrastructure and `NetworkX`, as anticipated before, to build the graph structure modeling the critical infrastructure.

Secondly, the function `.read_csv` has to be invoked to load the CSV file and convert it into a `DataFrame` object. Subsequently, an empty directed graph is built by instantiating the `DiGraph` class.

The following fragment implements the aforementioned actions:

```
import networkx as nx
import pandas as pd

df = pd.read_csv("data/ci.csv")

G = nx.DiGraph()
```

Now, it is possible to fulfill the empty graph with nodes and edges as they are reported in the adjacency lists in the dataframe `df`. In particular, the following fragment reports how to extract the nodes and their adjacencies from the dataframe `df`:

```
nodes = list(map(str,list(df["node"])))
adjs = list(df["adjs"])
```

The previous source code extracts the values in the columns `node` of `df`, converts them from integers (objects of the Python class `int`) to strings (objects of the Python class `str`) through the application of the `map` function and creates a new Python list (object of the Python class `list`) containing them. Moreover, the column `adjs` is extracted in order to create a Python list of string where each string reports the adjacencies for a given node. It is important to underline that in the created lists, a given index links a node with its adjacencies. In other words, the index equal to 0 corresponds to `nodes[0] == "1"` and `edges[0] == "2;3"`, therefore there are two edges starting from node `"1"`. The first one arrives to node `"2"` and the second one arrives to node `"3"`.

Once constructed the two lists, it is needed to adapt such lists to be used as input to fulfill the graph G. This is accomplished by executing the following code:

```
edges = list()
for i in range(len(nodes)):
    node = nodes[i]
    targets = str(adjs[i]).split(";")
    for t in targets:
        if t != "nan":
            edges.append((node, t))
```

The previous code fragment starts from the two lists constructed before and generates a Python list of edges. Each edge is represented by a Python tuple (s, t), where s is the source node and t is the target node. In this way, for each node $nodes[i]$ it is possible to create a set of edges $(nodes[i], t_1), (nodes[i], t_2), \ldots (nodes[i], t_k)$ where $adjs[i] ==$ "t_1; t_2; ...; t_k". Data in Table 6.3 are now transformed into two Python lists: `nodes` and `edges`. List `nodes` contains:

```
['1', '2', '3', '4", '5', '6', '7', '8'].
```

List `edges` contains:

```
[('1', '2'), ('1', '3'), ('2', '3'), ('2', '7'), ('3', '4'), ('4', '5'), ('4', '6'),
  ('5', '6'), ('6', '8'), ('7', '5'), ('7', '8')].
```

The last step for building the graph is to fulfill the graph object G by executing the following code:

```
G.add_nodes_from(nodes)
G.add_edges_from(edges)

print(len(G.nodes()), len(G.edges()))
```

In the previous fragment, the methods `DiGraph.add_nodes_from()` and `DiGraph. add_edges_from()` are used to achieve the aforementioned objective. The arguments of such methods are exactly the structures prepared before. The last instruction of the source code is a simple print command (producing 8 and 11 on the screen) to test the correct construction.

6.7.3 Calculating T Values

Once the graph is ready, it is possible to derive the values for T (see Eq. 6.5 by using the *Katz Centrality* to assign a score to the importance of each node in the critical infrastructure. The following source code has the objective of calculating such scores and attaching the right score to the right node in the graph:

```
from operator import itemgetter

centrality_dict = nx.katz_centrality(G)
nx.set_node_attributes(G, centrality_dict, 'centrality
    ')

sorted_centrality = sorted(centrality_dict.items(),
    key=itemgetter(1), reverse=True)

for b in sorted_centrality:
    print(b)
```

More in detail, the function `katz_centrality()` calculates the scores for all nodes and returns a Python dictionary where the keys are the names of the nodes and the values are such scores. Subsequently, the function `set_node_attributes()` is used to attach the calculated scores to the right nodes by using of the dictionary. Now, `G` has been enriched. Moreover, in order to print the scores, the function `sorted()` is used to sort the dictionary items with respect to the scores in descending order. Lastly, the `for` statement is included to iterate over the sorted dictionary items and print all of them. The result is the following one:

```
('8', 0.3772663346956877)
('6', 0.37725686056417757)
('5', 0.3738003306486869)
('3', 0.3697967460427693)
('4', 0.3425968200941689)
('7', 0.33923503149378015)
('2', 0.3361788600388812)
('1', 0.305617145489892)
```

The selection of a suitable centrality measure depends on the nature of the problem to face. In other words, in the context of other scenarios it will be possible to choose another function, in the place of `katz_centrality()`, like, for instance, `degree_centrality()`, `betweenness_centrality()`, `closeness_centrality()`, etc. In particular, the ordered results for the Degree Centrality are:

```
('2', 0.42857142857142855)
('3', 0.42857142857142855)
('4', 0.42857142857142855)
('5', 0.42857142857142855)
('6', 0.42857142857142855)
('7', 0.42857142857142855)
('1', 0.2857142857142857)
('8', 0.2857142857142857)
```

Lastly, it is possible to draw the infrastructure by using the `SocNetV` tool and open a serialized version of the graph built by using `NetworkX`. The serializa-

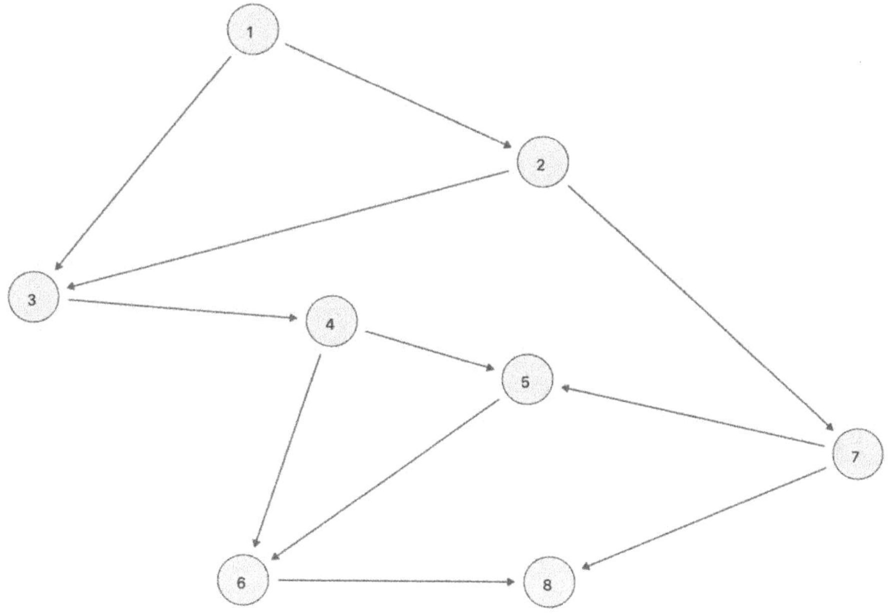

Fig. 6.5 Graph representing the infrastructure

tion process is accomplished by using the instruction `nx.write_graphml(G, "infra1.graphml")`. The result is shown in Fig. 6.5.

6.7.4 Building the Decision Table

Once the values for function `T` have been calculated, the construction of the decision table is due. In particular, it is needed to start from the Table 6.3 and add a column for values of function `v` according to the Eq. 6.5 with $\lambda = 0.5$. The following source code can be used to construct the decision table:

```
df["T"] = centrality_dict.values()
df["T"] = round(df["T"], 2)
df["F"] = df["funcs"]

df = df.drop(columns=["funcs", "adjs"])

lambdav = 0.5
df["v"] = round(lambdav*df["T"] + (1-lambdav)*df["F"],
    2)
```

The result of the previous code is an adjustment of dataframe `df`:

Table 6.4 Decision table for the critical infrastructure

Node	Adjs	Funcs
1	2;3	0.1
2	3;7	0.4
3	4	0.2
4	5;6	0.3
5	6	1
6	8	0.7
7	5;8	0.6
8		1

6.7.5 Applying 3WD

Once the decision table (see Table 6.4) has been created it is possible to apply evaluation-based three-way decisions for tri-partitioning data. In particular, for each infrastructure node, the value of column `v` represents the evaluation of the corresponding object (node). Such value must be compared to β and α in order to assign the object (node) to a specific region: `NEG`, `BND` or `POS` according to the notions provided in Eq. 3.15. The following source code implements the aforementioned application:

```
def eval(x, **kargs):
    v = kargs["lam"]*x["T"] + (1-kargs["lam"])*x["F"]
    return v

data = pd.read_csv("dt_ci.csv")

infoTable = data.values
tw = ValueBasedThreeWay(data)

beta = 0.3
alpha = 0.6

P, B, N = tw.calculate3WD(eval, [alpha, beta], lam
    =0.5)

print("POS: ", P)
print("BND: ", B)
print("NEG: ", N)

twview = ThreeWayVisualization((P,B,N))
twview.show()
```

The code assumes that Table 6.4 has been serialized in the file `dt_ci.csv` that is load and pre-processed by using `Pandas` functions.

In order to run the above code the definitions of the classes `ThreeWayVisualization` and `ValueBasedThreeWay` must be executed in a Colab cell.

The code for `ThreeWayVisualization` is already provided in Sect. 3.7. The code for the `ValueBasedThreeWay` class is the following one:

```
import numpy as np

class ValueBasedThreeWay:
    _itable = np.array([])

    def __init__(self, itable):
        self._itable = itable

    '''
        v - is the evaluation function
        _alphabetas - a tuple with alpha and beta
            values
        **kargs - the dictionary with parameters for v

        this method sends a row at a time to the
            function v
    '''
    def calculate3WD(self, v, _alphabetas, **kargs):
        POS = np.array([], dtype=int)
        NEG = np.array([], dtype=int)
        BND = np.array([], dtype=int)
        values = list()
        for x in range(len(self._itable)):
            value = v(self._itable.iloc[x], **kargs)
            values.append(value)

        for x in range(len(self._itable)):
            value = values[x]
            if value > _alphabetas[0]:
                POS = np.append(POS, x)
            elif value < _alphabetas[1]:
                NEG = np.append(NEG, x)
            else:
                BND = np.append(BND, x)
        return POS, BND, NEG
```

In particular `ValueBasedThreeWay` is used for the tri-partitioning. The method `calculate3WD` and the thresholds β and α are used to achieve the goal. Lastly, the class `ThreeWayVisualization` (already used previously) is exploited to present the tri-partitioning results.

Take care that in Fig. 6.6, object with index `0` corresponds to the infrastructure node `1`, object with index `1` corresponds to the infrastructure node `2` and so on. Therefore, it is possible to affirm that in the considered infrastructure nodes `5` and `8` are the most critical components of the system. Take a look to the definition of function `eval()`. Such function is passed as reference to the `calculate3WD()`

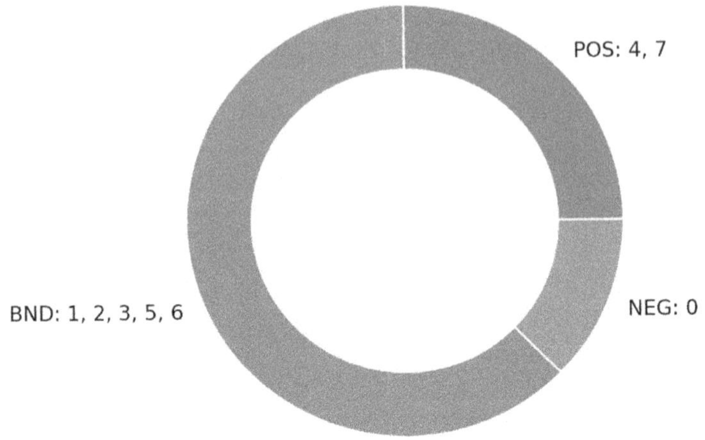

Fig. 6.6 Result of the application of evaluation-based three way decisions

method in order to apply a custom evaluation to for tri-partitioning data. The custom function `eval()` implements the Eq. 3.15.

The interesting aspect to consider is that if, for a given reason, the topology of the infrastructure changes, it is possible to have a different tri-partitioning leading to a different course of actions. In fact, if a link from node 3 to node 6 is added, the importance of node 6 grows. The modified infrastructure topology is reported in Fig. 6.7.

In such a case, the final result for tri-partitioning is provided in Fig. 6.8.

As it is possible to observe now node 6 (remember that it corresponds to the object with index 5) is included in the `POS` region. i.e., it is classified among the most critical components.

6.7.6 Implementing a Resilience Model

In order to assess the resilience degree of a whole Critical Infrastructure, represented as a directed graph, it is needed to provide an implementation for Eq. 6.3. For providing a simple tutorial for the readers, it is preferable to relax some complex aspects of such equation as it follows:

$$K_{s,t} = \frac{\sum_{p \in W_{s,t}} \sum_{u \in p} F(u)\pi(u)}{\sum_{p \in W_{s,t}} \sum_{u \in p} F(u)} \tag{6.6}$$

where $K_{s,t}$ is the resilience degree of the Critical Infrastructure when there is an attack with source node s and target node t, $W_{s,t}$ is the set of all paths starting from node s and ending at node t, $F(.)$ is the same `F` of Table 6.4 and $\pi(u)$ is the probability

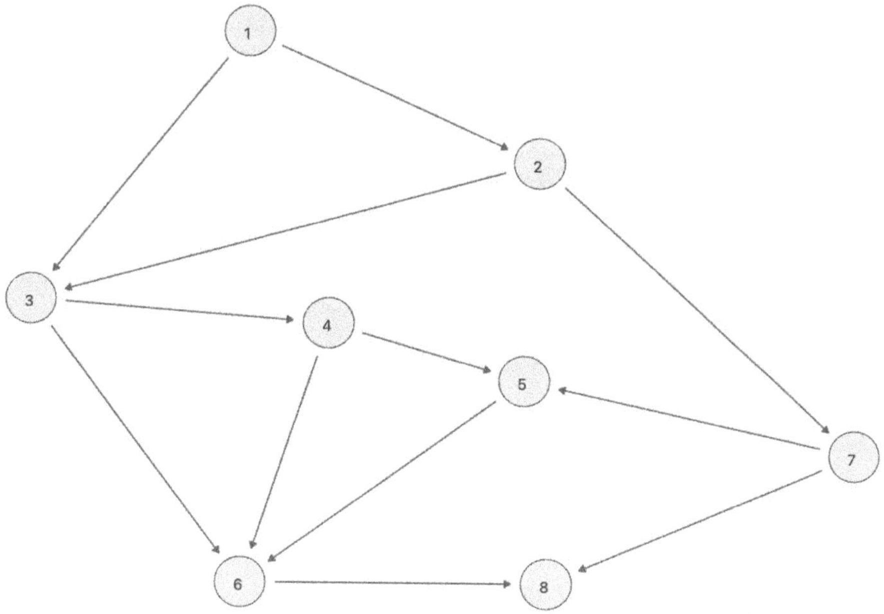

Fig. 6.7 Graph representing the infrastructure

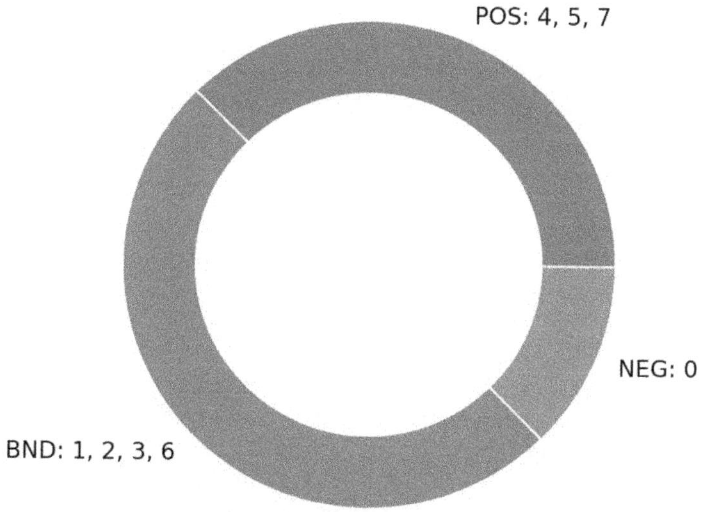

Fig. 6.8 Result of the application of Evaluation-based Three Way Decisions after a change in the infrastructure topology

that node u is active when an adverse event occurs. For the sake of simplicity, assume that values for π are pre-assigned on the basis of the occurring attack scenario.

The idea is that the analyst can simulate a specific attack scenario and calculate the resilience degree. If the obtained degree is not satisfactory, i.e., it is less than a fixed threshold, it is possible to adjust the three-way decisions thresholds to perform a better analysis aiming at finding the most critical nodes for which spending resources for better protection in order to increase the security level.

In terms of Python code, it is needed to consider the following script (that uses some results calculated in the previous code fragments of this section) and is used to assess the resilience when source node is `1` and target node is `8`:

```
actives = {"1": 0.7, "2": 0.7, "3": 0.7, "4": 0.7, "5"
    : 0.7, "6": 0.7, "7": 0.7, "8": 0.7}
relatives = { str(k): v for k, v in zip(list(df["node"
    ]), list(df["F"]))}

paths18 = nx.all_simple_paths(G, "1", "8")

sum_prods = []
sums = []
acc_prods = 0
accs = 0
for path in paths18:
    for i in path:
        acc_prods += (relatives[i]*actives[i])
        accs += relatives[i]
    sum_prods.append(round(acc_prods,2))
    sums.append(round(accs,2))

resilience_degree = round(sum(sum_prods)/sum(sums), 2)
print(resilience_degree)
```

In particular, π-values for all nodes are given by means the `actives` dictionary and F-values are assigned through the `relatives` dictionary. As you can note all the probabilities are set to 0.7. The second one is constructed starting from the dataframe, i.e., `df`), built before. The function `all_simple_paths` (from the `NetworkX` library) is used to extract all paths from `1` to `8` in the graph of Fig. 6.9.

Essentially, the external `for` statement is used to iterate the extracted paths and the inner `for` statement is used to extract individual nodes from such paths. Therefore, this part of code calculates the result of the formula in Eq. 6.6 in the case of $K_{1,8}$ and it provides the result $K_{1,8} = 0.7$. The Python built-in function `round` is used to round up the floating point numbers by using only two decimal digits.

Now, assume that the a different simulated attack scenario is performed still with source node `1` and target node `8`. In this case, the π-values could be modified. Assume that there is only a change: $\pi(6) = 0.2$. Thus, it is needed to run again the previous script with the new values for `actives`. The script result is $K_{1,8} = 0.6$. If such value is not satisfactory, the analyst could adjust the values for the Three-Way Decisions, i.e., β and α. In particular, assume that the analyst change the value of α from 0.6 to 0.55 and takes the same value (0.3) for β.

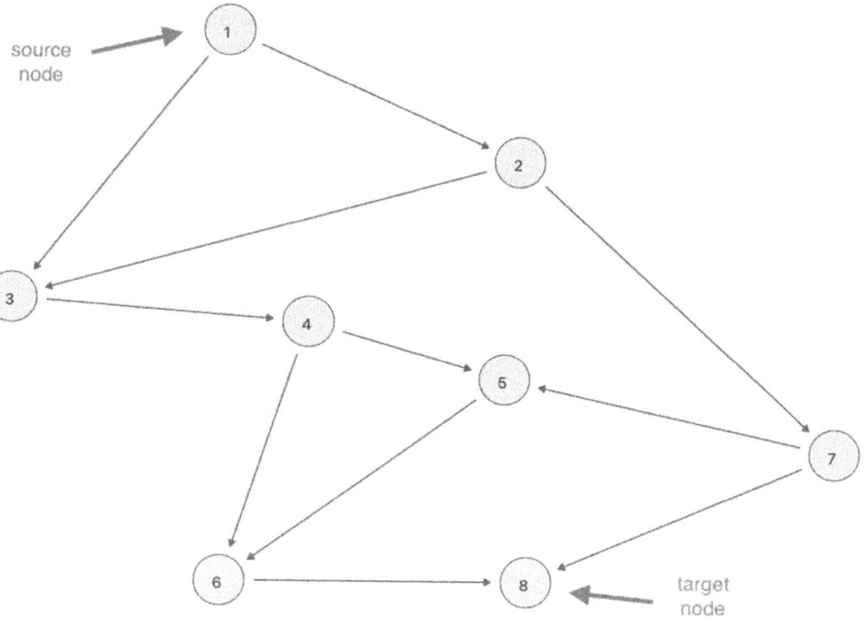

Fig. 6.9 Simulated attack scenario

Table 6.5 Table reporting results for two runs of evaluation-based three-way decisions

	run 1	***run 2***
	$\beta = 0.3, \alpha = 0.6$	$\beta = 0.3, \alpha = 0.55$
POS	5, 8	5, 6, 8
BND	2, 3, 4, 6, 7	2, 3, 4, 7
NEG	1	1

Let compare now the results of the Three-Way Decisions with respect to the previous execution and the current one in the Table 6.5.

It is interesting to note that if the analyst decrease the value for α of 0.05 node 6, whose probability to be active when an attack occurs is 0.2, is positioned in the positive region, i.e., it is classified as a critical node that should be better protected and enforced.

6.8 Useful Resources

- SocNetV, https://socnetv.org//. This is the official Web Site of SocNetV. The Site provides downloadable versions of the tool and the complete reference documentation.

- Graph Algorithms, http://www.martinbroadhurst.com/Graph-algorithms.html. The Site provides details about the implementation of many graph algorithms.
- Katz Centrality in NetworkX, https://networkx.org/documentation/stable/reference/algorithms/generated/networkx.algorithms.centrality.katz_centrality.html. This page provides knowledge about the usage of the Katz Centrality degree through NetworkX.
- GraphML and NetworkX, https://networkx.org/documentation/stable/reference/readwrite/graphml.html. This page provides information about the use of the format GraphML in NetworkX.

Chapter 7
Behaviour Modelling with Fuzzy Signatures

The approach to Intelligence Analysis proposed in this book leverages the concept of Situation and its application to intelligence cycles, as described in Chap. 4. In Chap. 5, the situation under analysis has been represented by means of granular structures (partitions lattices) constructed by performing granulation operations. This made it possible to reason on a *descriptive* perspective of a situation. In Chap. 6, a *relational* perspective based on the use of graphs has been added to this perspective. This made it possible to take into account the relationships that exist between nodes of a network to carry out resilience assessments.

In this chapter, a third perspective is introduced which is the *behavioral* one. This perspective can be defined by techniques useful for analyzing and abstracting the actions of objects within the environment. Specifically, each object of the universe under analysis is considered as the agent of a specific action directed towards a particular target and which uses particular resources.

The combination of descriptive, relational and behavioral perspectives offers a good conceptual overview of how a situation can be computationally represented.

The chapter applies the behavioral perspective to a concrete example of intelligence analysis: the assessment of hypotheses of terrorist attack. To do this, the behavior of known terrorist groups is modeled with a behavioral situational perspective: each group (object) can carry out an attack (action) towards a target using particular weapons (resources). This perspective is modeled with constructs from Fuzzy set theory described in Sect. 3.5.2.

7.1 Learning Objectives of the Chapter

This chapter contextualizes the analysis method of Chap. 4 to a counter-terrorism analysis. The Learning Objectives of this chapter refer to the levels 2 (Understand) and 3 (Apply) of the taxonomy shown in Fig. 1.2).

V. Loia et al., *Computational Techniques for Intelligence Analysis*,
https://doi.org/10.1007/978-3-031-20851-5_7

The Learning Objectives of this chapter are:

- Implementation and Execution of the methodology of Chap. 4 for a counter-terrorism analysis.
- Use of Fuzzy relations to construct behavioral models (i.e., fuzzy signatures) of terrorist groups.
- Use of a Three-Way decisions model to asses attack hypotheses.
- Experimenting the methodology with hands-on lab.

7.2 Topic Map of the Chapter

As shown by the topic map in Fig. 7.1, this chapter introduces a methodology aiming at supporting analysts to assess hypotheses of terrorist attacks. Such methodology is inspired to the scenario analysis method, widely adopted in counter-terrorism activities, and is defined by means of the integration of two main computational techniques: Fuzzy Signature and Three-Way Decisions. While Fuzzy Signatures are used to model the terrorist group behaviors, Fuzzy Similarity is used for measuring the similarity between the behaviors of two groups.

The techniques on which the methodology is based can be implemented by means of a set of Python-based tools and libraries indicated by the topic map and a precious dataset, namely Global Terrorism Database (GTD).

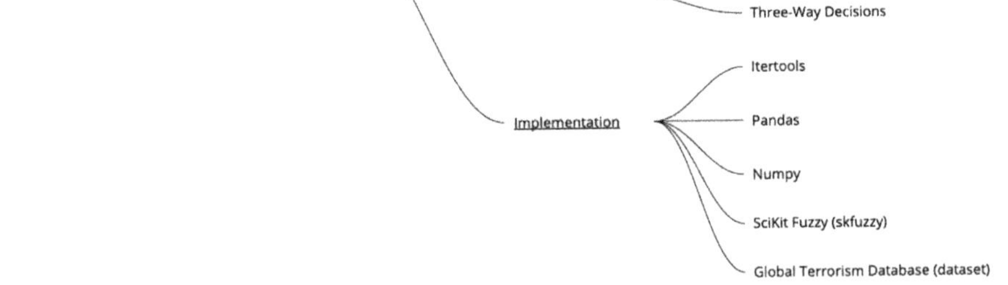

Fig. 7.1 Topic Map of the chapter

7.3 Case Introduction: Counter-Terrorism Analysis with the Global Terrorism Database

Terrorism is a phenomenon that has posed many challenges to governments and intelligence agencies in recent years. Correct intelligence is the basis for understanding and preventing the activities related to this phenomenon.

The case reported in this section aims at showing how counter-terrorism analysis can be executed with an open source database of terrorism events, i.e., the Global Terrorism Database (GTD)[1]. Counter-terrorism refers to practice, tactics, techniques, and strategies that governments, military, law enforcement, business, and intelligence agencies use to contrast terrorism organizations. Specifically, in this chapter, the focus will be limited to the analysis of the GTD to understand the behavior of terrorist groups and predict terrorist attack events.

GTD is an open source database which includes terrorist activities or events information all around the world since 1970. The dataset contains information on more than 180,000 terrorism events, and considers 9 main attributes and several sub-attributes. The main 9 are: (i) ID and Date; (ii) Incident Information, (iii) Incident Location, (iv) Attack Information, (v) Weapon Information, (vi) Target/Victim Information, (vii) Perpetrator Information, (viii) Casualties and Consequences, and (ix) Additional Information and Sources.

The GTD analysis is carried out to represent the behavior of terrorist groups in a computationally tractable way. Deriving a *signature* of a terrorist group is fundamental in many operational scenarios such as, for example, the construction and evaluation of hypotheses of attack. If, on the one hand, structured analytical techniques offer numerous diagnostic, contrarian and imaginative methods of analysis (such as competitive hypothesis analysis or high-impact/low-probability scenario analysis), on the other, a difficulty remains to correctly deduce the hypotheses and scenarios to be analyzed when they refer to human behavior, such as the terrorist phenomenon. To this end, the Fuzzy logic formalism described in Sect. 3.5.2 can be a useful support to take into account the uncertainty intrinsically associated with this type of analysis.

Downstream of the construction of such fuzzy behavioral models, the analysis envisages their use in a 3WD model to make predictions in relation to terrorist groups that may (or may not) perpetrate an attack based on intelligence information gathered in relation to the target type, weapon and intended attack strategy.

[1] https://www.start.umd.edu/gtd/.

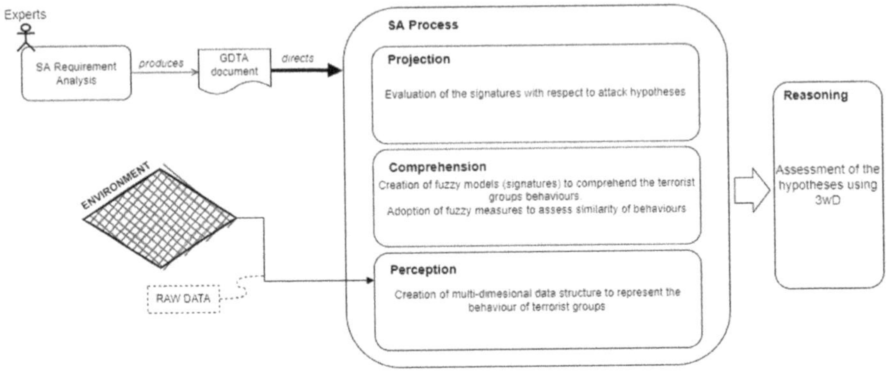

Fig. 7.2 The methodology for counter-terrorism analysis.

7.4 Methodology

The case described in the previous section can be executed following the methodology shown in Fig. 7.2. The starting point is the GDTA reporting the SA requirements. Raw Data refers to the GTD data.

At the perception level, the elements of the environment to perceive refers to terrorist groups. The purpose is to improve the comprehension of their behaviors and, thus, at this level aspects such as potential targets, attack strategies, weapons used and so on are of interest for the analyst. More formally, given a terrorist group, g, that can perform an attack, a, with a weapon, w, on a target, t. At SA level 1, the behavior of such groups can be described using a multi-dimensional data structure such as: $\langle G, A, W, T \rangle$ where G is set of a terrorist groups, A refers to a set of attack strategies, W to a set of weapon types and T to a set of target types. So, If a group, g_i, perpetrates an attack, a_j, towards a target, t_k, using a weapon, w_l, then a point $\langle g_i, a_j, t_k, w_l \rangle$ in $\langle G, A, W, T \rangle$ is marked.

At the comprehension level, the behavior of a terrorist must be made understandable by the analyst. It is, therefore, necessary to raise the level of abstraction of the information contained in the multi-dimensional data structure to obtain a behavioral signature that informs the analyst about what a particular target, and/or a particular attack strategy and/or a particular weapon characterize a group. To do this, the fuzzy set theory can be used which allows to include in the modeling a degree of uncertainty regarding the belonging of strategies, targets and weapons to terrorist groups. So, at this level, fuzzy sets for each of the elements of interests (e.g., targets, weapons, attack strategies) are derived and fused together by adopting the concept of fuzzy relation reported in Sect. 3.5.2.2. Specifically, for a group g_i three fuzzy sets are constructed, $\widetilde{T_{g_i}}$, $\widetilde{A_{g_i}}$ and $\widetilde{W_{g_i}}$. The elements of a fuzzy set, such as $\widetilde{T_{g_i}}$, are the targets of the group g_i with an associated membership degree. For instance, the element $\langle POLICE/0.75 \rangle$ of $\widetilde{T}$ informs that police is a target of g_i and this target belong to the behavior of g_i with a degree of 0.75. The same is for the elements of the other fuzzy sets. With these fuzzy sets, it is possible to derive a signature of g_i relating two or more fuzzy sets, e.g. $S_{WT}(g_i) = \widetilde{W}_{g_i} \times \widetilde{T}_{g_i}$, that models the behavior of g_i in terms of couple attack strategy - target type and a memberships degree, e.g. $\langle(EXPLOSIVE, POLICE)/0.54\rangle$ that informs that attack based on explosives towards a police target belongs to the behavior of g_i with a degree of 0.54. The signature just described is a fuzzy behavioral model of a terrorist group. Operations can be performed on this signature to improve situational awareness using fuzzy mathematical operators. As an example, the signatures of two groups can be compared using similarity measures.

At the projection level, the analyst has to project the fuzzy signature of a group with respect to an attack hypothesis. In other words, the analyst has to understand to what extend the group under analysis can perpetrate the attack. To this end it is necessary to construct an attack event in a similar way to what is done for group signatures. Suppose that the intelligence sources provide information about a possible terrorist attack carried out with a particular attack strategy, with a specific weapon and directed towards a specific target. Three fuzzy sets are constructed, $\widetilde{A}$, $\widetilde{W}$ and $\widetilde{T}$, which are not linked to a particular group but to the whole set of groups known to the analyst. If additional information is available, such as the geographic area of the attack, the analyst can proceed to reduce the set of groups to be used to derive the signature of the event. For example, suppose that intelligence sources report information such as this: attack toward civilians with firearms. This leads to the construction of a signature for an event, Ω, modeled as: $S(\Omega) = CIVIL/0.25 \times FIREARMS/0.47$ where $CIVIL/0.25$ is an element of $\widetilde{T}$ and $FIREARMS/0.47$ is an element of $\widetilde{W}$.

To assess the hypothesis of attack, i.e. to attribute the hypothesis to terrorist groups, an evaluation based 3WD (Sect. 3.6) can be used. The evaluation function compares the signatures of each group with that one of the event Ω. The function is reported in the next sections.

7.5 Computational Techniques

This section describes how to construct a fuzzy signature and how to assess the attack hypotheses using 3WD.

7.5.1 Fuzzy Signature

The computational approach to derive fuzzy signatures of terrorist groups is based in the concepts defined by (Yager,RonaldRand Marek ZReformat, 2012). Their contextualization is reported here for the case of counter-terrorism analysis described in this section. The starting point is the GTD which can be exemplified as in Tab. 7.1. Each row is an attack event described with categorical attributes related to attack

Table 7.1 Event dataset

	A	T	W	D
e1	3	2	2	g1
e2	2	4	3	g1
e3	3	2	2	g1
e4	3	4	3	g2
e5	3	2	1	g2
e6	2	1	3	g2
e7	3	3	2	g3
e8	3	4	3	g3
e9	3	3	2	g3
e10	1	4	3	g3

strategy (A), target type (T) and weapon type (W). Each event is perpetrated by a terrorist group (D).

Let us fix a group, e.g. $g1$, and evaluates the relative frequencies of each category of attack type, target type and weapon type. For instance, for $A = 1$ the relative frequency is 0, for $A = 2$ the relative frequency is $1/3$ and for $A = 3$ the relative frequency is $2/3$. Each relative frequency can be interpreted as a membership degree of a specific category of attack and a fuzzy set $\widetilde{A_{g1}} = \{A1/0, A2/0.33, A3/0.66\}$ can be constructed. This fuzzy set characterize the attack strategies of $g1$ and inform that the category 1 belongs to $g1$ with a membership degree of 0 (i.e., category 1 has never been used by $g1$ and can be omitted in the fuzzy set), category 1 belongs to $g1$ with a membership degree of 0.33 and category 3 belongs to $g1$ with a membership degree of 0.66. With the same procedure the fuzzy sets $\widetilde{T_{g1}}$ and $\widetilde{W_{g1}}$ can be derived. The same operations are repeated for all the groups under analysis.

From a computational perspective, the algorithm to derive the fuzzy sets from the GTD requires several partitions based on equivalence relations. Let us call U the subset of GTD consisting of all the events for which the group that perpetrated the attack is known. First, $\{U/D\}$ is evaluated to derive equivalence classes consisting of all the events perpetrated by a specific group. Let $[g_i]$ be an equivalence class. The elements of the fuzzy set $\widetilde{A_{g_i}}$ can be derived with the partition $\{[g_i]/A\}$: let $[A_j]$ be the jth parts then the corresponding element of $\widetilde{A_{g_i}}$ is evaluated as $\langle Aj/\frac{|[A_j]|}{|[g_i]|}\rangle$ where $\frac{|[A_j]|}{|[g_i]|}$ is the membership degree of the category Aj and $||$ is a cardinality measure.

Once the fuzzy sets of a group have been constructed, a signature can be derived using fuzzy relations among two or more fuzzy sets. For example, limiting to a signature with respect to attack strategies and target types: $S_{AT}(g_i) = \widetilde{A_{g_i}} \times \widetilde{T_{g_i}}$ where min can be used to evaluate the couples as reported in Sect. 3.5.2.2. Other signatures can be created using fuzzy sets of weapon types and target types, i.e., $\widetilde{W_{g_i}}$

and $\widetilde{T_{g_i}}$, to comprehend how g_i is characterized with respect to the couples weapons-targets. Lastly, all the three fuzzy sets can be related to to comprehend how g_i is characterized with respect to the triples attacks-weapons-targets.

7.5.2 Reasoning Based on 3WD and Fuzzy Signature

The fuzzy signatures of the terrorist groups are used by the analyst to predict the attribution of a hypothesis of attack to a known group. Let us see how to model the hypotheses of attack with the signature. Let us suppose two intelligence sources are in accordance on the possibility of an attack towards military units ($T4$) with a weapon based on radioactive material ($W3$). They diverge on the attack strategy, with the first that supposes for a bombing/explosion strategy ($A3$) and the second for an armed assault ($A2$).

The idea is to derive, from historical data such as the GTD, the signature of a target group (let us call Ω) that could be able to perpetrate the hypothesis of attack. The build this target group, the analyst can use just a subset of information of the GTD by considering, for instance, only the information about groups that are more active in the geographic area and time period under analysis. If, for example, the attack is planned in a particular geographic area, the signature of Ω will be built taking into account information on the most active terrorist groups in that particular geographic area.

After this filtering phase, the fuzzy sets $\widetilde{A_\Omega}$, $\widetilde{T_\Omega}$ and $\widetilde{W_\Omega}$ are constructed as explained before. By considering couples of attributes, 5 signatures can be derived for this example: Ω_{T4W3}, Ω_{T4A3}, $S(\Omega_{T4A2})$, $S(\Omega_{W3A3})$, $S(\Omega_{W3A2})$. By considering triples of attributes, other 2 signatures can be derived: $S(\Omega_{T4W3A2})$ and $S(\Omega_{T4W3A3})$. All these signatures model the behavior of the target group Ω with respect to the information derived from the intelligence sources.

With Eq. 3.15, it is possible to evaluate if one of the known group can be considered as the target group. By defining an evaluation function, $v([g_i], \Omega)$, capable to measure to what extent the behavior of a group g_i is contained or is part of the behavior of the target group Ω, it is possible to tri-partition the known groups into the three regions of 3WD model. If the known group belongs to a positive region then it can be perpetrator of the hypothesis of attack, if it belongs to a negative region then it can not be perpetrator otherwise it belongs to a boundary regions and it can not be decided on the possibility that the group is perpetrator of the hypothesis of attack. As evaluation function, the following one is reasonable: $v([g_i], \Omega) = \dfrac{|S(g_i) \cap S(\Omega)|}{|S(\Omega)|}$ where the signatures have to be consistent with respect to the attributes (omitted now for readability). This evaluation function is used to evaluate the extent to which the behavior of a known group is similar to the behavior of a target group. The function gives information on how much the profile of the know group g_i is similar to the profile of the target group Ω by comparing the common elements between these two profiles and referring this number to the elements of Ω. Let us note that in general $v([g_i], \Omega) \neq v(\Omega, [g_i])$. It is clear that $v([g_i], \Omega) = 1$ if and only if the signature of Ω is completely contained in the signature of g_i and this means that the behavior of Ω is fully compatible with that of the group g_i. The adoption of proper values of the thresholds, α and β, allows to include a level of flexibility in the definition of the three regions which can be useful for the analyst to evaluate the compatibility of behaviors (for example, the analyst can associate a group g_i with the target Ω if $\alpha \leq v \leq 1$ and not only if $v = 1$. More information on how to set and optimize the thresholds values will be given in Chap. 3.6.1 of the book.

7.6 Analytical Value

Predicting if and how a terrorist group may perpetrate an attack is a difficult analysis also considering that terrorism is mostly an human phenomenon. An approach can be to consider a brad range of alternative scenarios and then narrow the list down to those that are most attention deserving.

The computational technique proposed in this chapter leverages the Fuzzy Signature concept to model a behavior and predict whether this behavior is compatible with a hypothesis of attack using 3WD.

The use of the Fuzzy Set theory allows to create behavioral models of terrorist groups robust with respect to the information uncertainty typical of counter-terrorism scenarios where inaccurate and often incorrect information is the norm rather than the exception.

Furthermore, the Fuzzy Signature is flexible enough to allow the modeling of behavior of terrorist groups and hypotheses of attack in an incremental way, starting from a minimum set of information (such as those reported in the case study presented in this chapter) and refining it gradually when more information emerges from intelligence cycles.

7.7 Hands-on Lab

This tutorial shows how to build a fuzzy signature of a terrorist group starting from the GTD downloadable from the url https://www.start.umd.edu/gtd/contact/. Some additional operations on the obtained fuzzy signatures will be accomplished in order to perform reasoning tasks.

7.7.1 Building the Activity Matrix

The GTD is shared as a XLSX file. Pandas is able to support such format. Alternatively, it is possible to convert it into a CSV file, upload it in the Colab environment[2] and then load such a file into a Pandas DataFrame as shown in the next piece of code:

```
import pandas as pd

gtd = pd.read_csv("gtd_mod.csv")

gtd = gtd[["eventid", "gname", "iyear", "
    attacktype1_txt", "weaptype1_txt", "targtype1_txt",
     "success", "suicide"]]

gtd = gtd[(gtd.weaptype1_txt != "Unknown") & (gtd.
    targtype1_txt != "Unknown") & (gtd.attacktype1_txt
    != "Unknown")]
```

The previous source code loads (into a DataFrame) a reduced version of GTD (terrorist events from 2013 to 2016), extracts only three columns, i.e., eventid (the event identifier of the attack), gname (terrorist group's name), iyear (the year in which the attack occurred), attacktype1_txt (type of the attack), weaptype1_txt (type of the weapon used during the attack), targtype1_txt (type of the hit target), success (if the attack was successful), suicide (if the attack led to suicide) and, lastly, selects the rows in which weapon type, target type and attack type are all known. The dataframe is essentially a table where the rows are terrorism events (attacks) and the columns specify the descriptions of each event.

Once these preliminary operations have been executed, it is needed to filter data with respect to the terrorist group of interest and to the other context information. For instance if it is needed to obtain the fuzzy signature of the behavior of the group *Boko Haram* when its attacks led to success, when its attacks fail and without considering success or not, it is possible to consider the following filters:

```
gtd_boko_s = gtd[(gtd.gname == "Boko Haram") & (gtd.
    success == 1)]
gtd_boko_n = gtd[(gtd.gname == "Boko Haram") & (gtd.
    success == 0)]
gtd_boko = gtd[gtd.gname == "Boko Haram"]
```

The previous code extracts subsets of rows from the gtd dataframe applying the right filter as conditions.

The last step needed to build an activity matrix is to apply a pivoting operation over the filtered dataframe. For example, if it is requested the activity matrix for *Boko Haram* when its attacks have success it is possible to manipulate gtd_boko_s. An important aspect to consider the the choice of the two features to be exploited for the

[2] use the already explained files.upload() function.

Table 7.2 Partial activity matrix resulting from the application of pivoting

	Airports & Air.	Business	Educational Inst.	...
Chemical	0	0	0	...
Explosives	0	39	8	...
Firearms	1	14	17	...
Incendiary	0	2	4	...
...	...	...	...	...

fuzzy signature construction. Let consider `weaptype1_txt` and `targtype1_txt`. However, it is possible to replace `weaptype1_txt` with `attacktype1_txt`.

The data manipulation operation that allows to transform the attack table `gtd_boko_s` into an activity matrix for *Boko Haram* (when the attacks of this perpetrator are successful) is pivoting. Pivoting is now used to focus on the two selected features, i.e., `weaptype1_txt` and `targtype1_txt`, and counting the successful attacks of *Boko Haram* in all the possible cases represented by pairs of weapon type and target type. The source code to execute is the following one:

```
m_boko_s = pd.pivot_table(gtd_boko_s, fill_value=0,
   values="eventid", index="weaptype1_txt", columns="
   targtype1_txt", aggfunc=["count"])
```

The previous code fragment transforms a dataframe into a matrix with a row for each distinct value in the column `weaptype1_txt` (index) and a column for each distinct value for the column `targtype1_txt` (columns). The matrix values are calculating by counting for each weapon type how many attacks were perpetrated over a give target. Other aggregation functions could be used in the place of `count` by changing the value for the named argument `aggfunc`. A fragment of the result of the pivoting operation is reported in the Table 7.1.

For example, the result reports that *Boko Haram* has perpetrated 39 successful attacks to Business structures by using explosives, bombs or dynamite (Table 7.2).

7.7.2 *Defining the Fuzzy Sets*

In order to build a fuzzy signature from the activity matrix it is needed to define two fuzzy sets from such matrix. The first fuzzy set is `PopularWeapons`. The second fuzzy set is `AttactiveTargets`. The universe X of the first fuzzy set includes the labels of all rows in the matrix: { Chemical, Explosives, ... }. Moreover, the universe Y of the second fuzzy set includes the labels of all the columns of the matrix: { Airports & Aircraft, Business, Educational Institutions, ... }. Moreover, it is required to define membership functions for constructing the two fuzzy sets. In this case, the functions are defined by calculating their values for each element of the corresponding universe of discourse. Let start with `PopularWeapons`. In order to calculate the membership values it is possible to calculate the total numbers of attacks perpetrated by means of each different weapon type and divide these numbers by the max of them. Hence, the idea is to construct a vector including values stating the relative importance of each weapon type in the universe. The source code to accomplish the above task is the following one:

```
wattacksn = m_boko_s.sum(axis=1)
popular_weap = round(wattacksn / max(wattacksn), 2)
print(popular_weap)

tattacksn = m_boko_s.sum(axis=0)
attractive_targ = round(tattacksn / max(tattacksn), 2)
print(attractive_targ)
```

Such code produces the results reporting in Tables 7.3 and 7.4.

Table 7.3 Fuzzy set `PopularWeapons`

Weapon type	Membership value
Chemical	0.00
Explosives/bombs/dynamite	0.93
Firearms	1.00
Incendiary	0.16
Melee	0.03

Table 7.4 Fuzzy set `AttractiveTargets`

Target type	**Membership value**
Airports and Aircraft	0.00
Business	0.08
Educational institution	0.04
Government (diplomatic)	0.00
Government (general)	0.07
Military	0.22
NGO	0.00
Other	0.02
Police	0.14
Private citizens and property	1.00
Religious figures/institutions	0.10
Telecommunication	0.01
Terrorists/non-state militia	0.02
Tourists	0.00
Transportation	0.05
Violent political party	0.01

7.7.3 Constructing the Fuzzy Signature

Once the two fuzzy sets have been defined, it is needed to construct the fuzzy relation `PopularWeapons × AttractiveTargets` over them by using the `min` operator as shown in Section 3.7.4. After applying an α-cut to the fuzzy relation is possible to obtain the fuzzy signature of successful attack behaviour for *Boko Haram*. The following code fragment accomplishes the above task:

```
import numpy as np
import itertools
import skfuzzy as sf

popularWeapons_u  = list(popular_weap.index)
popularWeapons_m  = np.array(popular_weap.values)

attractiveTargets_u  = list(attractive_targ.index.
    droplevel(0))
attractiveTargets_m  = np.array(attractive_targ.values)

fuzzyr = sf.cartprod(popularWeapons_m,
    attractiveTargets_m)
fuzzys_m = np.array(fuzzyr).reshape(len(
    popularWeapons_m )*len(attractiveTargets_m), 1)

fuzzys_alphacut  = list()
index=0

for pair in itertools.product(popularWeapons_u,
    attractiveTargets_u):

     fr_mem  = fuzzys_m[index][0]

     if fr_mem > 0.2:
        fuzzys_alphacut.append((pair, fr_mem))
     index += 1

print(fuzzys_alphacut)
```

More in detail, the source code constructs the fuzzy relation by using the function `cartprod` (that applies the `min` operator over the pairs o membership values coming from the two fuzzy sets) of the module `skfuzzy`. The resulting values are provided as a matrix that must be reshaped by using the method `reshape` of the `numpy` module. Once the membership values have been calculated they must be associated to the correct pairs obtained by executing the Cartesian product over the universes of `PopularWeapons` and `AttractiveTargets`. The Cartesian product is executed by means of the function `product` of the `itertool` module that provides an iterable to explore through a `for` statement. Lastly, the `if` statement in the body of the `for` statement is used to apply an α-cut by using a threshold of 0.2. The result provided by the above code fragment is:

```
[
    (('Explosives/Bombs/Dynamite', 'Military'), 0.22),
    (('Explosives/Bombs/Dynamite', 'Private Citizens & Property'), 0.93),
    (('Firearms', 'Military'), 0.22),
    (('Firearms', 'Private Citizens & Property'), 1.0)
]
```

The previous result represents the fuzzy signature of the successful attacks of `Boko Haram`. If it is needed to compare such behaviour to the behaviour of the same perpetrator conducting to attack failures, it is possible to use the filtered data `gtd_boko_n` and repeat the previous steps starting from the pivoting operation. In this case the result, obtaining with an α-cut 0.3 is:

```
[
    (('Explosives/Bombs/Dynamite', 'Government (General)'), 0.37),
    (('Explosives/Bombs/Dynamite', 'Military'), 0.47),
    (('Explosives/Bombs/Dynamite', 'Private Citizens & Property'), 1.0),
    (('Firearms', 'Business'), 0.21),
    (('Firearms', 'Government (General)'), 0.37),
    (('Firearms', 'Private Citizens & Property'), 0.47),
]
```

It is interesting to note that unsuccessful behavior of `Boko Haram` is also characterized by attacks to government infrastructures.

7.7.4 *Projecting and Reasoning with Fuzzy Signatures*

In this tutorial, the objective is to show how practically it is possible to implement the methodology provided in Sects. 7.5.1 and 7.5.2. The idea is to get a subset of GTD (all attacks related to the year 2016) and partition the obtained dataset into two parts. The division line represents the current date (16 October 2016). Assume that, at the current date, the intelligence analyst provide a set of information: a new terrorist attack could occur in the `Sub-Saharan Africa` region and the potential target could be `Private Citizens & Property`. Therefore, it is possible to build the event Ω. The second step is building fuzzy signatures for potential perpetrators. For the sake of clarity, only four terrorist groups will be considered: `Boko Haram (BOKO)`, `Fulani extremists (FULANI)`, `Al-Shabaab` and `Islamic State of Iraq and the Levant (ISIL)`. The following code is useful to load the dataset and extract the needed columns and select the sub-datasets to build the Ω event and the four fuzzy signatures:

```
gtd = pd.read_csv("gtd_mod.csv")

gtd = gtd[["eventid", "gname", "iyear", "
    attacktype1_txt", "weaptype1_txt", "targtype1_txt",
    "country_txt", "region_txt"]]

gtd = gtd[(gtd.weaptype1_txt != "Unknown") & (gtd.
    targtype1_txt != "Unknown") & (gtd.attacktype1_txt
    != "Unknown")]
gtd = gtd[(gtd.iyear==2016) & (gtd.eventid <=
    201610160002)]

event = gtd[(gtd.region_txt=="Sub-Saharan Africa") & (
    gtd.targtype1_txt=="Private Citizens & Property")]

boko = gtd[gtd.gname=="Boko Haram"]
fulani = gtd[gtd.gname=="Fulani extremists"]
alshabaab = gtd[gtd.gname=="Al-Shabaab"]
isil = gtd[gtd.gname=="Islamic State of Iraq and the
    Levant (ISIL)"]
```

Consider that it is needed to import the same modules used in the previous section before using such source code. More in detail, the previous Python code gets only the needed part of the dataset by requesting all attacks of year 2016 with an `eventid` less or equal to `201210160002` corresponding to the day before the current date. The sub-dataset for defining the event Ω is obtained by selecting all the attacks perpetrated in the `Sub-Saharan Africa` region with `Private Citizens & Property` as target. Subsequently, the sub-datasets for building the four fuzzy signatures are obtained by selecting, in the right time interval, all the attacks perpetrated by the considered terrorist groups.

Now, for each sub-datasets (one for the event and four for the possible perpetrators) it is needed to build the fuzzy signature as shown in the previous section starting from the pivoting operation (to be executed for five times).

Firstly, execute the pivoting operation by considering `index="attacktype1_txt"` and `columns="targtype1_txt"`. In this way the event and the fuzzy signatures will consider the behaviors regarding attack types and target types. Once the pivoting operation and the other operations needed to build the signatures have been executed, the results are the following. For `BOKO`:

[
(('Armed Assault', 'Military'), 0.4),
(('Armed Assault', 'Private Citizens & Property'), 0.8),
(('Bombing/Explosion', 'Military'), 0.4),
(('Bombing/Explosion', 'Private Citizens & Property'), 1.0)
]

For `FULANI`:

```
[
  (('Armed Assault', 'Private Citizens & Property'), 1.0)
]
```

For `Al-Shabaab`:

```
[
  (('Armed Assault', 'Government (General)'), 0.36),
  (('Armed Assault', 'Military'), 0.63),
  (('Armed Assault', 'Private Citizens & Property'), 0.38),
  (('Assassination', 'Government (General)'), 0.24),
  (('Assassination', 'Military'), 0.24),
  (('Assassination', 'Private Citizens & Property'), 0.24),
  (('Bombing/Explosion', 'Government (General)'), 0.36),
  (('Bombing/Explosion', 'Military'), 1.0),
  (('Bombing/Explosion', 'Private Citizens & Property'), 0.38)
]
```

For `ISIL`:

```
[
  (('Bombing/Explosion', 'Military'), 0.6),
  (('Bombing/Explosion', 'Private Citizens & Property'), 1.0)
]
```

Moreover, the event Ω is the following one:

```
[
  (('Armed Assault', 'Private Citizens & Property'), 1.0),
  (('Bombing/Explosion', 'Private Citizens & Property'), 0.3),
  (('Hostage Taking (Kidnapping)', 'Private Citizens & Property'), 0.36)
]
```

The last step consists in comparing the four signatures of the possible perpetrators to the signature of Ω by using the similarity function explained in Sect. 7.5.2. Such function is implemented by the following source code:

```
def FuzzySimilarity(group, event):
    acc=0
    den=0
    done = False
    for eg in group:
        for ee in event:
            memb = 0
            if eg[0] == ee[0]:
                memb = min(eg[1], ee[1])
            acc += memb
            if not done:
                den += ee[1]
        done = True
    return acc/den

sim_boko = FuzzySimilarity(boko, event)
sim_fulani = FuzzySimilarity(fulani, event)
sim_alshabaab = FuzzySimilarity(alshabaab, event)
sim_isil = FuzzySimilarity(isil, event)
```

Such code defines the aforementioned similarity function and applies it to the four signatures of the possible perpetrators by comparing them individually to the signature of the event Ω.

The results are:

sim_boko = 0.6626506024096386
sim_fulani = 0.6024096385542168
sim_alshabaab = 0.4096385542168674
sim_isil = 0.18072289156626503.

It is possible to interpret the above results by affirming that Boko Haram and Fulani extremists could be the most important suspects for a potential terrorist attack during a reasonable time interval starting from 16 October 2016 in the Sub-Saharan Africa region with Private Citizens & Property target. According to the methodology described in Sect. 7.5.2 the similarity function can be considered an evaluation function for the application of the Three-Way Decisions method that supports the analyst to make decisions.

The results of the similarity function can be checked by counting the attacks (of year 2016) reported in GTD after 15 October 2016 for each terrorist group. In fact, the attacks respecting the characteristics of event Ω are distributed in the following way:

Boko Haram: 40 attacks
Al-Shabaab: 19 attacks
Fulani extremists: 17 attacks
ISIL: 0 attacks

The only anomaly is the preference of `FULANI` with respect to `Al-Shabaab` in the results provided by the similarity (evaluation) function. This is essentially due to the almost exclusive specialization of `FULANI` for attacks with the same characteristics of the event Ω.

7.8 Useful Resources

- Pivoting, https://www.analyticsvidhya.com/blog/2020/03/pivot-table-pandas-python/. This Site provides a comprehensive practical guide to build pivot tables starting from Pandas DataFrames.
- Reshaping, https://towardsdatascience.com/reshaping-numpy-arrays-in-python-a-step-by-step-pictorial-tutorial-aed5f471cf0b. The Site provides a step-by-step tutorial for reshaping numpy arrays.

Chapter 8
Concept Drift Analysis with Structures of Opposition

This chapter focuses on the adoption of structures of opposition to reason on situations that contains contradictions or, in general, elements of opposition. This kind of reasoning is adopted in several intelligence analysis techniques such as the Contrarian Techniques based on contrasting assumptions (e.g., Team A/Team B) and can be enriched by the support a structured way to model and represent contradictory and contraries situations.

A famous structure of opposition is the Aristotelian Square of opposition (see left hand side of Fig. 8.1) where each vertex represents a different statement involving two entities X and Y. As example, X can be an object of the environment to be perceived and Y can be an attribute. The point A (universal affirmative) is "Every X is Y", point E (universal negative) can be stated "No X is Y", point O (particular negative) can be expressed as "Some X is not Y" and, lastly, point I (particular affirmative) can be expressed "Some X is Y". Clearly, A and I are in opposition to O and E (and vice-versa), A implies I and E implies O. A and E are contraries and can be false together but not true together, and for I and O it is the converse.

In general, to reason whit a square of opposition the analyst has to be aware that:

- A and E are contraries, that is they cannot both be true but can both be false.
- I and O are sub-contraries, that is they cannot both be false but can both be true.
- A and O (E and I) are contradictory, that is they cannot both be true and they cannot both be false.
- A and I (E and O) are subalterns, that is the subaltern proposition (I or O) must be true if its superaltern proposition (A or E) is true, and the superaltern must be false if the subaltern is false.

The square of opposition becomes an hexagon of opposition (see right hand side of Fig. 8.1) by adding points U (disjunction of A and E) and Y (conjunction of I and O)

Applications of these structures relate to the expression of traditional quantification in the categorical judgments. However, several other applications have been proposed for these structures. (Beziau, 2018) proposes a different perspective for the structures of opposition. Starting from the consideration that traditional tables of

V. Loia et al., *Computational Techniques for Intelligence Analysis*,
https://doi.org/10.1007/978-3-031-20851-5_8

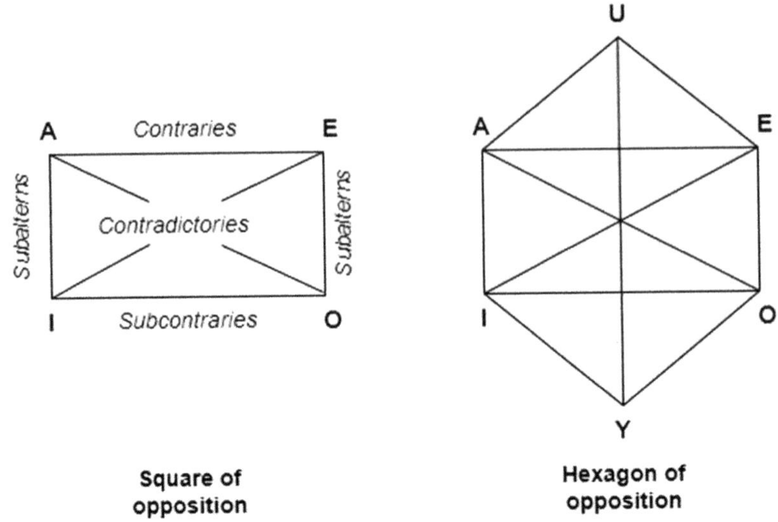

Fig. 8.1 Structures of opposition

opposites (such as the Pythagoras' table) "*sounds artificial*" a dichotomy Identity vs. Difference is analyzed and, in doing this analysis, Beziau constructs the analogical hexagon. In this structure, the point A refers to Opposition (to a given statement, sign, assumption), point E refers to Identity, point I to Difference, point O to Similarity, point Y to Analogy and point U to Non Analogy.

The application of this type of hexagon can be interesting for intelligence activities such as the key assumption check to support the evaluation of conflicting, different or similar assumptions or even in analysis activities based on contrarian techniques such as team A/team B.

8.1 Learning Objectives of the Chapter

This chapter contextualizes the analysis method of Chap. 4 to a particular concept drift analysis that is based on structures of opposition. Specifically, in this chapter the reader will learn how to model a concept (e.g., an opinion) and assess its drift (e.g., a change) on the basis of such structures.

The Learning Objectives of this chapter refer to the levels 2 (Understand) and 3 (Apply) of the taxonomy shown in Fig. 1.2).

The Learning Objectives of this chapter are:

- Implementation and Execution of the methodology of Chap. 4 for opinion change analysis based on structures of opposition.

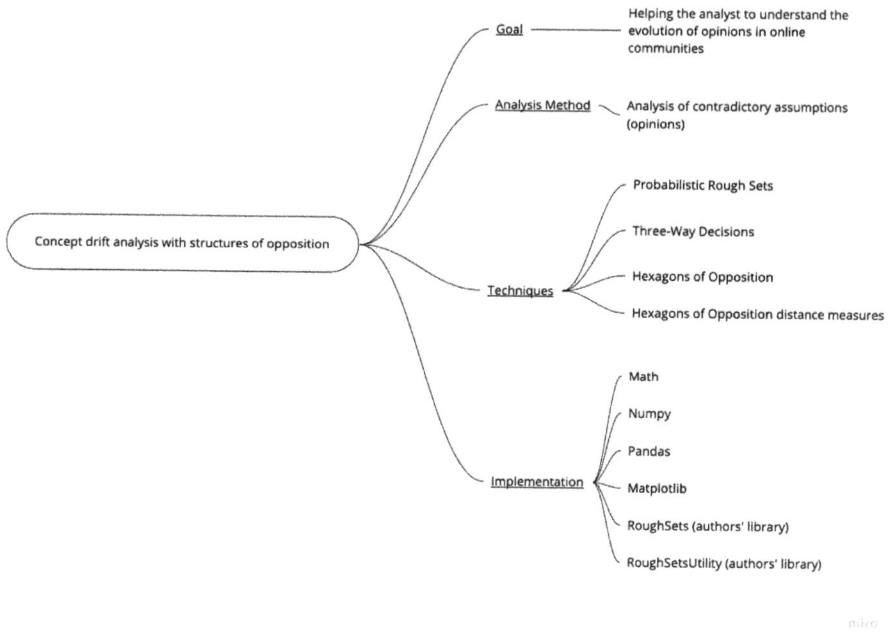

Fig. 8.2 Topic map of the chapter

- Use of Rough Set theory to construct structures of opposition such as Squares and Hexagons of opposition.
- Execute opinion change analysis with structures of oppositions.
- Use visualization methods (i.e., radars chart) to visualize structures of opposition.
- Examine opinion changes with the visualization of structures of opposition.
- Experimenting the methodology with hands-on lab.

8.2 Topic Map of the Chapter

As shown by the topic map in Fig. 8.2, this chapter introduces a methodology aiming at supporting the analyst (human operator) to better comprehend the evolution of opinions in online communities (useful in information warfare scenarios). Such methodology is based on the analysis of contradictory assumptions and is defined by means of Three-Way Decisions based on Probabilistic Rough Sets. The methodology provides the analyst with both intelligible structures called Hexagons of Oppositions and some distance measures to quantify the opinion drift between two time instants.

The techniques on which the methodology is based can be implemented by means of a set of Python-based tools and libraries indicated by the topic map.

8.3 Case Introduction: Opinion Changes

The case reports the adoption of hexagons of opposition to evaluate to what extent new information can support opinion changes. Opinion changes is a phenomenon by which a group of users, such as a community, modifies opinions and beliefs on the basis of new information that circulates in a social media. Let us consider, for instance, the effects of propaganda or other type of dis- and mal-information with a deliberated intention on influencing opinions.

The case refers to the study of on-line communities sharing and commenting news. The target concept of interest for the analyst is a subset of users expressing a particular opinion on these news. Let us label with *like* the specific opinion of this target concept.

By partitioning the universe of users, the analyst can use an hexagon of opposition to perform analysis on groups of users who have similar or different opinion. Let us consider the hexagon of Fig. 8.3 where the analyst fixes the target concept (that is a subgroup of users sharing a common opinion such as *like*) with the point A of the hexagon. The users having a contrary opinion (labeled with *dislike*) will fall in the point E of the hexagon. Contradictory opinions with respect to the target concepts of point A will fall in the point O (labeled with *do not like*) and contradictory opinions with respect to point E will fall in the point I (labeled with *do not dislike*). Point U consists of users with a clear opinion, that is users that like or dislike the news (labeled with *decided*) and point Y consists of users without a clear opinion (labeled as *undecided*).

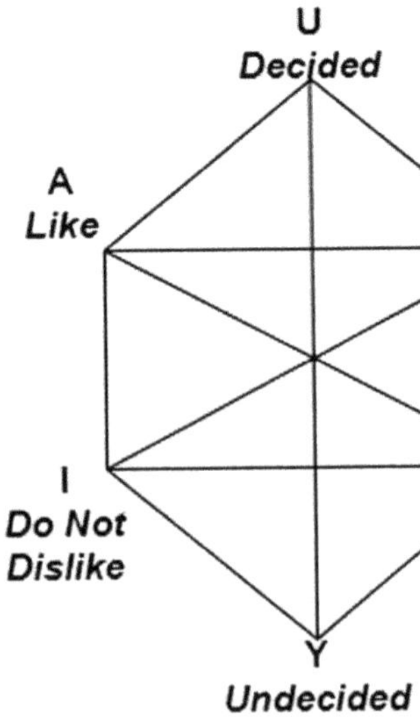

Fig. 8.3 Hexagon for opinion changes analysis

When new information circulate in a social media, the analyst can perform an analysis similar to the what-if described in Chap. 5 creating a new hexagon of opposition and using granular measures to evaluate the changes in the points of the hexagon. The following section describes the methodology.

8.4 Methodology

The case described in the previous section can be executed following the methodology shown in Fig. 8.4. The starting point is the GDTA reporting the SA requirements. An important requirement of the GDTA may be the indication of the target concept to analyze. Referring to the example reported in the previous section, the analyst could focus the attention on oppositions (e.g., contraries and contradictory) of a target concepts that is clearly stated in the GDTA such as: *users that have positive opinions on a specific topic*. Raw Data refers to tweet, comments, or other social media content that the users produce when sharing and commenting a news.

At the perception level, an information table is constructed starting from an universe of users, $U = \{u_1, ..., u_n\}$, who are described by a set of attributes $N = \{N, ..., N_m\}$ that represents the news shared and commented by the users. An information function, $I : U \rightarrow V_n$ for every $n \in N$, is used to evaluate attributes values. I is an evaluation function for sentiment analysis that can extract sentiment values from text of the users' comments attached to the news. An additional attribute, C, is the community to which the users belong. An example of information table is reported in Table 8.1 where P, D and N are categorical values for sentiment (e.g., positive, doubt and negative) and 1, 2 and 3 are categorical values for the community attribute that represent different communities (e.g., *scientist*, *journalist*, etc.).

At the comprehension level, the information table is transformed into a decision table and a target concept is fixed to build the hexagon of opposition. To build a

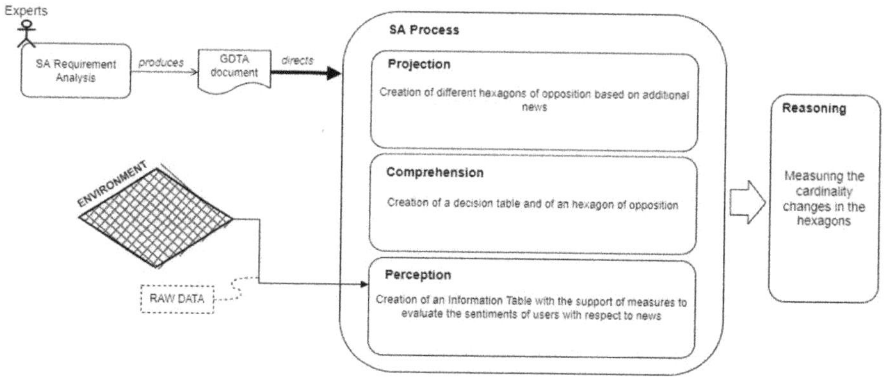

Fig. 8.4 The methodology for opinion changes analysis

Table 8.1 The information table

	N_1	N_2	N_3	...	N_m	C
u_1	P	P	D	...	P	1
u_2	N	P	N	...	D	2
...	...	...	...	...	...	...
u_n	P	N	P	...	N	3

Table 8.2 The decision table

	N_1	N_2	N_3	...	N_m	C	d
u_1	P	P	D	...	P	1	1
u_2	N	P	N	...	D	2	1
...	...	...	...	...	...	...	...
u_n	P	N	P	...	N	3	2

decision table from an information table such as Table 8.1 a decision attribute has to be evaluated. The decision attribute has to represent the overall opinion of an user on the set of news circulated so far. So, a simple way to derive this value is to aggregate the sentiment values of the information table. For an user u, the aggregate value can be calculated with an aggregation operator applied to the sentiment values:

$$d(u) = \bigoplus_{n \in N}(V_n), \tag{8.1}$$

where N is a set of news and $\bigoplus$ is an aggregation operator such as a simple average function or a more complex operator.

After this operation, Table 8.1 becomes a decision table such as Table 8.2 where values of d are categorical and represent the overall opinion of the users on the set of news (e.g., 1 means positive, 2 neutral, and so on).

After this phase, a target concept T has to be fixed by the analyst. The target concept can be any subset of users of interest such as all the users with a specific value of d. If in the GDTA it is clearly expressed that the target refers to users expressing positive opinions, the target concept is the subset of user expressing overall positive opinions. Once the target concept has been decided, the analyst can use a partition of U to allocate the users in the points of the hexagon of opposition as described before. The generic semantic of an hexagon of opposition based on partition is as shown in Fig. 8.5 where P is a part and T is a target concept and the analyst has to take decision on the affiliation of the parts to the target. If, for instance, T refers to all the users with a positive opinion (that can be labeled as *like*) the semantic of the hexagon of Fig. 8.5 is the same of Fig. 8.3.

At the projection level, the analyst has to assess how the opinion changes when new information, in terms of fresh news, is available. To this purpose, following the same

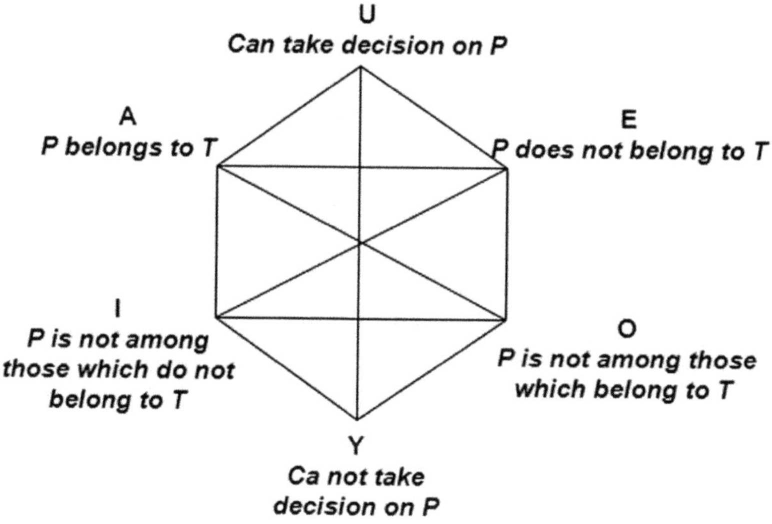

Fig. 8.5 An hexagon of opposition to assess partitions

approach above described, a new hexagon of opposition is created and compared with the previous one. An example is shown in Fig. 8.6 where the left-hand side shows an hexagon built at time t_0 and the right-hand side an hexagon built at time t_1. This last one takes into account the fresh news. A way to compare the two hexagons is to evaluate the difference of the parts that fall into the points of the hexagons. Let us consider, for example, the dashed arrow shown in Fig. 8.6. This arrow represent a shift of some parts belonging to the point Y of the hexagon built at time t_0 to the point A of the hexagon built at time t_1. Considering the semantic associated to these points, this means that the fresh news have had the effect to increase the number of users with a positive opinion on the news. In general, any shift that moves parts from the bottom to the top on the hexagon of opposition implies a polarization of opinions towards positive (in the right-hand side, i.e., points I or A) or negative (in the right-hand side, i.e., points O or E) opinion. The opposite can be argued, if the shift moves parts from the top of the hexagon to the bottom.

8.5 Computational Techniques

This section describes how to build hexagons of opposition with partition based on rough set theory. Let us consider the decision table of Table 8.2 and fix a target concept $T = \{u \in U \mid d(u) = 1\}$ where $d(u)$ is evaluated with an aggregation operator (see Eq. 8.1) and 1 represents positive opinions. In this case, the interpretation of T is that of a community of opinion, specifically the community with a positive opinion

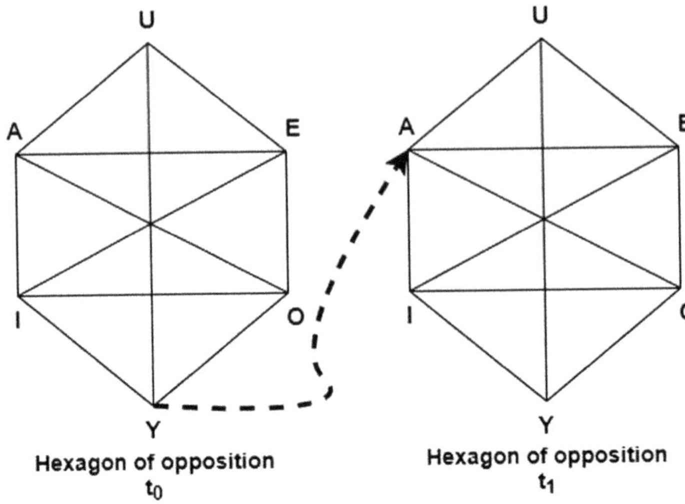

Fig. 8.6 Comparison between different hexagons of opposition

on the news. Let $C = \{c_1, ..., c_q\}$ be a partition of U. The parts of C are the original community to which the users belong to (e.g., *scientist, journalist*, etc.).

8.5.1 *Creating and Reasoning on Structures of Opposition Based on Rough Set*

Using rough set theory an hexagon of opposition can be built by evaluating the lower and upper approximations of a target concept or, alternatively, in terms of positive, boundary and negative regions.

Specifically, Eq. 3.3 represents the subset of parts contained in the target concept and this is exactly the meaning of point A of the hexagon of opposition (see Fig. 8.5). Equation 3.4 represents the subset of parts which have non-empty intersection with the target concept and can not be positively (i.e., unambiguously) classified as belonging to the complement of the target concept. Equation 3.4 refers to point I of the hexagon of opposition (see Fig. 8.5). Equation 3.5 informs on the fact that it is not possible to decide if a part belongs or does not belong to the target concept and refers to the point Y of the hexagon of opposition (see Fig. 8.5). By construction of the hexagon, points E, O and U are the complements respectively of points I, A and Y.

In terms of positive (POS), boundary (BND) and negative (NEG) regions of the target concept T:

- A corresponds to the $POS(T)$
- E corresponds to the $NEG(T)$

- Y corresponds to the $BND(T)$
- I corresponds to the $(NEG(T))^c = POS(T) \cup BND(T)$
- O corresponds to the $(POS(T))^c = NEG(T) \cup BND(T)$
- U corresponds to the $(BND(T))^c = POS(T) \cup NEG(T)$

A three-way decisions method based on Probabilistic Rough Sets can also be used (see Eq. 3.16) which, with the adoption of the thresholds α and β, allows a greater degree of flexibility in the creation of the three regions.

To reason on the influence that a new set of fresh news can have with respect to opinion changes, some measures based on the cardinality of the three-way regions can be applied. Let N_{t1} be the new subset of news, a simple way to assess if the fresh news polar e or negative opinions id to evaluate two measures:

$$\mu(N_{t1}) = |A(t_1)| - |A(t_0)| \tag{8.2}$$

$$\xi(N_{t1}) = |E(t_1))| - |E(t_1)| \tag{8.3}$$

where $|.|$ is a set cardinality measure and A and E are the points of the hexagons of opposition created at t_1 and t_0. The meaning of these measures is that of gains. In fact, if the universe of users does not change, $\mu > 0$ means that the fresh news allowed an increase of users with positive opinions and, similarly, $\xi > 0$ indicates an increase of users with negative opinions on the basis of the new information at t_1.

Obviously, the gains can be evaluated also on the other points of the hexagon which, however, provide less marked information than the analysis of points A and E but, nevertheless, can be useful for analyzing trends. For example, evaluating the gains on the I and O points allows us to understand variations in opinions, even if in a more nuanced way.

8.6 Analytical Value

Opposition reasoning is commonly used in Intelligence Analysis in numerous techniques that aim to challenge traditional assumptions and, in general, the analyst's current mind-set.

The computational technique presented in this chapter aims to support reasoning by oppositions through the use and visualization of opposition structures such as squares and hexagons.

From an analytical point of view, its added value consists in organizing the concepts by opposition in a coherent way (building structures of opposition with the operators of the Roguh Set theory) and allowing an immediate and intuitive visualization.

8.7 Hands-on Lab

The objective of this section is to show how to write Python code for constructing and visualizing hexagons of oppositions starting from the results of a Three-Way Decisions analysis. In order to achieve such objective, the present section is divided into two tutorials. Contextually, such tutorials will show how to reason on the temporal evolution of a given phenomenon by considering two decision tables, at time t_0 and t_1. These decision tables report the opinions of online users regarding to a specific topic by considering the sentiment values of their comments related to news articles dealing with the topic of interest. More in detail, the condition attributes report the sentiment values with respect to the considered news articles and the decision attribute report the sentiment value related to the whole topic (these values are calculated by means of an aggregation operators). If in the interval $[t_0, t_1]$ further news articles are shared, it is possible to analyze the evolution of the opinions (sentiment) of such users with respect to the overall topic. Before starting to execute the source code provided in the next sections remember to upload the needed datasets (`dt_t0.csv` and `dt_t1.csv`) into the Colab environment by means of the following instructions:

```
from google.colab import files
uploaded = files.upload()
```

8.7.1 Building Hexagons of Opposition

First of all, as anticipated in the premise for this section, it is needed to consider two decision tables that are stored in two CSV files: `dt_t0.csv` and `dt_t1.csv` constructing with tweets commenting news articles related to racism. Let analyze the structure of such tables by using the function `info()` of Pandas for the first decision table:

```
import pandas as pd

df0 = pd.read_csv("dt_t0.csv")
print("COLUMNS: ", list(df0.columns))
print("N. ROWS: ", len(df0))
```

The result of the previous source code is the following one:

```
COLUMNS: ['01R', '02R', '03R', '04R', '05R', '06R', 'community', 'id', 'decision']
N. ROWS: 151
```

In particular, the first six columns are the condition attributes whose values represent the sentiment of users with respect to news article dealing with the overall topic. Such column names are composed of a progressive number and a character that is `R` if the article is a real news and `F` if the article is a fake news. The column `community` reports a number that identifies a group or community which the users belong to. Such column is ignored within the tutorial. The column `id` is a value that identifies a user within the analysis process. In the case of this decision table there are `151` rows, hence corresponding to `151` different users. Lastly, the column `decision` provides an aggregated sentiment value corresponding to the opinion of specific users regarding to the overall topic (`1` a neutral sentiment, `2` a negative sentiment, and `3` a positive sentiment.).

In order to obtain the same information for the second decision table it is possible to execute the following code fragment:

```
df1 = pd.read_csv("dt_t1.csv")
print("COLUMNS: ", list(df1.columns))
print("N. ROWS: ", len(df1))
```

In this case the result is:

```
COLUMNS: ['01R', '02R', '03R', '04R', '05R', '06R', '07F', 'community', 'id', 'decision']
N. ROWS: 151
```

As it is possible to observe from the above result, in the interval $[t_0, t_1]$ one further news has been shared by the `151` users who remain the same across such interval.

Once prepared the decision tables, it is requested to perform a 3WD analysis to study a specific target concept that is defined by all the rows having value `2` for the `decision` column. In other words, the concept of `negative sentiment` (with respect to the overall topic) is characterized by using the sentiment values of users with respect to the shared news articles dealing with such topic. The 3WD is executed over the two decision tables by using the following script:

```
df0 = pd.read_csv("dt_t0.csv")
B0 = ["01R", "02R", "03R", "04R", "05R", "06R"]

df1 = pd.read_csv("dt_t1.csv")
B1 = ['01R', '02R', '03R', '04R', '05R', '06R', '07F']

B0_granules = RoughSetsUtility(df0, B0)
B1_granules = RoughSetsUtility(df1, B1)

B0_index = B0_granules.columns_index()
B1_index = B1_granules.columns_index()

infoTable0 = df0.values
infoTable1 = df1.values

d0_2 = df0[df0.decision == 2]
d0_2 = d0_2.index

d1_2 = df1[df1.decision == 2]
d1_2 = d1_2.index
```

```
nrs_B0 = RoughSets(infoTable0, B0_index)
regions_B0 = nrs_B0.calculate3WD(d0_2,\
    probability=True, beta=0.2, alpha=0.8)

nrs_B1 = RoughSets(infoTable1, B1_index)
regions_B1 = nrs_B1.calculate3WD(d1_2,\
    probability=True, beta=0.2, alpha=0.8)
```

The previous script applies 3WD (based on Probabilistic Rough Sets) over the two decision tables obtaining the tri-partitioning for time t_0 (`regions_B0`) and time t_1 (`regions_B1`). Both the results are tuple of three Python sets containing the ids of users in the three regions: positive (POS), boundary (BND) and negative (NEG). Now, it is possible to construct the two hexagons of opposition:

```
POS0 = regions_B0[0]
BND0 = regions_B0[1]
NEG0 = regions_B0[2]

POS1 = regions_B1[0]
BND1 = regions_B1[1]
NEG1 = regions_B1[2]

points0 = {"A": {}, "E": {}, "I": {}, "O": {}, "U":
    {}, "Y": {}}
points1 = {"A": {}, "E": {}, "I": {}, "O": {}, "U":
    {}, "Y": {}}

points0["A"] = POS0
points0["E"] = NEG0
points0["I"] = BND0
points0["O"] = NEG0.union(BND0)
points0["U"] = POS0.union(BND0)
points0["Y"] = POS0.union(NEG0)

points1["A"] = POS1
points1["E"] = NEG1
points1["I"] = BND1
points1["O"] = NEG1.union(BND1)
points1["U"] = POS1.union(BND1)
points1["Y"] = POS1.union(NEG1)
```

The above source code simply extracts regions (as Python sets) from the resulting tuples and uses such sets to construct the points of the hexagons of oppositions implemented as a dictionary with six key-value pairs. The keys (e.g., A, E, etc.) represent the points of the hexagon and the values are sets containing the ids of the users. The associations between the three regions and the six points are realized by means of rules described in Sect. 8.5.1. Take care to run the definitions of classes `RoughSets` and `RoughSetsUtility` before executing the tutorial code.

8.7.2 *Visualizing Hexagons of Opposition*

In this tutorial, that is the continuation of the tutorial provided in the previous section, the objective is drawing the hexagons of opposition by using radar charts. In particular, the Matplotlib library is used to draw the radar charts, therefore some import instructions should be executed:

```
import numpy as np
import matplotlib.pyplot as plt
import pandas as pd
from math import pi
```

A possible function to draw a radar chart representing an hexagon of opposition could be written in the following way:

```
'''
    Adapted from the source code provided at https://
        www.python-graph-gallery.com/392-use-faceting-
        for-radar-chart
'''
def make_spider( row, title, color):

    # number of variable
    categories=list(df)[1:]
    N = len(categories)

    # What will be the angle of each axis in the plot?
        (we divide the plot / number of variable)
    angles = [n / float(N) * 2 * pi for n in range(N)]
    angles += angles[:1]

    # Initialise the spider plot
    ax = plt.subplot(2,2,row+1, polar=True, )

    # If you want the first axis to be on top:
    ax.set_theta_offset(pi / 2)
    ax.set_theta_direction(-1)

    # Draw one axe per variable + add labels labels
        yet
    plt.xticks(angles[:-1], categories, color='grey',
        size=8)

    # Draw ylabels
    ax.set_rlabel_position(0)
    plt.yticks([10,20,30], ["10","20","30"], color="
        grey", size=7)
    plt.ylim(0,40)
```

```
    # Ind1
    values=df.loc[row].drop('time').values.flatten().
        tolist()
    values += values[:1]
    ax.plot(angles, values, color=color, linewidth=2,
        linestyle='solid')
    ax.fill(angles, values, color=color, alpha=0.4)

    # Add a title
    plt.title(title, size=11, color=color, y=1.1)
```

The aforementioned code has been adapted from the source code accessible at https://www.python-graph-gallery.com/392-use-faceting-for-radar-chart.

In order to use the previous function it is needed to execute the following instructions:

```
maxi = len(df0) # maxi = len(df1) is equivalent

values0 = []
values0.append(len(points0["U"])/maxi*30)
values0.append(len(points0["E"])/maxi*30)
values0.append(len(points0["O"])/maxi*30)
values0.append(len(points0["Y"])/maxi*30)
values0.append(len(points0["I"])/maxi*30)
values0.append(len(points0["A"])/maxi*30)

values1 = []
values1.append(len(points1["U"])/maxi*30)
values1.append(len(points1["E"])/maxi*30)
values1.append(len(points1["O"])/maxi*30)
values1.append(len(points1["Y"])/maxi*30)
values1.append(len(points1["I"])/maxi*30)
values1.append(len(points1["A"])/maxi*30)


# Set data
df = pd.DataFrame({
'time': ['t0', 't1'],
'U': [values0[0], values1[0]],
'E': [values0[1], values1[1]],
'O': [values0[2], values1[2]],
'Y': [values0[3], values1[3]],
'I': [values0[4], values1[4]],
'A': [values0[5], values1[5]]
})

# initialize the figure
my_dpi=96
plt.figure(figsize=(1000/my_dpi, 1000/my_dpi), dpi=
    my_dpi)
```

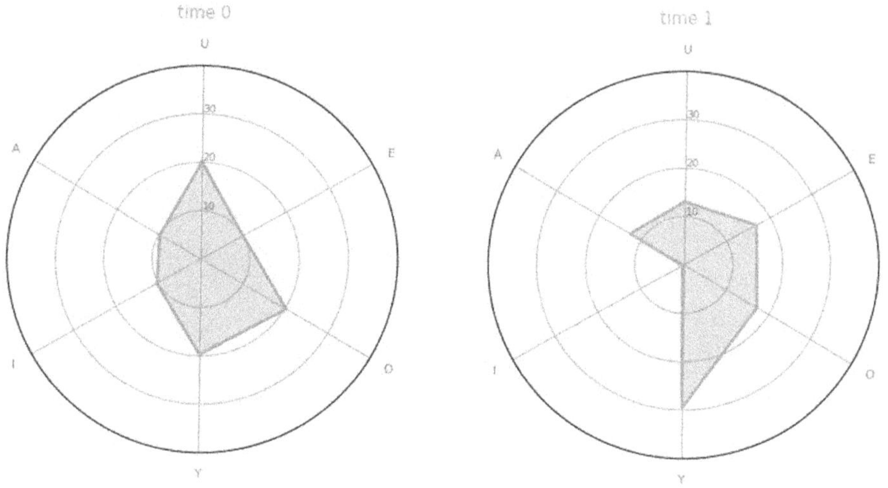

Fig. 8.7 Hexagon of opposition at time t_0 and t_1

```
# Create a color palette:
my_palette = plt.cm.get_cmap("Set2", len(df.index))

# Loop to plot
for row in range(0, len(df.index)):
    make_spider( row=row, title='time '+str(row),
        color=my_palette(row))
```

In the previous code the first code lines obtain the length of the six spokes (for both time instants) by considering the number of users included in each point of the hexagon. Such numbers are normalized by dividing by the total number of users and adapted to the layout by multiplying them for a constant value (30). Subsequently, a dataframe with the two set of data is prepared and passed (as arguments) to two invocations of function `make_spider()`.

The graphical result of the last code fragments is reporting in Fig. 8.7.

An immediate interpretation of the graphical results is that the sharing of a fake news in the interval $[t_0, t_1]$ leads to a growth (point Y) of precise opinions (negative or positive) with respect to the racism and to a decrease (point I) of uncertainty.

8.8 Useful Resources

- Radar Chart, https://www.python-graph-gallery.com/radar-chart/. This Site provides code samples to draw radar charts (and other types of charts) with different styles.

- An Intuitive Guide to Data Visualization in Python, https://www.analyticsvidhya.com/blog/2021/02/an-intuitive-guide-to-visualization-in-python/. This Site provides a good introduction to Data Visualization in Python.
- Python Data Visualization Tutorials, https://realpython.com/tutorials/data-viz/. This page offers links to tutorials useful to solve different Data Visualization problems in Python.

Part III
Methodological and Technological Insight

Chapter 9
Comparing Different Approaches for Implementing Probability-Based Rough Set Operators

In this section two implementations of probability-based rough set operators will be compared in order to show some good practices to develop real-world versions of such operations. In particular, firstly, two implementation approaches will be described. The first one (see Algorithm 1) is a trivial method based on nested loops. This solution is highly inefficient.

Algorithm 1 Calculate $\underline{B}(X)$ and $\overline{B}(X)$

```
Require: IS = ⟨U, A⟩, B ⊆ A, X ⊆ U
  D = dict(U, list[U])
  B̲(X) = set()
  B̄(X) = set()
  for all x ∈ U do
    for all y ∈ U do
      if f(x, a) = f(y, a), ∀a ∈ B then
        D[x] ← D[x] ∪ {y}
      end if
    end for
  end for
  for all key ∈ D do
    m = |D[key] ∩ X| / |D[key]|
    if m ≥ α then
      B̲(X) = B̲(X) ∪ D[key]
    end if
    if m > β then
      B̄(X) = B̄(X) ∪ D[key]
    end if
  end for
```

In Algorithm 1, input data U, B and X are lists. D is a dictionary in which each pair is composed of elements of U (keys) and lists of elements of U (values). The output

V. Loia et al., *Computational Techniques for Intelligence Analysis*,
https://doi.org/10.1007/978-3-031-20851-5_9

is represented by two sets $\underline{B}(X)$ (lower approximation) and $\overline{B}(X)$ (upper approximation). The algorithm core is represented by three nested loops. Such structure leads to an asymptotic complexity of $O(kN^2)$, where $N = |U|$ and $k = |B|$. The dictionary operations within such nested loops takes $O(1)$.

In order to optimize such design, it is possible to exploit better the potentialities of the dictionary data structure. In fact, let consider Algorithm 2.

Algorithm 2 Calculate $\underline{B}(X)$ and $\overline{B}(X)$

Require: $IS = \langle U, A \rangle$, $B \subseteq A$, $X \subseteq U$
  $D = dict(tuple, list[U])$
  $\underline{B}(X) = set()$
  $\overline{B}(X) = set()$
  for all $x \in U$ **do**
    $D[des_B(x)] \leftarrow D[des_B(x)] \cup \{x\}$
  end for
  for all $key \in D$ **do**
    $m = \frac{|D[key] \cap X|}{|D[key]|}$
    if $m \geq \alpha$ **then**
      $\underline{B}(X) = \underline{B}(X) \cup D[key]$
    end if
    if $m > \beta$ **then**
      $\overline{B}(X) = \overline{B}(X) \cup D[key]$
    end if
  end for

Input data are the same with respect to Algorithm 1. The dictionary D is structured in a different way. In fact, the keys are tuples and the values remain elements of U. In particular, tuples are composed of values corresponding to the attribute set B. The algorithm core changes and only one loop is necessary. In fact, dictionary keys are used to group the elements with the same values for all the attributes in B. This solution leads to a complexity of $O(N)$.

The insertions into lower and upper approximation sets are $O(N)$ for Algorithm 1 and $O(h)$ for Algorithm 2, where h is the number of obtained equivalence classes.

Some practical experiments have been executed in order to evaluate the two above solutions. In particular, Python implementations of the above two algorithms have been provided and evaluated over a specific dataset, namely *Connect-4 Data Set* [1], consisting of 42 condition attributes and one decision attribute. Table 9.1 reports the execution times of different runs of the approximation operators for the two provided algorithms over a different number of rows. The studied concept is constructed by using a specific value of the decision attribute.

[1] http://archive.ics.uci.edu/ml/datasets/connect-4.

Table 9.1

# rows	Algorithm 1	Algorithm 2
1000	1.08	0.22
4000	17.07	0.37
10000	107.74	2.37

Let consider Algorithm 2. The Python implementation related to such algorithm is essentially based on the capability of Python dictionaries to group values with respect to specific keys. In particular, the insertion operation into a dictionary (class `dict`) takes $O(1)$. The second part of both the algorithms, where lower and upper approximation set are constructed, is the same. A third interesting approach to implement probability-based rough set operators is represented by a solution based on functional programming. In particular, the adopted constructs are based on *map* and *reduce* functions. In particular, such solution is based on a custom pipeline of map and reduce operations. The first operation is a map and is useful to organize the description of an object $x \in U$ into the following pair:

$$(des_B[x], ([id[x]], [des_d[x]], lvalue), \tag{9.1}$$

where $des_B[x]$ (the key) is a tuple with all the values of $x \in U$ corresponding to the all the condition attributes in B, $id[x]$ is the unique identifier of x (the square brackets enveloping $id[x]$ means that a list of only one element is constructed), $[des_d[x]]$ is a list containing the value of x corresponding to the decision attribute d and, lastly, $lvalue$ is a list containing the value d_X if the concept to study is $X = \{x \in U | des_d[x] = d_X\}$, otherwise $lvalue$ is the empty list.

The second operation of the pipeline is a reduce that accumulates the pairs in Eq. 9.1 with the same key. In particular, such accumulation provides a new pair of the following shape only if $p_1[0]$ is equal to $p_2[0]$, otherwise the accumulation does not take place. The reduce operation is the following one:

$$\begin{aligned} p_1, p_2 \rightarrow (p_1[0], (p_1[1][0] + p_2[1][0], p_1[1][1] \\ + p_2[1][1], p_1[1][2] + p_2[1][2])) \end{aligned} \tag{9.2}$$

The key of the resulting pair is $p_1[0]$ or $p_2[0]$ given that such reduce accumulates results by key (i.e., for pairs with the same key). Moreover, the operators $+$ adopted for the value part of the resulting pair is a list concatenation operator. Such reduce operation is able to return a sequence of pairs containing the information related to the equivalence classes $[x]_B$ for all $x \in U$.

The third operation of the pipeline is a map. Such operation maps the sequence of all the pairs obtained by the reduce operation, i.e., there is a pair for each different key, into a sequence of tuples. The resulting pairs have the following shape:

$$p_s \rightarrow (p_s[0], p_s[1][0], p_s[1][1], p_s[1][2], len(p_s[1][2])/len(p_s[1][1])) \tag{9.3}$$

This map is useful to calculate the membership degree of each equivalence class with respect to the concept X.

The last operation of the pipeline is a new map that is able to assign a region to each equivalence class:

$$t \to (t[0], t[1][0], t[1][1], t[1][2], t[1][3], region), \tag{9.4}$$

where $region$ is equal to the string `POS` if $t[1][3] \geq \alpha$, otherwise $region$ is equal to the string `BND` if $t[1][3] > \beta$, otherwise $region$ is equal to the string `NEG`.

It is important to note that in this solution it is obtained a further result with respect to algorithms 1 and 2. In fact the above algorithms provides only upper and lower approximations. The solution based on functional programming is configured to return directly the regions obtained by applying the Three-Way Decisions.

A simple Python implementation of this solution offers great performance with respect the two aforementioned algorithms. In particular, for the same dataset *Connect-4 Data Set* and the same set of features, the solution based on map and reduce completes the computation in 0.006 for 1000 rows, in 0.022 for 4000 rows, in 0.06 for 10000 rows and in 0.25 for 40000 rows.

9.1 Useful Resources

- Python Data Structures, https://docs.python.org/3/tutorial/datastructures.html. This Site provides the Python official documentation and should represent the first resource to access when dealing with Python data structures.
- High Performance Python, https://www.oreilly.com/library/view/high-performance-python/9781492055013/. A book on how to increase Python code performance.
- Common Python Data Structures, https://realpython.com/python-data-structures/. A further resource on Python data structures. It is a knowledge repository on additional Python packages offering optimized data structures.
- Optimised Python Data Structures, https://python.plainenglish.io/optimised-python-data-structures-74c22a140cff. This Site provides a brief overview of the performance of Python data structures.
- Python most powerful functions, https://www.analyticsvidhya.com/blog/2021/07/python-most-powerful-functions-map-filter-and-reduce-in-5-minutes/. This Site provides a brief overview of the tools offered by Python to implement the Map-Reduce programming style.
- Python Map, Filter, and Reduce, https://towardsdatascience.com/python-map-filter-and-reduce-9a888545e9fc. This Site provides a good tutorial on how to use map, reduce, and filter functions in Python.

Chapter 10
Data Streaming Scenarios

In real-world scenarios, where data possibly comes from multiple wireless sensors, it is needed to handle huge volumes of streaming data. In such cases, the methodologies provided by this book should be deployed to software platforms supporting these aspects. For instance, the methodological approach provided in Chap. 5 has been illustrated by considering a fully defined decision table and also the temporal evolution of such table is simulated by providing, at a different time instant, a new decision table. But, what happens if we are in the Big Data conditions, records come with different velocities and the decision maker needs to have partial results in order to anticipate, where possible, decisions in the case of sufficient information? In such situations the answer is to define a solution that can handle streams of data. Streaming platforms, like Apache Spark (Salloum et al. 2016), support the aforementioned solutions and can be used to develop real-world applications also for methodologies like the one presented in Chap. 5. Spark streaming capabilities lays on a couple of core data abstractions called Discretized Stream (DStream) and Resilient Distributed Dataset (RDD). DStream is a high-level abstraction which represents a continuous stream of data as a sequence of small batches of data. Internally, a DStream is a sequence of RDDs, each RDD has one time slice of the input stream, and these RDDs can be processed using normal Spark jobs. In this way, computations can be structured as a set of short, stateless, deterministic tasks instead of continu- ous, stateful operators. This can avoid problems in traditional record-at-a-time stream processing (Salloum et al. 2016).

Figure 10.1 reports an example of a DStream bringing different RDDs. The first RDD on the right is the the first RDD arrived to be processed by the Spark application. In general the representation of RDDs is aligned with the timeline. In fact the second the RDD depicted into the middle of the DStream temporally follows the first one and so on. Thus, processing is re-applied as new data arrive in subsequent micro-batches (RDDs).

Stream processing mechanism of Spark is implemented on the top of its distributed capabilities. Therefore, also stream processing is parallelized and distributed over a cluster of computation nodes.

V. Loia et al., *Computational Techniques for Intelligence Analysis*,
https://doi.org/10.1007/978-3-031-20851-5_10

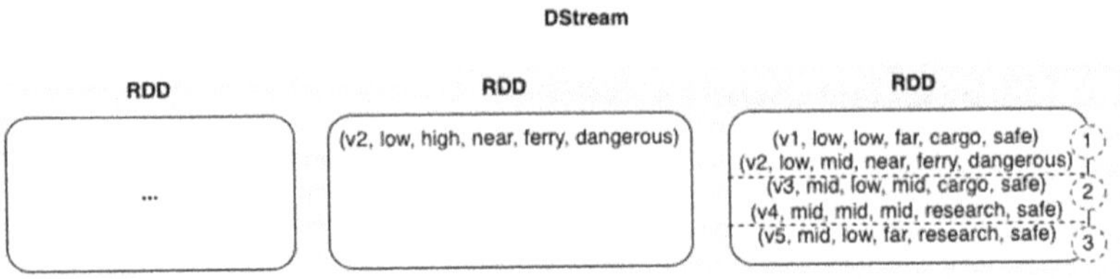

Fig. 10.1 Example of DStream bringing different RDDs

In brief, records into an RDD are grouped into different partitions. For instance, the first RDD in Fig. 10.1 foresees three partitions. Each partition is sent to a given node and processed by such node in parallel with the computation of the other nodes (which, in general, are responsible for the other partitions).

Definitely, Spark guarantees streaming processing and distributed computing. Moreover, the good news is that the data processing algorithms running on Spark do not need to consider such aspects that are, in some sense, transparent (except for some configuration useful to optimize the computation). Such algorithms need only to be written by using the constructs offered by Spark.

In particular, it is possible to adopt a functional programming style based essentially on functions similar to *map* and *reduce* previously introduced in Chap. 9. Hence, the implementation of Three-Way Decisions for streams of data can be defined by providing an algorithm based on the aforementioned style. There are two types of parallel operations that it is possible to execute on an RDD: transformations and actions (Zaharia et al. 2012). Transformations, are deterministic and lazy operations, used to applying a function that returns a new RDD without immediately computing it. With a narrow transformation (e.g., map, filter, etc), each partition of the parent RDD is used by at most one partition of the child RDD. With a wide transformation (e.g., join, groupByKey, etc), multiple child partitions may depend on the same partition of the parent RDD. Moreover, an action (e.g., count, first, take, etc) launches a computation on an RDD and then returns the results to the driver program or writes them to an external storage. When used in pipelines, transformations produce a concrete result only when an action is called. In the presence of such pipelines, Spark is able to break the computation into tasks to run in parallel, organized into multiple stages, on separate machines. These stages are separated by distributed shuffle operations for redistributing data (Salloum et al. 2016).

For the sake of clarity, it is opportune to provide an example based on the methodologies and the case study described in Chap.5. Therefore, the objective is to analyze, by means of Three-Way Decisions, the environment related to a set of vessels with respect to dangerous situations. The evolving scenario could consider new vessels introduced into the environment, fresh information related to a specific vessel replacing the old one, existing vessels disappearing from the environment and so on. In such a scenario, Three-Way Decisions must be executed over data streams through the execution of a data processing algorithms running on the streaming platform provided by Apache Spark.

To describe the aforementioned algorithm it is needed to assume that vessel information arrives already organized in records of the same length and structure. In particular, the vessel features serialized into records are `ID, Velocity, Drift Angle, Distance, Type, Dangerousness, Timestamp`. More in detail, `ID` identifies a given vessel, `Velocity` indicates a range of velocity of the vessel (LOW, MID, HIGH), `Drift Angle` reports the drifting angle of the vessel (LOW, MID, HIGH), `Distance` is the distance from the coast (NEAR, MID, FAR), `Type` is the type of the vessel (FERRY, CARGO, RESEARCH, etc.), `Dangerousness` is the decision attribute and states if the vessel is in a `SAFE` or `DANGEROUS` state and, lastly, `Timestamp` is the time in which the information reported into the record has been generated.

Before executing the data processing algorithm in Spark, it is needed to set environment. In particular, we would like to execute a Spark testing environment directly from Google Colaboratory. The following code lines must be used to accomplish the above task:

```
!apt-get update
!apt-get install openjdk-8-jdk-headless -qq > /dev/
    null
!wget -q http://archive.apache.org/dist/spark/spark
    -3.0.0/spark-3.0.0-bin-hadoop3.2.tgz
!tar xf spark-3.0.0-bin-hadoop3.2.tgz
!pip install -q findspark

import os

os.environ["JAVA_HOME"] = "/usr/lib/jvm/java-8-openjdk
    -amd64"
os.environ["SPARK_HOME"] = "/content/spark-3.0.0-bin-
    hadoop3.2"

!ls

import findspark
findspark.init()

import pyspark
from pyspark import SparkContext
from pyspark.streaming import StreamingContext
```

The above code must be executed into a Colab cell in order to obtain the result reported by Fig. 10.2 and will take some minutes.

Once the environment is ready, it is possible to define the data processing algorithm for Three-Way Decisions that aims at tri-partitioning with respect to the concept of `SAFE` vessel.

The following code is useful to get the context in which it is possible to execute our Spark application:

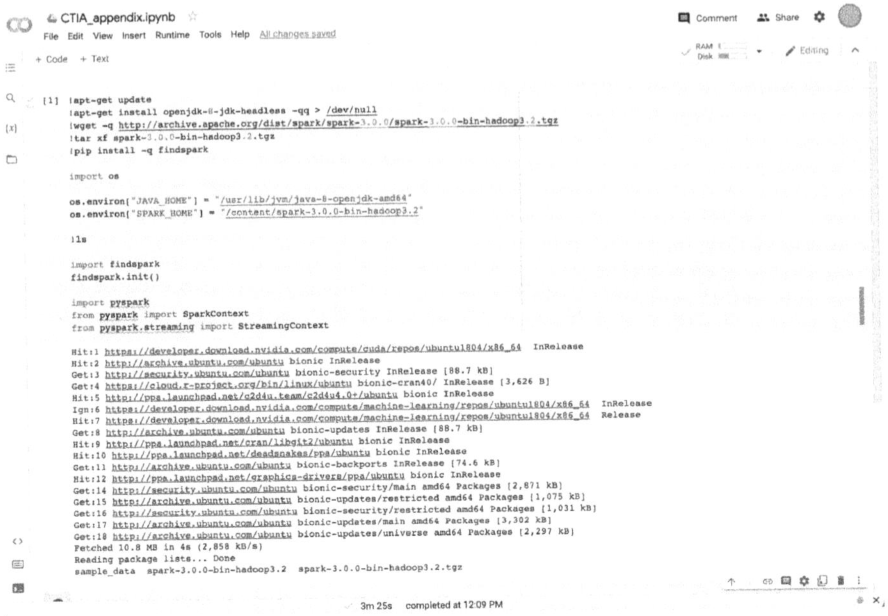

Fig. 10.2 Installation of Apache Spark into Google colaboratory

```
sc = SparkContext.getOrCreate()
ssc = StreamingContext(sc, 1)
```

Moreover, the algorithm to run into a Colab cell is the following one:

```
stream_data = ssc.textFileStream("/content/drive/
    MyDrive/CTIA/data").map(lambda x: x.split(","))

stream_data = stream_data.map(my_map_prepare)

stream_data = stream_data.window(30,5).reduceByKey(
    my_update)

# stream_data = stream_data.repartition(10)

stream_data = stream_data.map(my_restore)

stream_data = stream_data.map(my_map_angle)

stream_data = stream_data.reduceByKey(my_reduce)

stream_data = stream_data.map(my_map_bayes)

stream_data = stream_data.map(my_map_3WD)

stream_data = stream_data.flatMap(my_explode)
```

```
stream_data.pprint()

ssc.start()
ssc.awaitTermination()
```

The method `StreamingContext.textFileStream()` continuously reads file contents from the folder specified as argument. Note that we have created a specific subfolder `data` within the folder `CTIA` in GDrive. Thus, you need to do the same thing. Your GDrive must be mounted before by using the following code:

```
from google.colab import drive
drive.mount('/content/drive/')
```

Once mounted the GDrive, the computation can start. Let return to the description of the algorithm. The method `StreamingContext.textFileStream()` reads a CSV into a sequence of strings. Each string is transformed into a Python tuple by applying the split operator in the context of a `map` operation that allows to execute the split on each element of the sequence. According to the vessel features described before we obtain tuples of seven elements. The resulting tuples are inserted into the RDD structure (`stream_data`) used by Spark to distribute and parallelize the job. As introduced before, a set of transformations and actions will be applied to the RDD (the computation is distributed and executed, in general, by different nodes). The first one is the `.map(may_map_prepare)` that applies the following function:

```
def my_map_prepare(elem):
    return (elem[0], (elem[1], elem[2], elem[3], elem
        [4], elem[5], elem[6]))
```

to each tuple into the RDD. The goal is to reshape flat tuples into key-value pairs where the key is the `ID` and the value is a tuple with the remaining elements of the record.

The second step of the algorithm consists in replacing old data with new data belonging to the same vessel. This is accomplished by applying a `.reduceByKey()`, passing the `my_update` function, over the pairs coming from the previous step. The source code is the following one:

```
def my_update(e1, e2):
    if int(e2[5]) > int(e1[5]):
        return (e2[0], e2[1], e2[2], e2[3], e2[4], e2
            [5])
    else:
        return (e1[0], e1[1], e1[2], e1[3], e1[4], e1
            [5])
```

The previous function takes in input two pairs with the same `ID` (thanks to the `.reduceByKey()` method) and returns the pair with the greater `Timestamp`.

The method `.window()` is used to reset the characteristics of the window within the streaming computation based on micro-batches.

Subsequently, in order to optimize the distributed computation is possible to re-partition the RDD (in the algorithm source code such operation is commented).

The fourth step applies a `.map(my_restore)` method to reshape the records (in the RDD) to the original flat form. The `my_restore` function code is:

```
def my_restore(elem):
    return(elem[0], elem[1][0], elem[1][1], elem
        [1][2], elem[1][3], elem[1][4], elem[1][5])
```

Hence, the first four steps are useful to manage information updating. The remaining steps perform the Three-Way Decisions analysis.

Let describe the fifth step that is useful to reorganize the flat tuples into key-value pairs in which the key is a tuple constructed by using relevant condition attributes and the value is a tuple constructed with: (i) a list containing the `ID` of the vessel, (ii) a list containing the estimated `Dangerousness` value of the vessel, and (iii) a list that is empty if the vessel is `DANGEROUS` or contains the string `"S"` if the vessel is in a `SAFE` state. Such step is realized by means of the application of `.map(my_map_angle)` if the only the attribute `Drift Angle` is needed to determine the equivalence classes used to perform the analysis. Otherwise, it is possible to use `.map(my_map_velocity_angle)` to use also the attribute `Velocity`, and so on. For these functions let consider this possible implementation:

```
def my_map_angle(elem):
    if elem[5] == "S":
        return (elem[2], ([elem[0]], [elem[5]], [elem
            [5]]))
    else:
        return (elem[2], ([elem[0]], [elem[5]], []))

def my_map_velocity_angle(elem):
    if elem[5]=="S":
        return ((elem[1], elem[2]), ([elem[0]], [elem
            [5]], [elem[5]]))
    else:
        return ((elem[1], elem[2]), ([elem[0]], [elem
            [5]],[]))
```

Once the new pairs have been generated it is possible to reduce them in order to create the equivalence classes. Such operation is realized by means of the application of `.reduceByKey(my_reduce)`. The used function is defined as it follows:

```
def my_reduce(e1, e2):
    return (e1[0]+e2[0], e1[1]+e2[1], e1[2]+e2[2])
```

Thus, the sixth step groups the pairs with the same values for the relevant condition attributes. In this sample we are using only the attribute `Drift Angle`. The idea is to group two pairs at time by concatenating the lists included in the tuple representing the value and maintaining, of course, the key. For instance, two pairs like (LOW, ([25], ["S"], ["S"])) and (LOW, ([38], ["D"], [])) will be reduced for obtaining the pair (LOW, ([25, 38], ["S", "D"], ["S"])). The process is iterative and the result is a number of pairs containing the information of all the equivalence classes that partition the Universe by using the attribute `Drift Angle`.

After generating all the equivalence classes it is possible to calculate the conditional probability (see Sect. 3.5.1) for each one by executing `.map(my_map_bayes)`. The function `my_map_bayes` can be defined in the following way:

```
def my_map_bayes(elem):
    k = elem[1][0]
    p = len(elem[1][2])/len(elem[1][1])
    return (k, p)
```

that map each pair into another pair where the key is a tuple containing the identifiers (attribute `ID`) of the vessel in the equivalence class and the value is the rough membership of the class calculated as conditional probability as described before.

The seventh and last step consists in using the thresholds, α and β to assign each equivalence class to only one of the three region of the Three-Way Decisions. The source code for this step is the following one:

```
alpha = 0.63
beta = 0.25

def my_map_3WD(elem):
    p = float(elem[1])
    k = elem[0]
    if p < beta:
        return (k, "NEG")
    elif p <= alpha:
        return (k, "BND")
    else:
        return (k, "POS")
```

More in detail the method `.map(my_map_3WD)` transforms each pair into another pair where the key is the tuple containing the vessel identifiers in the equivalence class and the value is one of the strings `"POS"`, `"BND"` or `"NEG"` depending of the region in which the equivalence class falls.

An additional step is needed to complete the work. The method `.flatMap()` must be applied to the RDD with the function `my_explode` to expand the equivalence classes into single vessels. For instance, the pair ([25, 28, 14], "POS") will be transformed into the following set of pairs (25, "POS"), (28, "POS), (14, "POS"). The source code for accomplishing such operation is:

```
def my_explode(elem):
    granule=elem[0]
    v=elem[1]
    result=list()
    for obj in granule:
        result.append((obj, v))
    return result
```

Additional instructions to print the algorithm results (`.pprint()`) and the methods `StreamContext.start()` and `StreamContext.awaitTermination()` to start the computation and wait for results have to be provided.

In order to demonstrate how to launch the Spark application and obtain the results of the Three-Way Decisions analysis you need to prepare two CSV files (`data01.csv` and `data02.csv`).

The first file contains:

```
v1,LOW,LOW,FAR,Cargo,S,1
v2,LOW,MID,NEAR,Ferry,D,1
v3,MID,LOW,MID,Cargo,S,1
v4,MID,MID,MID,Research,S,1
v5,MID,LOW,FAR,Research,S,1
```

Moreover, the second one contains:

```
v2,LOW,HIGH,NEAR,Ferry,D,2
```

In order to launch the Spark application you need to execute the environment setting (with the installation script), to mount your GDrive, to define all the custom functions and, lastly, run the algorithm script in Colab cells.

Once the algorithm starts, Spark is listening for new data in the folder `CTIA/data` in the mounted GDrive. For simulating the arrival of new vessel information you can open a Terminal and copy the file `data01.csv` into the `data` folder and observe the result reported in Fig. 10.3 (all the records with timestamp 1 have been processed and there are two vessels in the boundary region). After a delay of few seconds you can copy the file `data01.csv` into the `data` subfolder and observe the result reported in Fig. 10.4 (a record with timestamp 2 replace old information for the same vessel and the boundary region disappears). At the end of the validity window in which the first records arrive the tri-partitioning results are up-to-date as demonstrated in Fig 10.5 (the records with timestamp 1 have been forgotten given the end of their validity window and the tri-partition includes only observations with timestamp 2).

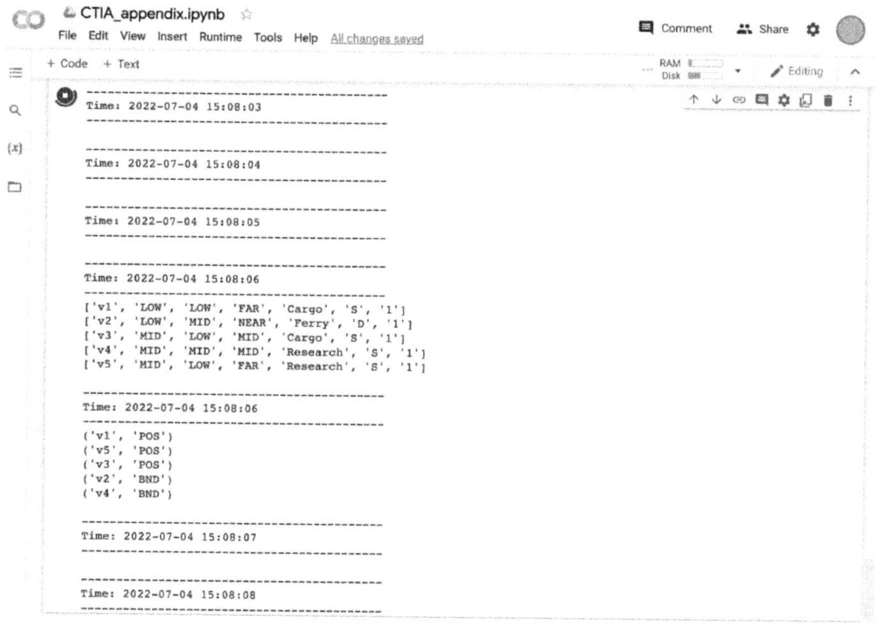

Fig. 10.3 Three-way decisions after the arrival of the first part of the records

Fig. 10.4 Three-way decisions after the arrival of the second part of the records

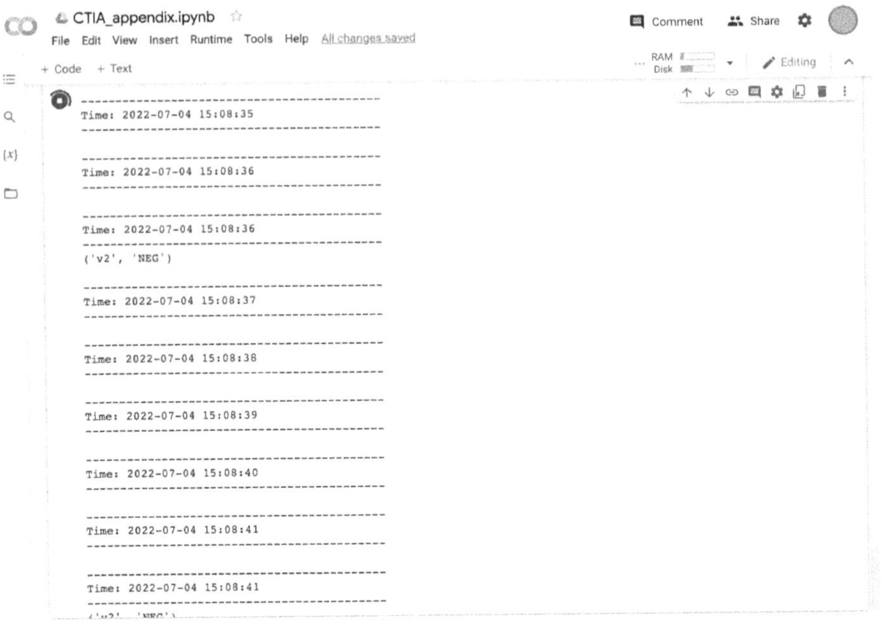

Fig. 10.5 Three-way decisions after that the first part of the records has been forgotten

10.1 Useful Resources

- RDD Programming Guide, https://spark.apache.org/docs/latest/rdd-programming-guide.html. This Site provides the official PySpark documentation for implementing data analysis algorithms by leveraging on the RDD abstraction.
- A Comprehensive Guide to PySpark RDD Operations, https://www.analyticsvidhya.com/blog/2021/10/a-comprehensive-guide-to-pyspark-rdd-operations/. This Site proposes a good tutorial for learning PySpark and, in particular, RDD programming.
- Streaming Programming Guide, https://spark.apache.org/docs/latest/streaming-programming-guide.html. This Site provides the official PySpark documentation for the streaming computing capabilities of Spark.
- A Beginner's Guide to Spark Streaming For Data Engineers, https://www.analyticsvidhya.com/blog/2020/11/introduction-to-spark-streaming-add-new-tag/. This Site provides a good tutorial to learn basic practical notions about spark stream capabilities.

Chapter 11
Dealing with Continuous Variables: Neighborhood and Dominance Based Rough Sets

The indiscernibility relation described in Sect. 3.5.1.1 allows the creation of information granules based on equivalence classes. This binary relation is a basic construct of Rough Sets and Probabilistic Rough Sets but it works on categorical data.

In some situations, when data are not categorical and it is not possible to discretize ordinal data, other binary relation can be used to build information granules and construct approximations. In this section, the neighborhood and dominance binary relations are presented.

Yao (1999) describes an approach for Granular computing using neighborhood systems. It is a set-theoretic framework where each element of a universe is associated with a nonempty family of neighborhoods. A neighborhood of an element is an information granule that contains the element and the elements that are close to it. Yao (1999) defines a neighborhood system as a family of granules.

For each element of an Universe, $x \in U$, and given a distance function $D : U \times U \to R^+$, the neighborhood of x is defined as:

$$n_d(x) = \{y | D(x, y) \leq d\} \tag{11.1}$$

where $d \in R^+$ is a threshold value.

Equation (11.1) is based on spatial proximity but is generic enough to enable other types of granulation. If, for instance, D is a similarity relation, i.e., $D : U \times U \to [0, 1]$ then Eq. (11.1) defines a granules of similar elements.

From Eq. (11.1), a neighborhood system is defined as a non empty family of neighborhoods:

$$NS(x) = \{n_d(x) | x \in U, d \in R^+\} \tag{11.2}$$

Lower and Upper approximations of a target concept can be constructed with neighborhoods with Eqs. (3.3) and (3.4). Neighborhood systems, such as Eq. (11.2) can be used to create multi-layer granular structures. A nested neighborhood system, $NS(x) = \{n_d(x_i)\}$ where $i = 1, 2, ..., j$ and $n_d(x_1) \subseteq n_d(x_2) \subseteq ... \subseteq n_d(x_j)$ produces a hierarchy.

V. Loia et al., *Computational Techniques for Intelligence Analysis*,
https://doi.org/10.1007/978-3-031-20851-5_11

Another approach that can deal with ordinal values is the Dominance based Rough Set approach (DRSA) proposed by Greco et al. (2001). This is an extension of rough sets theory for multi-criteria decision analysis. The idea is to use, instead of the indiscernibility relation, a dominance relation to deal with preference-ordered decision classes. Let us define a preference relation $\succeq_a$ s.t. $x_i \succeq_a x_j$ means that x_i is preferable to x_j with respect to the attribute $a \in A$. If $x_i \succeq_a x_j$ for every $a \in A$, x_i dominates x_j, i.e. $x_i D_A x_j$. For every object x_i, it is possible to defines two sets of objects.

Specifically, a set of objects that dominates x_i and a set of objects that are dominate by x_i. These are respectively formalized in Eq. (11.3).

$$\begin{aligned} D_A^+(x_i) &= \{x_j \in U | x_j D_A x_i\} \\ D_A^-(x_i) &= \{x_j \in U | x_i D_A x_j\} \end{aligned} \tag{11.3}$$

Let us define $Cl = \{Cl_p, p \in P\}$ with $P = \{1, 2, ..., j\}$ be these ordered set of decision classes.

With DRSA it is possible to find upward union classes, $Cl_p^{\geq} = \cup_{t \geq p} Cl_t$ that contain *all the objects at least of class* Cl_p, and downward union classes ,$Cl_p^{\leq} = \cup_{t \leq p} Cl_t$ that contains *all the objects at most of class* Cl_p.

It is possible also to find lower and upper approximations of these union classes. In this case, of course, the knowledge to be approximated (i.e., the target concept) is a collection of upward and downward unions of Cl and the granules of knowledge used for approximations are the dominance classes of Eq. (11.3).

Thus given a set of attributes A, the lower and upper approximations of $Cl_p^{\geq}$ are defined as follows:

$$\begin{aligned} \underline{A}(Cl_p^{\geq}) &= \{x | D_A^+(x) \subseteq Cl_p^{\geq}\} \\ \overline{A}(Cl_p^{\geq}) &= \{x | D_A^-(x) \cap Cl_p^{\geq} \neq \phi\} \end{aligned} \tag{11.4}$$

Similarly, the lower and upper approximations of $Cl_p^{\leq}$ are defined as follows:

$$\begin{aligned} \underline{A}(Cl_p^{\leq}) &= \{x | D_A^-(x) \subseteq Cl_p^{\leq}\} \\ \overline{A}(Cl_p^{\leq}) &= \{x | D_A^+(x) \cap Cl_p^{\leq} \neq \phi\} \end{aligned} \tag{11.5}$$

A measure of the quality of approximation is given by:

$$\gamma_A(Cl) = \frac{|U - ((\cup_p Bn(Cl_p^{\leq}) \cup (\cup_p Bn(Cl_p^{\geq})|}{|U|} \tag{11.6}$$

where, in Eq. (11.6), $Bn(Cl_p^{\leq}) = \overline{A}(Cl_p^{\leq}) - \underline{A}(Cl_p^{\leq})$ is the boundary class of $Cl_p^{\leq}$ and $Bn(Cl_p^{\geq})$ is the analogous for $Cl_p^{\geq}$. As in the traditional rough set theory, boundary classes contain objects that are doubtful. In fact, the quality of an approximation of Eq. (11.6) is perfect, i.e. $\gamma_A(Cl) = 1$, only if boundary classes are empty.

11.1 Strategies for Implementing Neighborhood Rough Sets

In this chapter, two strategies for the implementation of Neighborhood Rough Sets, introduce in this chapter, will be proposed. Both strategies will adopt, as usual for this book, the Python programming language. More in detail, the main difference between the two strategies is that the second one is based on NumPy and, thus, it offers better time performance.

Let start with the first strategy that is also the more intuitive among the two alternatives. With this kind of implementation, the idea is to build the neighborhood for each element in the universe of discourse and then test the neighborhood against the target concept in order to understand if updating both lower and upper approximations, only the upper approximation or to provide no change to the aforementioned sets. The source code for building neighbors, lower and upper approximations and, lastly, for tri-partitioning the universe is the following one:

```
from scipy.spatial.distance import euclidean, cosine,
    minkowski

class NRoughSets:

    '''
        Class variable containing a map between
            distance metrics names and function
            references.
        The considered functions are provided by the
            SciPy library.
    '''
    _distances = {"cosine": cosine, "euclidean":
        euclidean, "minkowski": minkowski}


    def __init__(self, itable, features):
        self._itable = itable[:, features]


    '''
        This private method builds the neighborhood of
            the element with index "xindex"
    '''
    def __neighborhood(self, xindex, function, delta):

        delta_set_x = list()

        for yindex in range(len(self._itable)):

            v=function(self._itable[xindex], self.
                _itable[yindex])

            if v <= delta:
```

```
                delta_set_x.append(yindex)

        return delta_set_x

    '''
        Three-Way Decisions from lower and upper
            approximations
    '''
    def calculate3WD(self, concept, function, delta, l
        =None, u=None, probability=False, beta=0.3,
        alpha=0.6):

        if (l==None) or (u==None):
            if not probability:
                l, u = self.approx(concept, function,
                    delta)
            else:
                l, u = self.papprox(concept, function,
                    delta, beta, alpha)

        POS = l
        NEG = set([i for i in range(len(self._itable))
            ]).difference(u)
        BND = u.difference(l)

        return (POS, BND, NEG)


    '''
        Lower and approximations based on
        Y. Y. Yao, "Granular computing using
            neighborhood systems" (1999)
    '''
    def approx(self, concept, function, delta):

        lower = list()
        upper = list()

        for x in range(len(self._itable)):

            N = self.__neighborhood(x, NRoughSets.
                _distances[function], delta)

            cap = set(N).intersection(set(concept))
            lencap = len(cap)

            if lencap > 0:
                upper.extend(N)
                if lencap == len(N):
                    lower.extend(N)

        return set(lower), set(upper)
```

```
    '''
        Probability-based extension for Lower and
            approximations
    '''
    def papprox(self, concept, function, delta, beta,
        alpha):

        lower = list()
        upper = list()

        for x in range(len(self._itable)):

            N = self.__neighborhood(x, NRoughSets.
                _distances[function], delta)
            membership = len(set(N).intersection(set(
                concept)))/len(set(N))

            if membership >= alpha:
                lower.extend(N)
            if membership > beta:
                upper.extend(N)

        return (set(lower), set(upper))
```

More in detail, the class `NRoughSets` provides an initializer that receives a 2D array (for the sake of simplicity a list of lists of numbers), namely `itable`, with the values in the information system and a 1D array (for the sake of simplicity a list of integers), namely `features`, including the indexes of the columns we need to consider as condition attributes. The initializer executes a slicing operation obtaining only the relevant columns from the whole dataset and storing such data into the object variable `_itable`.

The private method `__neighborhood()` constructs a set containing all the neighbors of the element (of the universe) with index `xindex`. Such set is built by implementing Eq. (11.1). In our simple implementation the distance function could be one of the following implemented in the SciPy package: *Cosine Distance*, *Euclidean Distance*, *Minkowski Distance*. The client of `NRoughSets` is able to provide its choice, related to the distance function, by using the name (as a string) of such function. `NRoughSets` implements a kind of distance function factory by using a Python dictionary, namely `_distances`.

The public method `approx()` returns two sets containing lower and upper approximations. The input parameters are: `concept` (a list of integers) containing the indexes of all the elements forming the target concept we are going to approximate, `function` (a string) containing the name of the distance function that will be used (remember that for this implementation we have a small set of alternatives), and `delta` (a floating point number) representing the diameter of the neighborhood. The behavior of the method is simple: for each element in the universe, a set of its neighbors is constructed. Each neighbor set is included into both lower and upper

Table 11.1 Sample dataset for neighborhood rough sets

a1	a2	a3	a4	a5
0	0	0	0	0
0.5	0.5	0.3	0.1	0
0.3	0.3	0.3	0.1	0
0.5	0.5	0.3	0.1	0
0.5	0.5	0.3	0.1	0
0.5	0.8	0.3	0.1	0
0	0	0	0	0
0.5	1	0.3	0.1	0
0.1	0.1	0.1	0.1	0.1

approximations if it is a subset of the target concept. Otherwise, if its intersection with the target concept is not the empty set it is included into the upper approximations.

An alternative to the previous method is represented by the public method `papprox()` that builds lower and upper approximations by using the conditional probability. In other words, it calculates the membership degree for each neighbor set and compares such degree to two thresholds (`beta` and `alpha` included into the input parameters) to check if such set must be included into both lower and upper approximations, only into the upper approximation, or neither of them.

The last public method provided by the class `NRoughSets` is `calculate3WD()` that is a sort of *façade* because uses the results of `approx()` or `papprox()` for tri-partitioning the universe. Such method returns a tuple containing three sets representing the three regions (`POS`, `BND` and `NEG`) of the Three-Way Decisions. In order to select the probabilistic or the traditional approach, the cliend of `calculate3WD()` needs to set the named parameter `probability`. In the case of probabilistic approach, also the thresholds must be provided. Let us now explain how to use (write a client) the `NRoughSets` class. Assume that you need to approximate the concept $X = \{0, 2, 4, 6, 8\}$ using the dataset `ndata.csv` (Table 11.1):
Thus, it is possible to use the following source code:

```
import pandas as pd

df = pd.read_csv("ndata.csv")

features = [0,1,2,3,4]
nrs = NRoughSets(df.values, features)

target_concept = [0,2,4,6,8]
l, u = nrs.approx(target_concept, "euclidean", 0.2)

print("LOWER: ", l)
print("UPPER: ", u)
```

```
regions = nrs.calculate3WD(target_concept, "euclidean"
    , 0.2, probability=False)
print(regions)
```

The previous code invokes the `approx()` method requesting the *euclidean* distance with $\delta = 0.2$. With such configuration, the result is:

LOWER: {0, 8, 2, 6}
UPPER: {0, 1, 2, 3, 4, 6, 8}
(POS, BND, NEG) <-
  ({0, 8, 2, 6}, {1, 3, 4}, {5, 7})

Furthermore, if it is needed to exploit the probabilistic approach, then it is possible to rewrite the previous code in the following way:

```
import pandas as pd

df = pd.read_csv("ndata.csv")

features = [0,1,2,3,4]
nrs = NRoughSets(df.values, features)

target_concept = [0,2,4,6,8]
l, u = nrs.papprox(target_concept, "euclidean", 0.2,
    0.35, 0.65)

print("LOWER: ", l)
print("UPPER: ", u)

regions = nrs.calculate3WD(target_concept, "euclidean"
    , 0.2, probability=True, beta=0.35, alpha=0.65)
print("(POS, BND, NEG) <- ", regions)
```

In this case the result is:

LOWER: {0, 8, 2, 6}
UPPER: {0, 8, 2, 6}
(POS, BND, NEG) <-
  ({0, 8, 2, 6}, { }, {1, 3, 4, 5, 7})

The above illustrated source code adopt a rudimentary implementation approach. If you need to provide an high-performance implementation it is possible to adopt a different strategy based on NumPy that allows to avoid loops that are replaced with special functions mostly having an inner implementation based on compiled languages and high-performance data structures.

Let us explain, step-by-step, the second implementation strategy. The first operations to execute allow to import the needed packages and load the dataset:

```
import pandas as pd
import numpy as np
from scipy.spatial.distance import cdist

df = pd.read_csv("data/ndata.csv")
T = df.values
print(T)
```

The result is the print screen of the values into the dataset:

```
[
    [0.0 0.0 0.0 0.0 0.0]
    [0.5 0.5 0.3 0.1 0.0]
    [0.3 0.3 0.3 0.1 0.0]
    [0.5 0.5 0.3 0.1 0.0]
    [0.5 0.5 0.3 0.1 0.0]
    [0.5 0.8 0.3 0.1 0.0]
    [0.0 0.0 0.0 0.0 0.0]
    [0.5 1.0 0.3 0.1 0.0]
    [0.1 0.1 0.1 0.1 0.1]
]
```

Once obtained the values, it is needed to apply the *euclidean* distance between all pairs of elements in the universe. This can be accomplished by using the function `cdist()` of the package `scipy.spatial.distance`. The result is then converted in a NumPy 2D array of floats in order to be ready to exploit the other functions provided by NumPy. The following code performs the above operations:

```
D = cdist(T, T, "euclidean")
Ns = np.array(D)
Ns = Ns.astype(float)
print(Ns)
```

The result is a matrix (2D array) in which the cell (i, j) contains the distance value between row i and row j of T:

```
[
    [0.00000000 0.77459667 0.52915026 0.77459667 0.77459667 0.99498744 0.00000000 1.16189500 0.22360680]
    [0.77459667 0.00000000 0.28284271 0.00000000 0.00000000 0.30000000 0.77459667 0.50000000 0.60827625]
    [0.52915026 0.28284271 0.00000000 0.28284271 0.28284271 0.53851648 0.52915026 0.72801099 0.36055513]
    [0.77459667 0.00000000 0.28284271 0.00000000 0.00000000 0.30000000 0.77459667 0.50000000 0.60827625]
    [0.77459667 0.00000000 0.28284271 0.00000000 0.00000000 0.30000000 0.77459667 0.50000000 0.60827625]
    [0.99498744 0.30000000 0.53851648 0.30000000 0.30000000 0.00000000 0.99498744 0.20000000 0.83666003]
    [0.00000000 0.77459667 0.52915026 0.77459667 0.77459667 0.99498744 0.00000000 1.16189500 0.22360680]
    [1.16189500 0.50000000 0.72801099 0.50000000 0.50000000 0.20000000 1.16189500 0.00000000 1.00995049]
    [0.22360680 0.60827625 0.36055513 0.60827625 0.60827625 0.83666003 0.22360680 1.00995049 0.00000000]
]
```

The third step is accomplished by using the function `argwhere()` that returns the indexes of the pairs whose distance value respects a given condition. In our case the condition is that the distance value must be less or equal to 0.2. The source code is the following one:

```
Ni = np.argwhere(Ns <= 0.2)
print(Ni)
```

The result is a list of pairs representing cells for which the previous condition is true:

```
[
    [0 0]
    [0 6]
    [1 1]
    [1 3]
    [1 4]
    [2 2]
    [3 1]
    [3 3]
    [3 4]
    [4 1]
    [4 3]
    [4 4]
    [5 5]
    [5 7]
    [6 0]
    [6 6]
    [7 5]
    [7 7]
    [8 8]
]
```

If you consider the previous result as a matrix (list of lists), the next step is obtaining the unique elements in the first column (`Ni[:, 0]`) by considering the source code that follows:

```
U = np.unique(Ni[:, 0], return_index=True)
print(U)
print(U[1][1:])
```

Once executed, the previous code returns the following result:

```
(
    array([0, 1, 2, 3, 4, 5, 6, 7, 8]),
    array([ 0, 2, 5, 6, 9, 12, 14, 16, 18])
)
```

In other words, the result is a tuple of two 1D NumPy arrays. The first array contains all unique elements of the first column of the result of the previous step `Ni`. The second array contains the indexes of such unique elements. In particular, if we read, at the same time, the two arrays we can affirm that the element 0 is at index 0, element 1 starts from index 2, element 2 starts from index 5, and so on. The second `print` operation in the previous code returns such print screen:

[2 5 6 9 12 14 16 18]

This is a list obtained from the second array in `U` by excluding the first element.

Let us continue with the next step. In particular, we need to invoke the `split()` function (offered by NumPy) to split an array into multiple sub-arrays. In particular, we need to split `Ni` into sub-arrays containing the elements of the second column of `Ni`. The partitioning is realized by considering the indexes of the unique elements of `Ni` included in the variable `U` that is opportunely sliced by using the instruction `U[1][1:]`. The code fragment is the following one:

```
R=np.split(Ni[:,1], U[1][1:])
print(R)
```

The above code provides the following result:

[
  array([0, 6]), array([1, 3, 4]), array([2]),
  array([1, 3, 4]), array([1, 3, 4]), array([5, 7]),
  array([0, 6]), array([5, 7]), array([8])
]

In particular, the above result is a list containing 1D arrays representing the neighborhood obtained from the original dataset. As you can note, there are some duplicates. Hence, we need to drop such a redundancy.

The last step is able to eliminate duplicates in neighborhoods and to use such sets to build lower and upper approximations of a given target concept (e.g., `[0, 2, 4, 6, 8]`). The following code realizes the last step:

```
def arrayToTuple(x):
   return tuple(list(x))

neighborhoods = set(map(arrayToTuple, R))
lower = list()
upper = list()
for N in neighborhoods:
   cap = set(N).intersection({0,2,4,6,8})
   lencap = len(cap)

   if lencap > 0:
      upper.extend(N)
      if lencap == len(N):
         lower.extend(N)
```

```
print("LOWER: ", lower)
print("UPPER: ", upper)
```

In particular, the idea is to eliminate the duplicates by transforming the list of neighborhoods into a set (this exploits the capabilities of Python sets to maintain only unique elements). Before executing such transformation we need to map each element of type NumPy array in the list into a tuple. Such mapping is needed because Python sets require immutable element types. The next code lines iterate over the set of tuples (neighborhoods) and perform the test to correctly update lower and upper approximations. The result of the above code is:

LOWER: [2, 8, 0, 6]
UPPER: [2, 8, 0, 6, 1, 3, 4]

11.2 Useful Resources

- SciPy Documentation, https://docs.scipy.org/doc/scipy/. This Site provides the official SciPy documentation.
- NumPy Documentation, https://numpy.org/doc/. This Site provides the official NumPy documentation.
- SciPy distance computation documentation, https://docs.scipy.org/doc/scipy/reference/spatial.distance.html. The official documentation of the sub-package `spatial.distance` of SciPy.
- NumPy Tutorial: Your First Steps Into Data Science in Python, https://realpython.com/numpy-tutorial/. This Site provides a good tutorial on NumPy for Data Science.

References

Anderson LW, Krathwohl DR (2001) A taxonomy for learning, teaching, and assessing: a revision of Bloom's taxonomy of educational objectives. Longman
Ariew R, Garber D (1989) GW Leibniz philosophical essays
Bargiela A, Pedrycz W (2016) Granular computing. In: Handbook on computational intelligence: volume 1: fuzzy logic, systems, artificial neural networks, and learning systems. World Scientific, pp 43–66
Beitler SS (2019) Imagery intelligence. In: The military intelligence community. Routledge, pp 71–86
Beziau J-Y (2018) An analogical hexagon. Int J Approximate Reasoning 94:1–17
Bonwell CC, Eison JA (1991) Active learning: creating excitement in the classroom. 1991 ASHE-ERIC higher education reports. ERIC
Chang W et al (2018) Restructuring structured analytic techniques in intelligence. Intell Nat Secur 33(3):337–356
Clark RM (2019) Intelligence analysis: a target-centric approach. CQ Press
Coffman T, Greenblatt S, Marcus S (2004) Graph-based technologies for intelligence analysis. Commun ACM 47(3):45–47
Cutter SL et al (2013) Disaster resilience: a national imperative. Environ Sci Policy Sustain Dev 55(2):25–29
Deng X, Yao Y (2012) An information-theoretic interpretation of thresholds in probabilistic rough sets. In: International conference on rough sets and knowledge technology. Springer, pp 369–378
Endsley MR, Bolte B, Jones DG (2003) Designing for situation awareness: an approach to user-centered design. CRC Press
Endsley MR (1995a) A taxonomy of situation awareness errors. In: Human factors in aviation operations, vol 3(2), pp 287–292
Endsley MR (1995b) Toward a theory of situation awareness in dynamic systems. In: Human factors, vol 37(1), pp 32–64
Fujita H et al (2018) Resilience analysis of critical infrastructures: a cognitive approach based on granular computing. IEEE Trans Cybern 49(5):1835–1848
Gaeta A, Loia V, Orciuoli F (2021) A comprehensive model and computational methods to improve situation awareness in intelligence scenarios. Appl Intell 51(9):6585–6608
Greco S, Matarazzo B, Slowinski R (2001) Rough sets theory for multicriteria decision analysis. Eur J Oper Res 129(1):1–47

V. Loia et al., *Computational Techniques for Intelligence Analysis*,
https://doi.org/10.1007/978-3-031-20851-5

Haines GK, Leggett RE (2003) Watching the bear: essays on CIA's analysis of the Soviet Union. Central Intelligence Agency
Herbert JP, Yao JT (2011) Game-theoretic rough sets. Fundamenta Informaticae 108(3–4):267–286
Heuer RJ (1999) Psychology of intelligence analysis. Center for the Study of Intelligence
Jorgensen JE et al (1995) The learning factory. In: Proceedings of the fourth world conference on engineering education, St. Paul, Minneapolis, USA
Klir G, Yuan B (1995) Fuzzy sets and fuzzy logic, vol 4. Prentice Hall New Jersey
Krebs VE (2002) Mapping networks of terrorist cells. Connections 24(3):43–52
Lallie HS, Debattista K, Bal J (2020) A review of attack graph and attack tree visual syntax in cyber security. Comput Sci Rev 35:100219
Latora V, Marchiori M (2005) Vulnerability and protection of infrastructure networks. Phys Rev E 71(1):015103
Liang J (2011) Uncertainty and feature selection in rough set theory. In: International conference on rough sets and knowledge technology. Springer, pp 8–15
Lim K (2016) Big data and strategic intelligence. Intell Nat Secur 31(4):619–635
Liu Q, Liu Q (2002) Approximate reasoning based on granular computing in granular logic. Proceedings international conference on machine learning and cybernetics 3:1258–1262. https://doi.org/10.1109/ICMLC.2002.1167405
Marchio J (2014) Analytic tradecraft and the intelligence community: enduring value, intermittent emphasis. Intell Nat Secur 29(2):159–183
McConnell JJ (1996) Active learning and its use in computer science. In: Proceedings of the 1st conference on integrating technology into computer science education, pp 52–54
Odom WE (2008) Intelligence analysis. Intell Nat Secur 23(3):316–332
Pawlak Z (1982) Rough sets. Int J Comput Inf Sci 11(5):341–356
Pawlak Z, Polkowski L, Skowron A (2001) Rough set theory. KI 15(3):38–39
Pawlak Z, Skowron A (2007) Rudiments of rough sets. Inf Sci 177(1):3–27
Pedrycz W, Al-Hmouz R et al (2015) Designing granular fuzzy models: a hierarchical approach to fuzzy modeling. Knowl Based Syst 76:42–52
Pedrycz W, Homenda W (2013) Building the fundamentals of granular computing: a principle of justifiable granularity. Appl Soft Comput 13(10):4209–4218
Pherson RH, Heuer RJ Jr (2020) Structured analytic techniques for intelligence analysis. CQ Press
Phythian, Mark (2013). Understanding the intelligence cycle. Routledge London
Primer AT (2009) Structured analytic techniques for improving intelligence analysis. CIA Center for the Study of Intelligence
Salloum S et al (2016) Big data analytics on Apache Spark. Int J Data Sci Anal 1(3):145–164
Skowron A, Jankowski A, Dutta S (2016) Interactive granular computing. Granular Comput 1(2):95–113
Trudeau RJ (1993) Introduction to graph theory. Courier Corporation
Tversky A, Kahneman D (1974) Judgment under uncertainty: heuristics and biases. Science 185(4157):1124–1131
Wang G-Y, Yao Y-Y, Yu H et al (2009) A survey on rough set theory and applications. Chin J Comput 32(7):1229–1246
Weinbaum C, Shanahan JNT (2018) Intelligence in a data-driven age. Joint Force Q 90(3):4–9
Willems N et al (2013) Visualization of vessel traffic. In: Situation awareness with systems of systems. Springer, pp 73–87
Wong SKM, Ziarko W (1987) Comparison of the probabilistic approximate classification and the fuzzy set model. Fuzzy Sets Syst 21(3):357–362
Yager RR, Reformat MZ (2012) Looking for like-minded individuals in social networks using tagging and e fuzzy sets. IEEE Trans Fuzzy Syst 21(4):672–687
Yao JT (2010) Novel developments in granular computing: applications for advanced human reasoning and soft computation: applications for advanced human reasoning and soft computation. IGI Global

Yao JT, Vasilakos AV, Pedrycz W (2013) Granular computing: perspectives and challenges. IEEE Trans Cybern 43(6):1977–1989
Yao Y (2005) Perspectives of granular computing. In: 2005 IEEE international conference on granular computing, vol 1. IEEE, pp 85–90
Yao Y (2007) Decision-theoretic rough set models. In: International conference on rough sets and knowledge technology. Springer, pp 1–12
Yao Y (2009) Three-way decision: an interpretation of rules in rough set theory. In: International conference on rough sets and knowledge technology. Springer, pp 642–649
Yao Y (2011) The superiority of three-way decisions in probabilistic rough set models. Inf Sci 181(6):1080–1096
Yao Y (2016) Three-way decisions and cognitive computing. Cogn Comput 8(4):543–554
Yao YY, Wong SKM, Lin TY (1997) A review of rough set models. In: Rough sets and data mining, pp 47–75
Yao YY (1999) Granular computing using neighborhood systems. In: Advances in soft computing. Springer, pp 539–553
Yao Y (2020) Set-theoretic models of three-way decision. Granular Comput 6:133–148
Yao Y, Greco S, Slowinski R (2015) Probabilistic rough sets. In: Springer handbook of computational intelligence. Springer, pp 387–411
Ye J, Dobson S, McKeever S (2012) Situation identification techniques in pervasive computing: a review. Pervasive Mobile Comput 8(1):36–66
Zadeh LA (1965) Information and control. Fuzzy Sets 8(3):338–353
Zadeh LA (1997) Toward a theory of fuzzy information granulation and its centrality in human reasoning and fuzzy logic. Fuzzy Sets Syst 90(2):111–127
Zaharia M et al (2012) Resilient distributed datasets: a fault-tolerant abstraction for in-memory cluster computing. In: 9th USENIX symposium on networked systems design and implementation (NSDI 12), pp 15–28
Zimmermann H-J (2011) Fuzzy set theory-and its applications. Springer Science & Business Media

www.ingramcontent.com/pod-product-compliance
Ingram Content Group UK Ltd.
Pitfield, Milton Keynes, MK11 3LW, UK
UKHW020239061126
16351UKWH00016B/50
* 9 7 8 3 0 3 1 2 0 8 5 2 2 *